JOURNAL FOR THE STUDY OF THE OLD TESTAMENT SUPPLEMENT SERIES
68

Editors
David J.A. Clines
Philip R. Davies

BIBLE AND LITERATURE SERIES
14

General Editor
David M. Gunn

Assistant General Editor
Danna Nolan Fewell

Consultant Editors
Elizabeth Struthers Malbon
James G. Williams

Almond Press
Sheffield

The Triumph of Irony in the Book of Judges

Lillian R. Klein

The Almond Press · 1989

Bible and Literature Series, 14

General Editor: David M. Gunn
(Columbia Theological Seminary, Decatur, Georgia)
Assistant General Editor: Danna Nolan Fewell
(Perkins School of Theology, Dallas, Texas)
Consultant Editors: Elizabeth Struthers Malbon
(Virginia Polytechnic Institute & State University, Blacksburg, Virginia)
James G. Williams
(Syracuse University, Syracuse, New York)

First published by Almond Press 1988
Paperback edition 1989

Published by Almond Press
Editorial direction: David M. Gunn
Columbia Theological Seminary
P.O. Box 520, Decatur
GA 30031, U.S.A.
Almond Press is an imprint of
Sheffield Academic Press Ltd
The University of Sheffield
343 Fulwood Road
Sheffield S10 3BP
England

Typeset by Sheffield Academic Press
and
printed in Great Britain
by Billing & Sons Ltd
Worcester

British Library Cataloguing in Publication Data

Klein, Lillian R.
    The triumph of irony in the Book of Judges.
    1. Bible. O.T. Judges—Critical studies
    I. Title   II. Series
    III. Series
    222'.3206

    ISSN 0309-0787
    ISSN 0260-4493

    ISBN 1-85075-100-5
    ISBN 1-85075-099-8 Pbk

CONTENTS

PREFACE

This book has developed out of conversations with Paul Ricœur, and though it has taken an emphasis far removed from that initially projected, I am indebted to Professor Ricœur for the impetus of that discussion. The responsibility for the outcome is entirely my own.

Rather than proposing an interpretation of Judges, I have attempted to set forth the ironic and literary structure of the book and to show how they function in the text. A close analysis of the kinds and modes of irony used and to what effect awaits further studies.

I feel a word about the translations is in order. In attempting to convey implicit meanings, I have rendered the text in a manner *counter* to contemporary translation theory, which advocates phrase translation. I have translated word for word, including redundant pronouns where pronoun number is important. For readability, words which seem redundant in English translation have been placed within parentheses, and words which have been added for clarity in brackets. I acknowledge that my translations do not reflect the aesthetic quality of the Hebrew text and hope that the discussion based on these translations will somewhat compensate and perhaps encourage reading in the original.

For those students of Hebrew who can profit by following the translations closely, I have made constant reference to the two standard Hebrew-English Lexica: those by Benjamin Davidson and Brown–Driver–Briggs. Biblical references follow those of the Hebrew text.

The use of gender-specific nouns and pronouns has posed a problem. Though I heartily welcome contemporary assumption of both male and female participants in all aspects of life, I do not feel justified in projecting this equality on the literature of the Bible, where 'man' often means just that: woman is not implied in the word. To translate 'man' as 'humankind' would not only distort the meaning of the Hebrew word and world but also would often distort the implications of the text. However, the contemporary reader belongs to humankind, non gender-specific, and is so referred to in the text. I ask the reader's tolerance of this variable.

The *Bayerische Staatsbibliothek* in Munich provided a friendly and helpful milieu, the resources necesary for research, and the seclusion for writing, for which I offer sincere thanks. Of the many individuals to whom I am indebted, I first would like to mention my special thanks to David Gunn for his editorial guidance. It is a pleasure to acknowledge my appreciation to Dr David Marshall, who patiently read the first drafts; to my student assistant Michelle Zamora, who checked the references with scholarly care; and and to my dear friend and colleague, Diane Ewing, who offered valuable editorial comments on the last version.

Lillian Rae Klein
University of Maryland
Munich Campus
Munich, West Germany

ABBREVIATIONS

AB	Anchor Bible
ABC	Abingdon Bible Commentary
AHCL	*Analytical Hebrew and Chaldee Lexicon*
BASOR	*Bulletin of the American Schools of Oriental Research*
BDB	Brown–Driver–Briggs–Gesenius Hebrew/Aramaic Lexicon
CB	Century Bible
CBC	The Cambridge Bible Commentary on the New English Bible
CBQ	*Catholic Biblical Quarterly*
EI	*Eretz Israel*
GUOS	*Transactions of the Glasgow University Oriental Society*
HUCA	*Hebrew Union College Annual*
IB	Interpreter's Bible
ICC	The International Critical Commentary
IEJ	*Israel Exploration Journal*
Interp	*Interpretation: A Journal of Bible and Theology*
ITL	International Theological Library
JBL	*Journal of Biblical Literature*
JETS	*Journal of the Evangelical Theological Society*
JNES	*Journal of Near Eastern Studies*
JSOT	*Journal for the Study of the Old Testament*
JTS	*Journal of Theological Studies*
LBS	The Library of Biblical Studies
NOAB	New Oxford Annotated Bible: Revised Standard Version
PT	*Prooftexts*
RB	*Revue Biblique*
SBT	Studies in Biblical Theology
TOTC	Tyndale Old Testament Commentaries
VT	*Vetus Testamentum*
ZAW	*Zeitschrift fur die alttestamentliche Wissenschaft*

In loving memory of my mother,
Helen Rothbin Klein Frank

Chapter 1

INTRODUCTION

The book of Judges is generally regarded as a sequence of narratives with some bridging material appended before and after—a pastiche rather than a unified work of art.[1] A typical instance of this view is the preface to Judges in *The New Oxford Annotated Bible* (1972:293). In spite of tradition to the contrary, my basic premise is that the book of Judges is a structured entity in which elements are shaped to contribute to the integrity and significance of the whole; that is, it is organized through narrative form—exposition, main narrative and resolution—and a dominant (though by no means sole) structural device of opposing perspectives: irony.

Each of the narratives within the book likewise reveals narrative structure.[2] In the exposition of the book, the Othniel narrative establishes a paradigm which shapes the following 'major' judges narratives; the exposition in individual narratives may be reduced to that paradigm, as in the Ehud narrative (3.15), or more fully developed, as in later narratives. The resolution of individual narratives, however, is more regularly curtailed.[3]

Various redactors have left their imprints in the language and the concepts of the book of Judges; and recent studies have contributed greatly to our knowledge of the evolution of the book. One hand, nevertheless, must have given it its present form; whether it was the late Ephraimic redactor, whom C.F. Burney credits with the most significant literary force, or another is, for the purposes of this study, not of particular relevance (1970:xlvi). I am proceeding from the premise that 'the author, the craftsman of a book . . . *is not precisely anybody*. One of the functions of language, and of literature as language, is to destroy its user and to designate him [sic] as absent' (Blanchot, quoted by Genette, 1982:66). I regard the work as an entity and credit the work of perhaps many hands to a single author, whom I call just that.[4]

Whereas I am not concerned to identify the author, I am concerned to identify the separate 'voices' of the book. The author is 'absent', but the omniscient narrator is indeed present, despite the apparent detachment. The narrator's is practically the only reliable voice in the book, verified by the narrator's function as spokesman. I do not therefore assume Yahweh's sanction when unprincipled and undependable characters claim divine support, even when they act on behalf of Israel.

I
Overview

Using Meir Sternberg's criteria (see Appendix I, p. 193), the reader can determine that the initial passages of Judges are expositional: they define the time and place of the action.[5] Although the book of Joshua ends with the death of that leader-figure, the book of Judges opens with a brief glance backward to the moment when Joshua brought the descendents of the sons of Israel to the promised land. In the first fifteen verses, the Judges text depicts relatively long periods in brief spans of reading time. This expositional time ratio is, for the most part, distinctly contracted compared to the 'time norm'[6] of the central narrative sequence (3.12-16.31). In the same vein, when specific events are introduced in expositional narrative material they are neither developed nor do they enter into the 'dynamics' of the plot.[7] The brief episode of Adoni-bezek is narrated in three verses and effects no change in the direction of action; the narrative of Achsah and Othniel takes only four verses and is likewise non-developmental.[8] (The Achsah-Othniel narrative does, however, contribute the symbol of Israel as a bride, a recurrent figure in the ensuing narratives.) Although specific and concrete, this material can be recognized as expositional. The balance of the first chapter continues in this vein: the time-ratio basically adheres to that already established. An additional brief but specific episode (1.22-26) similarly covers a long period of represented time and introduces no actional dynamics, thus marking it as another expositional unit.

With ch. 2, the text returns chronologically to the beginning of the book—a flashback to the same characters and events as 1.1—and amplifies the exposition described above in a second expository passage (2.1-3.11), marked by a second beginning with Joshua (Judg. 2.6-3.11). Whereas the first expositional unit introduces the cohabitation of the Israelites with the non-Yahwists, this second unit stresses anti-Yahwist behavior (worship of other gods), the two units enunciating the *causes* of the dynamics of the main narratives. With the exception of 2.1-5, which depicts Yahweh's confrontation with the Israelites, the balance of the chapter is narrated exposition. The time-ratio of the entire chapter basically adheres to that already established in ch. 1, the ratio of represented to representational time remaining contracted and thus expositional.

Two expositional narratives are dramatized rather than narrated: Joseph's model destruction of Luz (1.22-26) and the story of Achsah and Othniel (1.12-15). Although they serve as foils for later situations and/or characters, these narratives are considered to be expositional because they maintain the expositional time norm and their actions do not bring about the dynamic action characteristic of main narrative. A third important expositional narrative concerns Othniel as judge (3.9-11). This narrative is regarded as expositional because it is narrated, not dramatized, and its time ratio is condensed compared to that of the main narrative sequence.[9]

In addition to establishing specifics of the *mise en scene* of the narrative, the exposition also establishes the point of view. In this respect the book of Judges is worthy of notice, for its point of view *shifts* between Israel and Yahweh. The opening verses (1.1-15) disclose Israel in the first phases of conquest and settlement. These initial verses emphasize the goodness of Yahweh as compared to heathen gods, and the potential of Israel to be a fertile bride to a powerful Yahweh. The following verses (1.16-36) shift in focus to the human condition, to Israel's tendency to compromise its covenant with Yahweh. Chapter 2 opens with a flashback. This striking temporal shift alerts the reader to possible structural significance— and indeed the point of view shifts once again, from Israel's to Yahweh's. Verses 11-19 return to Yahweh, to a concise, divine view: obedience, regression, affliction, remorse. Taken together, these passages introduce opposing perspectives.

To summarize: the book opens with an initial promise of Yahwist occupation of the land. The following verses describe the beginning of occupation, first from the point-of-view of the Israelites and then from that of Yahweh. It is this contrast of perspective which introduces the potential for irony.

Expositional passages may foreshadow the main narrative by introducing motifs and/or paradigms. The book of Judges does both.

In the expositional passages, Israelite laxity in driving out the non-Israelites is summarily narrated, not dramatized. This motif or failure to drive out non-Israelites is recapitulated in the main narrative sequence, and its consequences are developed anew in each narrative.

A significant expositional motif is the 'major' judge paradigm. In the exposition, the cyclical pattern of the main (major) narratives is both described (2.16-19) and dramatized (3.7-11). By virtue of the gap created by the flashback to the book of Joshua, Othniel is re-introduced, this time specifically in the role of a judge of Israel (3.2-11). Othniel's story employs phrases which become characteristic of the recurring sequence described in the main judges' narratives and is therefore often regarded as a 'pragmatic' scheme, providing a basis for analogy in the succeeding narratives.

The expositional paradigm of the 'major' judges is well-recognized, unlike other archetypal motifs embedded in the exposition. I suggest the conquest of Luz is a model of Yahwist war and occupation. The first dramatized narrative of the exposition, the story of Achsah and Othniel (1.12-15), offers a feminine model and a model of relations between the sexes; the last, of Othniel (3.2-11), is a complementary masculine model of leadership.[10]

Whereas the exposition of the book of Judges is a complex and subtle structure, the resolution of the book is clearly marked, the text directing the reader's attention from the main narrative to resolution in several ways. Most obvious is the abrupt disappearance of individuals who serve as judges. The protagonists of the concluding narratives are not leaders of their people; they are—like the other personae—'leaders' unto themselves.

A second motif of resolution is the refrain

17.6	In those days Israel had no king; everyone did as he saw fit in his own eyes.
18.6	In those days Israel had no king.
19.1	In those days Israel had no king.
21.25	In those days Israel had no king; everyone did as he saw fit in his own eyes.

which frames and links the narratives of resolution and underscores the lack of leadership, of judge and judgment, in the resolution.

There are further, subtle indicators of a shift in narrative form. In the last four chapters, protagonists are no longer judges, and they lose tribal designations, patriarchal line of descent, even names. The consistency with which this stripping-away occurs supports its functioning as consequence: resolution of the earlier narrative conflicts. The central narratives—the cycles of Israel's sinning and Yahweh's forgiveness—have been generated by Israel's repeatedly forsaking Yahweh for other gods, for Baalim (2.11-23), due to the influence of the non-Yahwists in whose midst she lives. After the last of the judges, the Israelites intensify their evil practices. They are so far from Yahweh that they build idols to him and believe that they— and the idols—are Yahwist. They slaughter a peaceful town and build a temple to Yahweh, complete with forbidden idols—made of silver stolen twice over. Finally, they maintain the tribal number by trickery, by abduction, and by rape. The resolution depicts the consequence of the main narratives of the book of Judges as anti-Yahwism in the name of Yahweh.

The major judge paradigm, introduced in the expository narrative of Othniel, functions as a pattern for the main narrative sequence of the book. After the central and critical narrative of Abimelech, a secondary paradigm is introduced: that of the 'minor' judges.[11] The motifs of these two paradigms vary and shift; in later chapters the Jephthah narrative contains elements of both 'major' and 'minor' paradigms and the Samson narrative two (highly developed) 'major' and one 'minor' motif.[12] There is no closure to these paradigms; the structure is left unresolved. But these paradigms, modified and interwoven in the main narrative sequence, receive a 'coda' paradigm—'In those days. . .'—in the resolution. This last paradigm is less freely varied: the first and last statements are complete, effecting an inclusion of the resolution (and the entire book). The intervening statements are abbreviated.

In brief, the 'major' judge paradigm is fully stated in the Othniel narrative, in the exposition of the book. This paradigm commands the initial narratives of the main narrative succession, becoming intermingled with and infiltrated by the 'minor' judge paradigm toward the end of the sequence. The 'coda' or 'resolution' paradigm is restricted to the resolution of the book.

The three paradigms warrant comparison. The 'major' judge paradigm posits a Yahwist ideal for the occupation of the promised land. The 'minor' judge paradigm states bare, implicitly negative facts about a judge figure. The 'resolution' paradigm is pessimistic, and a full statement of this paradigm concludes the book.

II

In Genesis 49, Jacob/Israel blesses his sons as founders of the twelve tribes of a great people. The tribes are a multifaceted symbol of the people—unified in the name of the *father*, subdivided and differentiated in the names of the *sons*—evolved in the interim generations, but both significations—'Israel' (or 'tribes of Israel') and 'sons of Israel'—retain their currency. In the interim generations, the sons evolved into that people. The book of Judges first introduces the 'people of Israel' (1.1), which term shortly becomes interchangeable with 'Israel' (2.10) and the names of the separate tribes, each symbolized by the name of it eponymous ancestor (1.16-36). In the exposition, the people, the tribes, are presented in narrated or partially dramatized episodes which individualize the tribal occupation of the promised land, but not all of the original twelve tribes are specifically named. On the other hand, the exposition shows the 'house of Joseph' had proliferated into the 'tribes' of Manasseh and Ephraim. The original tribal designations have evolved, but 'Israel' remains intact, as attested by Yahweh's messenger-speech to his nation: 'And it happened, when the angel of Yahweh spoke these words to all the sons of Israel . . . ' (2.4). The ensuing shifting between individual and aggregate names is considered intentional; the action of any particular narrative protagonist functions literally and as a complex symbol—the protagonist symbolizes both the particular tribe and the people as a whole.[13] Thus Israel can be recognized as the protagonist of the book, symbolized by the individual protagonists.

The main narrative of Judges recapitulates, in expanded and dramatic form, the involvement of the individual tribes. Even Issachar and Gad, neglected in the expository summary, are given judges to represent them. Burney's suggestion that the minor judges were introduced in order 'to raise the number of the Judges to *twelve*, and, so far as possible, to make them representative of the twelve tribes of Israel' supports the view that the people of Israel are the protagonist. In order to stay within twelve, Burney eliminates Shamgar as judge, although 'he too delivered Israel' (3.31) (1970:290).

Recognition of the expository structure automatically removes the story of Othniel from the central text, and the central section of the book is shown to be concerned only with judges who are *not* obedient to the covenant and Yahweh. Furthermore, both Joshua and Othniel belong to the tribe of Judah, which reinforces the division of the tribes and the structure of the book according to separateness/

cohabitation (or Yahwist obedience/disobedience).

Leader-Judge	Tribe
Exposition	
Joshua	Judah
Othniel	Judah
Main Narrative	
Ehud	Benjamin
Shamgar	--
Deborah/Barak/	Issachar/Napthali
Gideon	Manasseh
Abimelech	--
Tola	Issachar
Jair	Manasseh
Jephthah	Gad
Ibsan	Asher?
Elon	Zebulun
Abdon	Ephraim
Samson	Dan

Including the protagonists of the post-judge narratives, the macro-structure of the book emerges:

Resolution	
Micah	Levi
(Jonathan)	Dan
	Levi
	Benjamin

The main narrative section names twelve judges, but the complete book names twelve different tribes, Ephraim and Manasseh replacing Simeon and Reuben. Benjamin, the first tribe to the characterized in the main narrative , is also the last of the book, and the 'sons of Israel' (21.24) culminate the sequence begun by 'the sons of Israel' (1.1).

This cursory delineation of the composition of Judges suggests it is a traditionally structured narrative, with exposition, main narrative and resolution. Its other patterns of organization are integrated within this traditional framework.

III

All narrative develops around a protagonist. I propose the protagonist of the book of Judges is the people—the potential nation—of Israel, each judge symbolizing an aspect of Israel, a weakness, a particular quality which leads to the narrative consequences of that episode and contributes to the resolution of the book. James Martin notes that the book extends the image of local battles to include all of Israel, which could not have been *politically* unified (1975:6-7); I, instead, submit a *spiritual* entity had evolved in the desert. George E. Mendenhall finds that 'early Israel until the establishment of the Monarchy actually constituted the sovereignity of Yahweh as the functional system that enabled [Israel] to exist at all as a distinct social group' (1973:1).[14] In this frame, internal divisive pressures were surmounted by conflict with enemies and especially by faith in Yahweh. The text supports the relevance of local events to the people as a whole: the judges are identified as national rather than tribal leaders. On this basis, each of the judges may be seen as a symbol of Israel; furthermore, each serves to reveal a new aspect of the people's relationship to Yahweh.[15] I suggest each judge is a chosen protagonist, whether chosen by Yahweh or by man; and that Israel, the chosen people, is protagonist. So long as a judge represents Yahweh and is obedient to Yahweh, there is no conflict. But when this link fails, when human perception elevates power over ethic, conflict ensues.

> The conflict between ancient Israel and the non-Israelite popula-
> tion . . . was a conflict with an old political regime or system of
> regimes which were rightly dying out all over the civilized world
> because they valued power more than ethic, and valued property
> and wealth more than persons (Mendenhall, 1973:225).

When Israel devalues ethic and elevates man's judgment above Yahweh's, Yahweh causes Israel to suffer. With this in mind, I propose that the antagonist to the political, non-ethical, mundane values of Israel—as characterized and symbolized by the behavior of her judges—is Yahweh or ethical Yahwist values. ('Protagonist' and 'antagonist' describe the conflicting parties; no value is attached to the terms.) When protagonist and antagonist are in harmony, there is a 'wedding' of values and behavior, and Israel is a 'bride' to Yahweh.

Obedience, allegiance, love: these are the essence of biblical faith. The opening verse of the book of Judges pictures the sons of Israel in a desirable relationship to Yahweh: Israel asks and Yahweh answers. The avenue of communication is open; no idolatry of foreign gods intervenes. Although the second verse implies the potential of rift, Yahweh is with Israel and brings victory to his people. The reader

can perceive unity at the opening of the book. The spiritual and the earthly act in harmony.
 Against this background of unity, the polarity which evolves and develops in the sequences of the main narrative is composite:

> *Judge of Israel as chosen agent of Yahweh*:
>
> A: Covenant
>   Law
>   Yahwist practices
>
> *Judge of Israel as individualist/opportunist leader*:
>
> B: Baalim/idols
>   Plunder
>   Anti-Yahwist practices

This basic conflict is dramatized in each of the judge stories (major and minor), each narrative simultaneously highlighting one aspect of the polarity and increasing the distance between the poles: Israel and Yahweh.[16] In each narrative, the initial conflict tends *not* to be resolved by integration of the conflicting forces. With few (but significant) exceptions, the development of each major judge narrative leads to a decline of the Yahwist antipode—even during the judge's lifetime. Typically, after becoming a leader of the people and eliminating the source of oppression, the judge leads the people away from Yahweh. Even though he has lost touch with Yahweh and led the people away from Yahwist practices, the judge succeeds in integrating the people and maintaining peace (usually for forty years) so that the human-oriented, social aspect of the judgeship gains ascendance. Yahweh and the sons of Israel become isolated from each other within the narration, and the narratives of the individual judges generally fail to resolve the initial opposition. The human-social element remains dominant at the conclusion of each narrative, but only until the judge dies, anti-Yahwist practices intensify, and the cycle resumes.
 There is integration *after* each of the judge narratives, after the death of the judge. This integration is achieved not by a coming together in harmony of the social and spiritual conditions, but by a 'falling' of the social to the level of the spiritual: collapse. In terms of irony, Israel is 'victim' of its own ignorance and Yahweh's knowledge. There is no movement toward Yahweh until the people have been oppressed by Yahweh through the foreign nations. When all else fails, Israel turns to her god. The 'cycle' of the narratives, then, presents

opposition between worldly power and ethical Yahwism. In the first narratives of the judges (Othniel, Ehud, Deborah), the separation from Yahweh originates among the people—'they did evil'. With Gideon, the turn from Yahweh issues from the judge himself, and the people continue their earlier pattern. Instead of teaching the people, the judge 'learns' from them. Finally, with the last judge, Yahwism has become empty covenant and empty vow, meaningless to Israel.

The separation motif also shapes a larger sphere. The unified tribes of the opening chapter, under Yahweh and led by Joshua, splinter into tribes and clans and individuals, separated from Yahweh and, through internecine wars, from each other. As the refrain of the resolution makes clear, 'everyone did as he saw fit in his own eyes'. The cumulative narrative cycles describe a descent, a 'widening gyre', the sequence dramatizing ever more extreme sins against Yahwist ethics and the separation between Yahweh and his people becoming ever greater.

IV

Despite Wayne Booth's admonition that 'The critic who asks us to ironize our straight readings may seem to be corrupting a beloved object and repudiating our very souls'; and his warning that 'If I am wrong about irony, I am wrong at deeper levels than I like to have exposed' (1974:44), I submit the book of Judges may be perceived as a *tour de force* of irony, touching on every level from non-ironic to multi-layered irony, and that this ironic development is progressive. The opening chapters, the exposition, are basically non-ironic in *content*; however, these chapters establish an ironic structure of opposing perceptions. There are puns in the first brief dramatization (1.5-7),[17] but the ambiguity of word play is integrated into the story line; it neither generates action nor serves as a structural device within the miniature narrative, even if there is meaningful irony implicit in the juxtaposition of passages (1.4-7, 8-11, 12-15). Significantly, the paradigm narratives of Achsah and Othniel have no suggestion of irony, though the images of 'leader' and 'bride' are used for ironic purposes in subsequent narratives.

Irony—both of speaker and of situation—comes to the fore in the first post-expositional narrative, that of Ehud. The Deborah narrative ironically presents a woman judge who directs a male warrior to victory, and there are ironic elements in the Jael episode. But the irony of these chapters is expressed by *contrast* of the judge with another character; it is not invested in the *character* of the judge. In the subsequent chapters, the irony is intensified. From the Gideon narrative on, the irony is manifested in the persona of the judge. He may be a coward called to lead the people: one who, as he conquers his fear, loses his contact with the source of his power, Yahweh. He may be a bastard and a bandit, sincerely Yahwist, but one whose ignorance makes him sin against himself and Yahweh. He may be Yahweh's own conception, *in utero* dedicated as nazir, but one who does nothing better than submit to his passions, be they sexual or vengeful. These are ironic inversions of leaders, of judges.

Just as the exposition is practically without irony, the resolution is thick with it. The initial unity (non-ironic) of Yahweh and Israel under the leadership of Joshua is increasingly splintered under the influence of individualists, Yahwist in name only, until even Yahweh's words suggest irony in the last narrative (20.18, 23). The elements of separation multiply, ironic opposition having gained in intensity and complexity in the development of the book.

Biblical literature describes a society whose values are established, if not always heeded; and Yahweh repeatedly responds to the cries of the Israelites with compassion. The judges are individuals, but they also represent Everyman and Israel; the irony is 'specific' to that particular circumstance. However, because that situation is held to be symbolic, the reader is invited to judge and gain in perception. The irony does not become 'General', but the reader is importuned to generalize.[18]

These introductory comments attempt to suggest a framework of narrative form and irony, aspects basic to the structure of the book of Judges. The following chapters are organized according to narrative form: exposition, central narrative and resolution. Within this configuration, the individual narrative explications include discussion of irony which arises from the structure of the narrative. Each of the narrative units is followed by a short section directed specifically to occasions and patterns of irony.

Chapter 2

EXPOSITION

The Major Judge Paradigm

The situation at the opening of the book is critical. Joshua, who had taken over as leader of the people at the death of Moses, had only begun the conquest of the land; the 'promise' is still to be realized. The language and tripartite structure of the opening verse concisely depicts the situation of the Israelites: it establishes *first* the death of Joshua and *last* the need to attack the Canaanites. Between these statements of condition is the reaction of the Israelites—they 'inquired of Yahweh'. The structure of 1.1 is thus a paradigm of acceptable behavior for the people: submission to the will of Yahweh is central—between established fact (the death of Joshua) and recognized need (to attack the non-Yahwist dwellers in the land). In the second verse, Yahweh answers in the imperative ('Judah shall go up'), saying 'I gave the land into his power'.[1] Yahweh tells Israel (here Judah) specifically what to do, but Israel only partially heeds Yahweh's command: Judah immediately establishes a battle pact with his brother Simeon. Thus, from the outset, Israel exerts self-determination, evidencing automatic trust in *human* perception. These verses may be regarded as introducing the ironic configuration of the book—the implicit difference in perception between Yahweh and Israel and Israel's insistence on following human perception.[2]

Because of the brothers' pact, there is a disparity between what Yahweh has done and what men wish to do. Yahweh has, in his frame of time-reference (his past), already determined the human future: he has given the land to Judah. The distinction is upheld: consistently, only Judah's name is mentioned when land (or cities) are taken: Jerusalem (1.18), the wilderness of Judah (1.16), Gaza, Ashkelon, Ekron (1.18), and the hill country (1.19). Even though Simeon has joined him, specifically '*Judah* went up and the Lord gave the Canaanites and the Perizzites into their power' (1.3). Judah may

conquer peoples or lands; however, Judah *and* Simeon may conquer
only peoples together.[3]

Judah Conquers:

People		*Land*	
1.4, 5	Canaanite and Perizzite	1.8	Jerusalem
1.4	men at Bezek	1.18	Gaza and territory
1.4, 5	Bezek-Adoni		Ashkelon and territory
1.9	Canaanites of hill-country		Ekron and territory
	of Negev	1.19	hill country
	of foothills		
1.10	Canaanites of Hebron		
1.10	Sheshai, Ahiman, Talmai		
1.11	Dwellers of Debir		

Judah and Simeon Conquer:

1.17	Canaanites of Zephath

Although the text clearly states that 'Simeon went with him' (Judah)
(1.31), it also pointedly does not mention Simeon in any of the battles
but one, a battle with the Canaanites (a people) living in Zephath
(1.17). And although this city is taken, the narration describes the
destruction of the city as consequent upon the attack upon the
people. This is not the case when Judah fights alone: Judah 'took'
Jerusalem and Gaza (1.8,18) and 'possessed' the hill country (1.19).
The distinction between Yahweh's will (deed) and man's intentions is
emphasized in 1.19: 'Yahweh was with Judah' when he took
possession of the hill country. Judah and Simeon 'destroyed' Zephath
but did not 'take' the city. The men of Judah 'took' the cities and the
land; the men of Simeon and Judah only 'destroyed' the city. Yahweh
did not give the land to the consortium, and they do not 'take' the
city.

The human freedom of self-determination is not punished, even
though it does not adhere to Yahweh's will; however, no *anti*-Yahwist
practice is involved. Men may make pacts among themselves, the
text allows, but what Yahweh has done man cannot modify. The land
goes to Judah, not to Simeon. (The tribe of Simeon seems to have
been small and was absorbed by Judah.) On the other hand, this
minor disparity is not punished. This is the first of many instances of
Yahweh's tolerance with regard to man's insistence on self-determination, so long as no anti-Yahwist practice is involved.

The success of the first battle is measured by the use of a 'round number' of epic proportions: ten thousand men are struck. This battle leads to the first of a series of pre-judge episodes, the curious tale of Adoni-bezek at Bezek. Burney (1970:5) suggests that 'Adoni-bezek' ('God of pebble') may be an intentional perversion of 'Adoni-sedek' (possibly 'the God is righteous') to make fun of the idol as helpless, merely dumb stone.[4] The mutilation of Adoni-bezek was possibly intended to degrade the captive, reducing him to the level of a dog and a certain dog's death. Implicit in Adoni-bezek's interpretation of his fate is a note of irony: as he had done to others, so has his God requited him.[5] Concerned with righteousness, the narrative illustrates the anticipated recompense of the god among the non-Israelite peoples, among idol-worshippers: measure for measure, *quid pro quo*. This contrasts with the image of Israel as a people united under a saving (not vengeful) God to whom they turn for guidance, a people on the threshold of realizing its promise as described in 1.1-2.

With Adoni-Bezek dead, the men of Judah attack Jerusalem, destroying everything non-Yahwist. After a sequence of successful excursions against the Canaanites, Judah goes against Debir (Sepher), and the first narrative emerges.[6] Caleb promises his daughter Achsah to the man who strikes and captures the city. One Othniel, a relative, fulfills the conditions, and, subsuming the actual marriage, the narrative continues: Achsah 'incites him to ask from her father a field'. The bride provokes her husband to ask her father for land.

This reading supports rather than deviates from the Masoretic text ('And it happened as *she* came and *she* incited *him* to ask from her father. . .') as do the Septuagint and Vulgate 'corrections' of the text: 'and she came and *he* persuaded *her* to ask', justified so that 'the request does not come from Achsah' (Burney, 1970: 13) or 'to preserve the image of the first savior judge' (Boling, 1975: 57).

The narrative epitomizes the biblical style Erich Auerbach has made us aware of: the undefined but heavily present background and suggested depths of meaning. The entire sequence of the bride's wish, her husband's reaction, the request for land, and the granting of it is compressed into the wish, moving without transition—in the same verse—to the next event, so that Achsah's arrival before her father and even her alighting from her donkey are suppressed and only her prostration before Caleb is conveyed by the verb *tiṣnach*, 'dropped down'. The Hebrew is so concentrated that it almost sounds like Achash falls off her donkey before her father. That she gets down from her donkey is unimportant; what matters is that she shows her father utmost respect, 'dropping down' before him. Caleb, like most fathers, is not used to having his daughter prostrate herself before him and is apparently puzzled by her behavior: he asks, 'What is the matter with you?'[7] Achsah asks for a blessing and, acknowledging that Caleb had given land in the Negev ('southern'), she asks for a spring of water; and 'Caleb gave to her the upper spring(s) and the lower spring(s)'. Caleb is depicted in a position of authority and abundance: he offers his daughter to the hero who can prove his worth. The daughter is not only a reward; she is an individual, named and capable of initiating and completing actions. It is she who persuades her husband to ask for land, and she asks for the wells herself.[8] Achsah prods—even provokes—her husband to ask for a field—a place to plant his seed—and the young bride dramatically, but not seductively, asks for a source of water to make sure the seeds will grow. Woman is presented as exercising power in specific ways: not seducing but provoking, asking in order to gain her desire. That desire is not merely sensual-sexual, but reproductive; not of the moment, but of time, generation. The implications extend the significance of Achsah's request for a 'blessing' from a gift to something more. And Achsah emerges as an image of ideal Yahwist womanhood.

This short passage is taken practically word for word from Josh. 15.13-19; the variations from that text, all in 1.15, make clear who is addressed and name the donor of the gift. 'And she said *to him*, Give me a blessing since the land of the Negev you have given me . . . and *Caleb* gave'.[9] These alterations all call attention to the naming of Caleb as the donor. Caleb is in the fortunate position to give generously—the upper spring(s) and the lower. The promised bride, land and water are all there just for the fulfilling of the conditions set forth by Caleb, who has the power and authority to prescribe terms. The narrative of Caleb, Othniel and Achsah suggests a standard or example of the potential of Israel to ask for land and receive it, and to be fruitful, if only Israel fulfill the condition of her covenant with Yahweh. Here is perhaps the first biblical suggestion of Israel as bride, a recurrent metaphor in the Bible. The bride is a reward to the hero who proves his worth, she leads to honorable occupation of the land, and she asks for life-giving water.[10]

The implications of this episode only become apparent when it is put into juxtaposition with that of Adoni-bezek. The first narrative of battle and conquest contrasts the situation of the people of Israel with that of the Canaanites, especially with regard to the relationships between each people and its god; the second, a personal narrative, shows how well the Israelites can fare, what promise they have. Reading these two dramatized passages in juxtaposition, reveals two kinds of compensation: that for a follower of stone idols and that for followers of Yahweh. The former is disfigured and brought to Jerusalem to die; the latter is given land and water. The structure of these verses is striking:

1.4-7   Judah: conquers Adoni-bezek, idol-worshipper
1.8-11 Judah: conquest of land and peoples
1.12-15 Judah: Caleb gives Achsah as reward to Othniel

These three passages, each four verses in length, narrate tales of conquest and reward by the tribe of Judah, as foretold by Yahweh. The sequence enacts a three-part shift of focus: from a foreign leader (1.4-7), via foreign cities, areas, peoples, even leaders, none individualized (1.8-11), to individual Israelites (Caleb, Othniel and Achsah) (1.12-15). Contrast of the first and third passages ironically opposes idol-worship and Yahweh-worship, death and marriage; the intervening passage presents a Yahwist vision of the occupation of the land through conquest and destruction of the non-Yahwist culture. The capture of Jerusalem—not substantiated by Joshua, the facts of history, or even Judges 19—emphasizes the powerlessness of those who worship idols. The coherence of this structure is augmented by the harsh fate of the idol-worshippers (first and second passages), which is in contrast to the good fortune of the Yahwists (third passage). There is irony in Judah's conquest of the land although he invited his brother Simeon to join him, there is irony in the Adoni-bezek tale and ironic opposition between the first and third passages, but there is no irony in the bride-narrative. Furthermore, this last narrative of the passage is 'comic' in structure, concluding in integration.

With the close of this twelve-verse unit (1.4-15), the exposition introduces a second level of deviation from prescribed Yahwist behavior, and thereby a further turn from the good. Judah did not strictly follow Yahweh's command when he invited his brother Simeon to join him in battle. This was merely a first step in self-assertion. The contrast between 1.4-15 and the balance of the exposition suggest the essential conflict of Judges: occupation of the land *under* the covenant or *outside* it according to human determination. These two aspects—covenant-oriented versus human-oriented occupation of the land, which increasingly separate during the course of the book—are introduced early in the exposition, anticipating the course of the main narratives. With 1.16, the occupation of the land takes a new turn: instead of conquering the inhabitants, the men of Judah and their Kenite followers settle among the people (the Amalekites). In the following two verses, Judah is successful in his conquests and Yahweh is with him; but in verse 1.19 Judah is unable—for technological reasons—to dispossess the inhabitants of the valley, so the people remain. In 1.21, the inhabitants remain in Jerusalem, living with the children of Benjamin. After Judah, the Benjaminites live with the Jebusites in Jerusalem. Thus Judah first, and then the other tribes, is shown not overthrowing the local peoples (and their idolatry).

The tribe of Joseph is more successful, conquering Bethel, formerly named Luz. The germ of the strategy used to overcome Luz indicates that the Israelites, although invaders and conquerors, are capable of dealing kindly with those foreigners who have been helpful. There is even the suggestion that no real harm has been done since the man who is let go, with his family, builds another city in the land of the Hittites, which he names Luz. In other words, the city is rebuilt elsewhere, outside the promised lands.[11] Among the tribes named, only Joseph remains true to the covenant, destroying Luz but sparing the man who helped them in their conquest.

With 1.27, the so-called 'negative account of the conquest' is in full swing, and a new, more serious compromise is introduced: the children of Manassah do not drive out the inhabitants of the villages they attack; but 'when Israel grew strong', instead of purging the Canaanites, it *enslaves* them. The implication is that Israel could drive out the inhabitants at first, certainly when it is strong enough to enslave them. That it does not leads to its own 'enslavement'—in the spiritual sense, suggested here and later reinforced by Israel's worship of the Canaanite gods.

The following verses of ch. 1 tell of the remaining tribes of Israel, none of which drives out the native peoples from the various regions, but either lives among them or subjects them to forced labor. Even the 'house of Joseph' uses its strength to effect slavery (1.35).[12] Chapter 1 concludes this account of non-conquest with reference to the tribe least successful in realizing its potential in the promised land: the Danites. The Amorites keep the Danites in the hills, out of the cities; nevertheless, even the Amorites are eventually enslaved, thus implying eventual Danite 'enslavement'.

The dissemination of non-Yahwist practices among the Israelites is an irregular but clearly progressive sequence, indicated below by a scale of 'levels'. The course of backsliding is identified both with specific tribal names and with Israel as collective of the tribes (1.28):

Verse	Scale	Tribe
1.1-2	Level 0: obedient	Judah
1.3	Level 1: disobedient	Judah, Simeon
1.16	Level 2: live among people	Judah, Kenites
1.21	Level 2: live among Jebusites	Benjamin
1.25	Level 0: Luz conquered, destroyed	Joseph
1.27-8	Level 2: did not force people out	
	3: forced labor	Manasseh
1.29	Level 2: live among Canaanites	Ephraim
1.30	Level 2: live among Canaanites	
	3: forced labor	Zebulun
1.31	Level 2: live among Canaanites	Asher
1.33	Level 2: live among Canaanites	
	forced labor	Napthali
1.35	Level 3: forced labor	Danites (Joseph)

The focus in these verses is on the individual tribes; the perspective depicts the actions of the Israelites from within the community. The progression is continued in the remaining text of the exposition (to 3.11), but with a different thrust: all-Israel is shown in relationship to individual non-Israelites; Israel is seen as a community, from the outside. With the second chapter, anti-Yahwism, Level X, is introduced:

Verse	Scale	Tribe
2.11-13	Level X: serve Baals,	
	forsake Yahweh	Israelites
3.5-6	Level 2: live among Canaanites,	
	Hittites, Amorites,	
	Perizzaites, Hivites	
	Jebusites	
	Level 4: give children in marriage	
	Level X: serve their gods	Israelites[13]

Chapter 1 begins with a prophecy of fulfillment: Yahweh's promise and Israel's *obedience* to Yahweh, that is, conforming to the moral order of the covenantal world. Irregularly but consistently, the chapter intensifies the scale of non-covenantal, non-Yahwist behavior.

In its parts and its entirety, ch. 1 provides a background for the main narrative: a promise of obedience and the first stages of deviance—the behavior which will dominate the rest of the book, at first primarily in the intervals between judges but finally permeating the narrative unit. As in the resolution of the book, the Danites are the focus of the last verse of this expositional unit. The opposing perspectives of ch. 1 are potential for irony, and through the sequence of main narratives the reader is gradually invited to share Yahweh's view, to 'look down' on humanity's presumptive ignorance.

But the exposition of the book does not end with ch. 1. It is amplified by a second passage of exposition (2.1–3.11), marked by a second beginning with Joshua (2.6-11). The second expositional unit introduces a flashback to the opening of the book: with 2.6, the text returns chronologically to the beginning of the book, to the same characters and events as 1.1. In ch. 2, Israel's behavior becomes notably more *anti*-Yahwist, and the tribes individualized in ch. 1 are fused as 'sons of Israel' or 'Israel'. This parallel structure supports the equivalent identity of separate tribes with the communal name. If ch. 1 implicitly offers the ironist's view of the circumstances and events, ch. 2 is explicit: it states directly, in a first-person statement, Yahweh's evaluation of the occupation thus far.

The initial verse of ch. 2 moves the sanctuary, symbolized by Yahweh, from that associated with Joshua at Gilgal to a new site, Bethel/Bochim.[14] (This sanctuary-moving in the exposition is ironically balanced by that in the resolution, from Micah's house to the city of Dan.) Gilgal was the headquarters of Joshua and the Israelites during the invasion of the hill country and the initial settlement in the land. The transfer of the Ark is symbolic of movement away from the values of Joshua's generation; it further symbolizes the movement of the people into the land of Canaan. Whereas Gilgal is presumed to be on the shore of the Jordan, Bethel is in the heart of the land.

Yahweh's reprimand recalls the promise of obedience associated with the figures of Moses and Joshua, but here the analogy emphasizes the negligence of the following generations, especially the present one. Unexpectedly, the distribution of each tribe to its inheritance is passed over in one verse (2.6). Not the occupation of the land but the failure of the people to remain true to their God is the theme of this section—and of the book. Before they lived among the local inhabitants, the people appealed to Yahweh directly and he answered in his own person (1.2). In this passage, they no longer appeal and Yahweh addresses them through his messenger, though referring to Yahweh's deed in the first person (2.1). This device simultaneously indicates immediacy and distance, an interim stage between Yahweh's direct speech and strictly messenger-speech. Yahweh first reviews the conditions of his covenant with Israel, concluding with the restriction against making a covenant with the inhabitants and the command to break down their altars. In a touching if rhetorical question, Yahweh asks the people 'What (is) this you have done?'

Once more Yahweh speaks in the past tense of his actions when referring to the future of the Israelites (2.3), 'and also I have said' (*weĝam 'amar'tî*). This phrase leads into a three-part sentence that can be taken as a warning of the consequences of further complicity with the idolators. In the first clause, Yahweh withdraws from helping to clear the land ('I shall not drive them out before you'); in the next two he uses imagery of the people being hindered, even trapped. The exact translation of *ṣiddîm* is unresolved, but possible interpretations and emendations all stress painful hindrance: 'as thorns in your sides', 'as a scourge on your sides', 'as adversaries to you'. The last clause of the verse clearly states that their 'gods shall become a snare to you'. In one sense, because the Israelites have not driven the other nations out, they themselves will be like animals. Yahweh's declaration brings about the repentance of the sons of Israel, who weep, name the place 'Weepers', and sacrifice to Yahweh, thus fore-shadowing the subsequent cycles of sin and repentance.

The period of Joshua has served as an image of a desirable relationship between Yahweh and the Israelites in the preceding chapter, and this chapter begins with a flashback to the period of Joshua, drawing directly from that book. The differences between Josh. 24.28-31 and Judg. 2.6-10 are small but significant. The most obvious is a change in sequence:

Joshua 24.28 Joshua sent	*Judges* 2.6 Joshua sent
29 Joshua died	7 People served
30 Joshua buried	8 Joshua died
31 Israel served	9 Joshua buried.

By ending with the death of Joshua and the generation that followed, the Judges version of this passage re-focuses the conclusion of the tale of Joshua to serve as an introduction to the sequence of judges. Josh. 24.28 corresponds exactly with Judg. 2.6 except that 'the people' becomes 'the sons of Israel', reinforcing the idea of the unity of the people despite the lack of land-based national unity.[15] More significant is the substitution of 'saw' for 'knew': retrospectively, the knowledge of the generation of Joshua is considered not to have been merely intellectual ('knew'); it was first-hand experience ('saw'). The Judges text also emphasizes the work of Yahweh which was seen in the time of Joshua by describing it as 'great', again a departure from the original text.[16] In Judg. 2.10, the following generation does not even know Yahweh or his works. The distinction between 'saw' and 'knew' becomes more pointed at this point, where Yahweh is not 'known', and in Judg. 3.1-2, which drums on the verb 'know'. Biblical narrative style, usually remarkably condensed, repeats 'not know', 'might know' to emphasize the gap which had developed between this generation and that of Joshua, which 'saw'. Unseen, unknown, the 'works' of Yahweh are unmodified in this verse.

Verse 10 develops from the Joshua passage to express what is implicit in v. 7: the generation that has no contact with Yahweh has no awareness of him; it forsakes its God and adopts others, those of the inhabitants, bowing to these gods, which angers Yahweh. The key words are repeated in summary in v. 13: 'forsook Yahweh . . . served *Baalim*'; the effect is intensified by the addition of female goddesses, *Ashtoroth*. These Canaanite deities of fertility were associated with temple prostitutes of both sexes, decidedly contrary to the precepts of Yahweh as established in the Pentateuch. The reference to female goddesses also serves to foreshadow the following verses, which allude to *Ashtoroth* in Israel's 'prostitution' after other gods.

Chapter 2, a re-play of the same time-span as ch. 1, introduces a shift in point of view to that of Yahweh; and verses 11-19 focus on a concise, divine view of the cyclical pattern. Verse 17 ushers in the important theme of the Israelites literally 'pursuing other gods like a prostitute', or 'whoring after other gods', an expression which embodies two complementary ideas. Practice of cultic prostitution is in a real sense prostitution, and Israel has already been represented as a bride (1.12-15).[17] When she turns from worship of Yahweh to worship of other gods, Israel becomes a prostitute.

The juxtaposition of human and divine actions in these two passages (2.11-13 and 2.14-19) exposes limited human potential and intensifies the force of divine action. The people 'did evil', 'served', 'went after', 'bowed themselves', and 'angered Yahweh'. The verbs in

Yahweh's passage are stronger ('burned', 'plundered', 'sold', 'distressed') than those of the people, and the attitude of his language is more complex. Not only does Yahweh have various tactics of punishment, but he also has compassion: he shows pity when the people suffer under oppression.

Divine and human points of view may be seen as juxtaposed in another set of verses: 2.20-24 and 3.1-3. In the earlier passage, the narrator reports direct speech by Yahweh, wherein Yahweh imputes his punishment (religious probation) of the Israelites to their transgressing their covenant with Yahweh. In the second passage, the narrator interprets Yahweh's intent. Not even an indirect quotation, it is a human vision of divine purpose: to teach the younger generation the experience of war (practical training). True, the tactical justification is followed by an ethical one—'to test the Israelites to see if they would obey the commands Yahweh had given to their fathers' (3.4). Nevertheless, the weight of the charge is on military readiness. Yahweh's testing—what he specifically stipulates as spiritual probation—is understood as combat training.

In the former passage, Yahweh punishes the people by not expelling that which is within; in the latter, his punishment allows them to be attacked by that which is external: the surrounding nations (with the exception of the Canaanites), in accordance with 2.11-19. Once again, the disparity between the points of view is ironically perceived and the reader may share the ironist's knowledge.

Verse 3.5 harks back to the point of view of 2.20-23, the races within Canaan. The Israelites are left to make their own way, spiritually and territorially. They must get rid of their enemies within and without. Ultimately, as 3.4 makes clear, the earthly conquest is part of the spiritual. The nations which are to test Israel by teaching war are simultaneously testing to see if Israel will observe Yahweh's commandments.

Through the gap created by the flashback to the book of Joshua, Othniel is recalled, this time specifically in the role of a judge blessed with the spirit of Yahweh. In this second narration of Othniel's story, what was an allegory of Yahweh's ideal relationship to his people (1.12-15) is retold, this time characterizing Othniel as a leader of the Israelites and embodying a pattern which will serve as paradigm for the judge narratives to follow. Comparison of the two Othniel narratives reveals that the first (1.12-14) quickly shifts focus to

Othniel's bride, Achsah, establishing an image of Israel as bride to Yahweh and a feminine criterion as foil for female characters in the ensuing narratives. In the second narrative (3.7-11), Othniel is presented as a model judge-leader, a standard for the judges that follow. These narratives defining feminine and masculine exemplars of ethical Yahwist behavior are the first and last narrative units of the exposition.

The 'pattern' elements in this passage have often been compressed into three or four designations.[18] It is, nevertheless, valuable to review the individual components. In a condition of peace, Israel *does wrong* in the eyes of Yahweh, which *angers* him. Yahweh *subjects* the people to a foreign power and Israel *cries* to her God. Yahweh then *raises up* a judge, and a notable *personal detail* about that individual is given—specifically, a detail which would appear to make that individual an unlikely choice to be a judge of the people.[19] The *spirit of Yahweh* comes upon the judge, he takes action to *deliver* the people, the land has *rest* (often forty years, a 'round number'), and the *judge dies*. With the death of the judge, the cycle begins again. This sequence is paradigmatic for the successive narratives of the 'major' judges, and any deviation from the pattern therefore suggests significance.

In the story of Othniel, the pattern is complete. In addition, nonparadigmatic details provide other references for later narratives. One such detail is that Othniel is the son of a younger brother. In a society strongly influenced by primogeniture, the likelihood that the offspring of a younger (literally 'smaller' with implications of 'unimportant') brother will become the leader of the elder's descendants warrants attention. Sternberg notes that 'the "unnatural" rise of the younger above the elder brother throughout Genesis... [is] rendered increasingly providential...' (1985:269). In Judges, the 'younger brother' motif works in two directions: it 'exposes' the pattern of younger brothers taking over in the sequence of Judges narratives and it reaffirms the providential.

The most particularized element of this narrative is the word play in the name of the oppressor, '*kûšan-riš'ātayim*'.[20] We encountered such word play as a means of belittling the enemy in the name of Adoni-Bezek in 1.15. Despite these details, the action of Othniel's story is only summarized; the story provides a narrated link between Joshua and the dramatized series of judges, and in so doing, establishes the type pattern for the main narratives of the book.

To recapitulate, the exposition opens in harmony. The two units of exposition reveal two perceptions of the occupation: the human perception of the conquest, and that of Yahweh. In two passages which cover the same time period, the exposition moves from the initial condition under Yahweh (1.1-2) to the human perception of the events (1.3-36), to the divine perception of the same events (2.1-3.11): from initial spiritual and earthly fortune, to human weaknesses and exposure of moral apostasy—vivified previews of the narrative to ensue. The ideal is left behind, but the divergence of human and divine perceptions in the exposition alerts the reader to the ironic opposition of two 'voices' of the book: Yahweh's knowing voice and humanity's ignorant one.

Irony
Minor instances of irony, such as that of Adoni-Bezek, may be found in the exposition, but irony is not its primary focus. The exposition establishes a basis for later irony by creating a clear distinction between two visions of Israelite occupation of the promised land: that of the people and that of Yahweh.

The sons of Israel and Yahweh—protagonist and antagonist—are in harmony in the first verse and so the book begins in integration, without irony. The focus of the remainder of the first chapter is on occupation of the land by the various tribes, as indicated by the many verbs of conquest: 'attacked', 'took', 'advanced', 'defeated', 'captured', 'destroyed', 'possessed', 'drove out', 'dislodged', and 'forced labor'. Through flash-back, the second chapter re-directs the focus from the Israelites to Yahweh. Yahweh's messenger reviews the events leading up to the covenant with the sons of Israel and remarks on three particularly relevant aspects: 'I will never break my covenant with you' (2.1), 'you shall not make a covenant with the people of this land', and 'you shall break down their altars' (2.2).

The exposition secures, through the opposition of perspectives, an opposition of divine and human wills. Yahweh is 'with' the judges he raises up, as stated clearly in 2.18, and Yahweh protects the people as long as this leader lives. A deliverer-judge may receive Yahweh's spirit, his charisma; however, the spirit of Yahweh is not clearly given to all the judges, and it is not equally recognized by all the individuals so graced. The will (word) of Yahweh will come to pass, but human nature distinctively shapes the expression of that will. This 'play' between divine will and human self-determination shapes the action—and the irony—of the book of Judges.

The disparity between the Israelite (human) and Yahwist (divine) perceptions shows the people to be narrowly fixed on occupation of the land at whatever cost; in contrast, Yahweh is concerned with the integrity of the covenant. Accordingly, the human perception dwells at great length on details of occupation, while in Yahweh's perception the occupation is passed over in one verse (2.6) and emphasis is given to the change in the relationship between Yahweh and his people during the generations that followed Joshua. The human and divine perceptions are subtly reinforced. The verbs which dominate this chapter are those of the 'evil' done by the people: 'did evil', 'served the Baals', 'forsook the Lord', 'whored after' and 'worshipped other gods', 'provoked the Lord to anger'; or those of Yahweh's reaction: 'handed them over to marauders who plundered them', 'sold them to their enemies', 'distressed them'. The Yahwist vision concludes with a two-fold rationale of Yahweh's punishment of Israel—the Yahwist and the Israelite: 'to test Israel's adherence to the covenant' (2.22, 3.4) and 'to teach warfare to the inexperienced descendants' (3.1-2). Irony is concentrated on the interpretation of 'to test', to which Yahweh and Israel attach differing perspectives.

The two points of view established in the exposition create an ironic potential which becomes increasingly significant in the course of the book and which constitutes a major structural device of the following narratives.

Chapter 3

THE FIRST JUDGES

Ehud

The story of Ehud (3.12-30) is the first dramatized narrative complete with the specific action by which Israel is restored to righteous prosperity under a Yahweh-elected judge. Comparing this narrative to the paradigm elements of the Othniel narrative, we find that three of the elements are missing: Yahweh does not 'raise up' but simply 'gives' Ehud to Israel as deliverer; the spirit of Yahweh does not come upon Ehud,[1] and though Ehud, like Othniel, is a 'deliverer', a *môšî'a*, he does not 'judge' *šāfaṭ (wayišpaṭ)* as Othniel does (3.10). When Ehud is 'given' as a deliverer, he is identified first as a Benjaminite—literally, 'son of the right hand'—which calls attention to the significance of the right hand for wielding power,[2] and then as a left-handed man. That Ehud is an unlikely choice is immediately suggested: he is not a judge, and he is 'bound' or 'impeded' in his right hand. A left-handed warrior? More pointedly, a left-handed 'son of the right hand'? Multiple—and ambiguous—meanings present themeselves at the outset of this text.[3] Ehud is to deliver Israel single-handed, and left-handed. A further play on left-handedness is suggested in the final clause of 3.15: 'the sons of Israel sent a tribute/present *by his hand* to the king of Moab, Eglon'.

In this narrative, left-handedness seems to have connotations of being peculiar and unnatural that are upheld by Ehud's actions. When Ehud presents a gift, he gains Eglon's confidence; however, Ehud leaves and returns alone, apparently unprotected (but with a hidden weapon); and he says that he has a 'word' for Eglon (but he really has a 'thing' for him). Hebrew allows this pun because *dabar* means both 'word' and 'thing'. Deception is so prominent that Robert C. Culley uses the Ehud narrative to illustrate 'deception story' as a type (1976:5). Ehud goes so far as to use the name of his god (Elohim) deviously. He first tempts Eglon's curiosity by saying that he has a *secret* word (thing) for him, but after the attendants have been dismissed and they are alone, Ehud tells Eglon that he has a 'word (thing) *of Elohim*' for him, shifting modifiers of the already ambiguous *dabar*. Eglon is led to anticipate a divine revelation, a 'secret word/thing of Elohim', while Ehud actually has a deadly secret of human origin. Beside the obvious disparity, Ehud's substitution of 'Elohim' for 'secret' implies that the two words are correlative, which is only part of the truth. A secret may be good or bad, but god is good; unlike the willful witholding of a secret, god is unknowable. The divine name is used as a lure. Ehud's 'playing' with the name of god underscores that Yahweh has, indeed, been absent from the action. He has given Israel a deliverer, but the divine spirit has not come upon Ehud. In his actions, Ehud has valued ends over means; implicitly, Yahweh is not in accord. Yahweh withdraws his help in conquering the Moabites, but Ehud is a good leader and manages on his own. However, the deeds of humankind and god are kept separate. Here, as in the following narratives, Yahweh's spirit is never involved in duplicity, even to the advantage of Israel.

That Ehud's actions are successful but dishonorable is reinforced by a central passage: the immediate aftermath of the stabbing of Eglon.

3.22   And he *went out*   the *feces*
         wayāṣā'   *hapars*ᵉ*dōnāh*

3.23   And he *went out* Ehud the *portico* toward
         wayāṣa'   *Ehûd*   *hamisd*ᵉ*rōnāh*

Although the verses are not parallel, lacking sufficient noun pairs, the repetition of the verb in such different contexts, underscored by a cluster of consonance, assonance and word stress in the concluding word of each clause, does warrant attention. 'The feces' is the subject of its clause and requires no further notation, but 'the portico' requires some linguistic link of relationship. 'The portico' could be the object of a prepositional phrase, taking an inseparable preposition 'to' (*li*) prefixed to the noun. The prefix, of course, would destroy the echo of the previous line. Instead, the noun 'portico', has *āh* as a locative suffix to signifiy direction. But *both* nouns have the same ending, *āh*. The first noun, of 3.22, has *āh* as a feminine ending even though the root of 'feces' is masculine.[4] The echo of the two nouns seems to be intentional. This effect, taken together with the stress afforded by the repeated verb, suggests the reader might regard 'the feces' as parallel to 'Ehud the portico toward'. Both went out, one uncontrollably and the other in control. Ironic, the comparison is not honorable to Ehud.

The abundance of details about the stabbing and the king's resultant incontinence are a departure from the usually terse style of the Bible; they serve to colorfully depict the unworthiness of the king. Eglon's corpulence suggests uncontrolled appetites which allow him to be more curious than prudent when tempted by a 'secret word', and his final condition, made vivid by the hesitation of the servants, makes him an object of derision.[5] When Ehud has escaped, he summons the Israelites to battle, and once more he uses a divine name for his own purposes. This time Ehud invokes Yahweh:

> 3.28   And he ordered them, Follow me! For Yahweh gave your enemy, Moab, into your hand.

Ehud is clever in his use of the divine names. He uses 'Elohim' (roughly, 'god of gods') when he speaks to Eglon, but the insider's name, 'Yahweh', to his Israelite troops. Yahweh, however, does not bestow his spirit on Ehud and is silent.

The men do battle and take possession of the Jordan fords to Moab.[6] Without a king, the Moabites easily fall prey to the invading Israelites, who once more subdue a round number (again 10,000) of the enemy. The episode closes with a doubling (80) of the typical round number (40) for the years of rest in the land, probably to include those of Shamgar, a minor figure of one verse whose story continues the witty tone of Ehud's.

Shamgar

This mini-narrative does not participate in the major judge paradigm and though Shamgar evidences no anti-Yahwist action, the judgeships of Ehud and Shamgar are held to be merged. This is supported by the substitution of 'Ehud' for 'Shamgar' in the death reported in 4.1. Shamgar's narrative is notable only in his unusual method of delivery: he uses a 'goad' of an ox, *malmad*, which is formed on the causative stem of *lmd*, 'to learn': literally, 'instrument of instruction or learning'. In his one verse Shamgar 'teaches' the enemy a thing or two.

Despite Ehud's duplicity, at this stage of the book Israel's fortunes are not utterly low. Ehud has acted in a less-than honorable manner, but he has not demonstrated *anti*-Yahwist behavior. There seems to have been a continuance of leadership under Ehud–Shamgar, so that the people have eighty years without unrest. In this narrative section, immediately following the paradigmatic pattern of the Othniel narrative, the Yahweh–Israel relationship is ambiguous. Yahweh, silent throughout, is only involved when he gives Ehud to Israel as deliverer. The results of Ehud's actions may be advantageous to Israel, but the actions themselves are not ethically Yahwist: they are less than honorable.[7] Typically, when Israel's actions are counter to Yahweh's will, Yahweh withdraws into silence. Also typically, Yahweh provides impetus only when needed by his covenantal people; otherwise men and women act out their own fate. Should those actions be wholly within the covenant, harmony between Israel and Yahweh and a successful settlement prevails. When Israel acts in an unethical or anti-Yahwist manner, Yahweh leaves the individual and the people to their own devices, to work out their own fate; he does not interfere with humanity's free will. Ehud, for instance, is able to succeed in overcoming the Moabites despite Yahweh's withdrawal. Yahweh sets the stage, as it were, and allows the people the freedom to interpret the script. Ehud's actions are devious and Yahweh is uninvolved for the majority of the narrative. But Ehud's transgression is relatively minor and Yahweh once again is willing to overlook human weaknesses (as with Judah–Simeon, subsequent to 1.2-3). Yahweh allows Ehud to conquer Moab, but Yahweh does not fight the battle.

Deborah

The cycle and the pattern resume: the people do evil (4.1), Yahweh oppresses them (4.2), the sons of Israel cry to Yahweh (4.3), and Deborah is judge in Israel. Integrated among elements of the pattern are the distinctive details of this story: that Sisera is the enemy captain, and that he has chariots of iron, indicating a degree of technology advanced over that of the Israelites. Most distinctive is that this judge, who has been offering judgment to the sons of Israel, is a woman, a prophetess, 'wife of Lappidot'. 'Lappidot' is usually translated as 'torches', and this is the only time in the Bible the word occurs. No other information about Deborah's husband is provided.

Deborah is said to be the wife of Lappidot, but the narrative discloses her in association with another man, her military leader. The name of that man, Barak, means 'flash of lightning'.[8] Thus Deborah seems to function on the social level (as wife) and on the spiritual (as prophetess), uniting both as judge; and she does so between two poles of light or fire.

Like Othniel and Ehud, Deborah is an unexpected choice for a judge. A woman judging Israel, to whom 'the sons of Israel went . . . for judgment' (4.4) is at least as much an improbability in patriarchal Israel as a younger son or a left-handed warrior. Even the most casual reader is directed to the fact that this judge is a woman by the feminine endings on her name, by her calling, and by the fact that she is a wife.

As with Ehud, the spirit of Yahweh is not given to Deborah; neither is she 'raised up' by Yahweh to save the people. Thus *two* elements of the pattern established in the Othniel narrative are missing in this third narrative. Ehud, who proved himself deceptive, did not receive the spirit of Yahweh. The suspicion that Deborah may prove analogously unworthy of the divine spirit is contradicted by the fact that she is, and has been, judge. Thus the omission of the 'raised up' element is positive rather than negative. Deborah has been functioning on behalf of Yahweh; thus there has been no need to 'raise up' a judge when one is available. The same argument can be used to justify the fact that Yahweh's grace is not specifically bestowed upon Deborah. Deborah is called a 'prophetess', which suggests that Deborah is inspired or already has the grace of Yahweh.[9] That Deborah speaks through the spirit is shown in 4.9 ('Yahweh shall sell Sisera into the hand of a woman'), where she speaks with accurate foreknowledge and gives Yahweh full credit, and in 4.14, where she tells Barak to rise, for 'this [is] the day in which Yahweh has given Sisera into your hand'. In this narrative, the seemingly missing pattern elements are recognized as a positive portent.

Finally, 'Deborah' means 'bee'. It is curious that the book which celebrates an abundance of milk and honey mentions the source of that honey, the bee, only once in the singular (Isa. 7.18), three times in the plural (Deut. 1.44; Judg. 14.18; Ps. 118.12), and as the name of two women: Rebecca's nurse and Deborah the judge.[10] The four references to the bee, furthermore, are unusually negative, associating the bee of clean habits with the notoriously filthy fly or depicting bees as vanquishers and attackers of men. Only the reference to bees in Samson's exploit associates bees with honey, but even in that passage the bee is stigmatized as living and producing in decaying flesh, totally contrary to the facts of nature. Heinrich Margulies, who advanced this argument, suggests that biblical redactors have taken care to eradicate or denigrate references to bees because of their association with another matriarchal figure, the Mother Earth of Aegean, especially Cretan, mythology (1974:48).[11]

The presentation of Deborah is altogether enigmatic: as deliverer, she catalyzes others to acts of delivery. She apparently has the Yahweh-given spirit to judge the Israelites and calls men to her, hardly servant roles; but she needs Barak, a male, to fulfill her prophecies. She accompanies Barak to the battlefield but not to battle; she 'draws' the fighting forces of men together (4.6, 7) so that Yahweh can act through them (4.15). And though Barak eliminates every single man of the enemy army, it falls to another woman, Jael, to kill the enemy leader, Sisera.

Jael accomplishes this by saying to him, 'Turn aside, my lord, turn aside to me' (4.18). When Sisera follows the word of a woman, his fortunes turn. As Ehud was devious with power, Jael is devious with sexuality; furthermore, she breaks the code of host. The guest is so honored in the nomad tent tradition that Lot offers his virgin daughters rather than allow his guests (who happen to be messengers of Yahweh) to be molested by the townspeople (Gen. 19.8).[12] Jael first appears to observe the code: she considerately covers her weary guest with a 'fly net'[13] and brings him a choicer drink than the water he requests. In this passage it is milk that she offers, but in the older poetic version (5.25) it is ḥem'āh, curds, delicious and refreshing but soporific. Offering such a drink appears to be appropriate to a good host but has elements of treachery. And once her weary guest is asleep, Jael drives a tent peg through his skull. This passage is particularly interesting because it uses the same verb, tiṣnaḥ, that was used to describe Achsah's act of respect before her father, and the verb is unique to these two passages. 4.21: 'And she struck the tent peg in his temple and she dropped down to the earth and he sank down senseless and he died.' The pronoun 'she' before 'dropped' has no clear antecedent: it could refer to the mallet (feminine) Jael used or to Sisera's temple (feminine); and it could infer Jael's 'dropping down', tiṣnaḥ evoking Achsah's respectful action and inviting comparison with Jael's contraventions of her role as woman. Like

Ehud, Jael gains advantage for Israel by transgressing social and ethical codes, by acting in forbidden ways: she is seductive and she takes matters into her own hands. Finally, Jael not only acts directly, without the intermediary of a male figure, but she acts against the interests of her husband, who is friendly with Sisera. She values her people over her husband and acts upon her own values.

We may assume Jael is an Israelite because the text takes care to identify even half-assimilated non-Israelites such as Jael's husband. Kenites have travelled with the Israelites and accepted Yahweh as their God but they do not belong to any Israelite tribe. Jael is not so identified and her actions define her allegiances: she acts for Israel— against the interests of her husband's friendship with Sisera—and is therefore presumed to be an Israelite.

Jael is not a judge, and there is no indication that she acts under the spirit of Yahweh. She is a woman who breaks the codes, and though her actions seem a gain for Israel, they are devious. Jael acts, but Yahweh is silent. Yahweh's name is not mentioned in direct conjunction with Sisera or Jael's deeds, as it is with those of Barak. In this narrative, Israel recalls both the victory of its God, through Deborah, and that of Israel, through the trickery of a woman. Though Deborah is a judge through whom Yahweh acts, her name is associated with that of Jael—a woman who acts treacherously—and the figure of duplicity is the more memorable.

The Song of Deborah celebrates the events of ch. 4 in a victory ode. Although this song has long been acknowledged as one of the oldest and finest examples of literature in the Bible and still conveys the excitement and immediacy of presence, it too has been subjected to modern 'revisions'. Fortunately, the cut-and-paste phase of elucidation is giving way, and Alan Hauser's interpretation of the poem unifies the apparently 'damaged, choppy, and non-poetic' text not by 'doing major surgery on the received text', but by trying to recapture the poetic devices used by the poet (1980:25). In Judges 5 he finds 'that parataxis is best suited as a key to understanding the poet's style'.

Hauser observes that the rapid, sequential narration of events in the foregoing chapters is modified, in the song, for dramatic effect. The song does not open with the heroes of the war, but with the 'leaders' of the peoples, 'kings' and 'potentates', on the one hand, and 'Yahweh'. The royalty are commanded (in the imperative) to 'listen' and 'give ear'; Yahweh is to be sung to. The verse which commands

(5.3) moves from the kings, through the poet, to Yahweh; and although the poet is emphasized ('I, even I will sing; I will sing praise'), the end of the verse focuses on Yahweh.

The following unit (5.4-5) presents a dramatic change of scene as Yahweh's cosmic power is celebrated with special emphasis on water imagery. Although this entire verse exalts Yahweh, his name is particularly stressed in the closing lines, thus echoing 5.1-3; furthermore, Yahweh is given prominence, in the second section, as champion of Israel.

The oppression of the people as cause for war is the concern of the third unit, and individual names are introduced: Shamgar (probably of the past) and Jael (who will yet play a role); central to the verse is the turning point, '*until* I arose, Deborah, I arose' (my italics). The repeated first person is immediately freed of any potential *hubris* by the appellative 'as a mother'. Once again, the last words of this unit repeat the pattern of emphasis on the name of Yahweh.

That the song is to be repeated in the places of wealth (and, presumably, power) is the object of 5.10. These affluent people are directed to 'consider' the humble and devout of Israel (5.11a). A transition to the final verse of this initial segment of the poem moves these people to the city gates, the place of justice (5.11b). The next verse (5.12) repeats the imperative of the opening, thus marking a structural unit of the song sung *by* Deborah (and Barak). This part of the song reinforces the image of Deborah proferred by the narrative: one who speaks and acts in the spirit of Yahweh.

The poem shares an important element with the narrative text: variable perspectives. The song sung by Deborah focuses on and celebrates Yahweh. After a one-verse exhortative call to Deborah and Barak (5.12), the following verses (5.13-18), are a song of the people, a chorus. With the shift in 'singer' comes a shift in focus. Deborah's verses constantly stress Yahweh; in the choral section he is invoked only once, and then in a construct-genitive form ('people of Yahweh'). (Only in the final verse of the poem [5.31] is the name of Yahweh once more used as a substantive.) On the other hand, the names of individuals and tribes abound in the song of the poeple; it is bustling with verbs of human activity as they respond to the call to arms. Even three of the four tribes who fail to join the battle are mentioned, and Hauser notes that the failures to participate are each 'ascribed to a watery cause' (1980:31), thus building tension as to whether Israel will be able to mount an army, and later intensifying Yahweh's victory.

With v. 19, battle is joined, recounted by a narrator's voice. The Israelite army has been assembled, but Yahweh fights the battle. Initially, the foreign kings are stressed, but instead of Israelite heroes or tribes, only 'waters' are named: 'by the waters of Megiddo' and 'the torrent Kishon'. The earlier allusions to Yahweh's power over the natural elements, symbolized by water (5.4, 19, 21) and stars (5.20), culminate in these verses in which battle is won without mention of human participation.

In 'cursing' Meroz, a non-participating village, v. 23 concentrates three of the five references to Yahweh. This verse further serves as closure to the battle narration and creates a contrast to Jael's single-handed deed. The concentration of references to Yahweh also draws attention to the absence of his name in the following seven verses, all concerned with Jael's activities. She is called 'most blessed' with superlative force, is praised by men for her assistance, and her 'blessedness stands in bold contrast to the inhabitants of Meroz' (Hauser, 1980:35); nevertheless, she—unlike Deborah—is not named in the same breath with Yahweh.[14] Only in the concluding verse of the poem does the narrator once again invoke Yahweh directly.

Jael's section is, however, dramatic. In contrast to the marching and rushing turbulence of the tribal scenes, these verses use extensive parallelism and chiasm for retardation and suspension. The actual murder scene is drawn out over two verses in frame-by-frame slow- and play-back motion, relishing each moment. The poetic version of the incident does not include Jael's invitation to Sisera to come into her tent, thus diminishing her treachery, but it cannot eliminate her murder of a guest, even if he is an enemy of Israel.

The conclusion of the poem focuses on another woman, an enemy woman: the mother of Sisera. The personal and selfish concerns of this mother contrast with the image of Deborah as a mother in Israel, and Deborah's wisdom contrasts with that of the 'wisest ladies' of Sisera's mother. Whereas the Israelites took 'no spoils of silver', no booty, in accordance with Yahweh's strictures, Sisera's mother impatiently awaits her son's return, comforting herself for his delay with speculation on the spoils he will bring. It is an intimate scene, one which gives more power to the reader's knowledge that Sisera has himself been 'plundered', and by a woman.

Woman wield power to an unusual extent in this narrative, as the song makes clear. The first passage is Deborah's. After the battle-scene, in which the only man named is Barak (5.15), the reader is offered Jael's story and a glimpse of the enemy through the eyes of a woman. This sequence, like that of the entire book, describes a decline in ethical merit from the Israelite point of view: Deborah, (some tribes of Israel), Jael, and at the last, Sisera's mother—foreign woman. Even though the narrative of the judge is positive in that Deborah remains true to Yahweh and he conquers the enemy, the sequence of figures in this narrative and song subtly diminish with respect to Yahwist beliefs and ethics.

Essentially, the Song of Deborah corroborates the relationship between Yahweh and his people established in the narrative version. Deborah speaks and acts as mediator of Yahweh, it is Yahweh who conquers the enemy; and Jael, though she is called 'most blessed', acts in verses without Yahweh's name. Compared to Ehud's narrative there has been some increase in Yahweh's involvement. Although Deborah, like Ehud, does not specifically receive Yahweh's spirit, Yahweh's voice is presumably heard by Deborah, and Yahweh is given credit for the battle victories. Thus there has been a minimal increase in Yahweh's active participation and, despite the final stress on Jael's treacherous victory, an advance of the occupation of the land. Once again, the threat expressed in the exposition seems stilled. Deborah continues the example of achieving a typical duration of peace for the land.

Irony

Variation of motifs is, perhaps, the only stylistic 'constant' in Judges. The irony of the Ehud narrative is invested in the *action* of Ehud, made possible by his character and thereby differentiating him from Othniel. Yahweh has chosen a warrior impeded in his fighting arm— a 'crippled', left-handed warrior—an 'unnatural' warrior. As an agent of divine power, of course, Ehud's infirmity is of no significance. But, apparently unwilling to rely on Yahweh, Ehud practices deception and trickery, achieving the Israelite goal of freedom from oppression but ironically negating the higher goal: contact with Yahweh. The one-verse Shamgar narrative offers a further element of ironic contrast: whereas Ehud led troops to conquer ten thousand men of Moab (a round number), Shamgar 'smote six hundred men of the Philistines' with a primitive instrument and apparently without troops. Shamgar's narrative is too brief to allow any generalizations, but the irony of contrast is invited by textual comparison of Ehud and Shamgar in 3.30 and 4.1.

Ehud's verbal irony is, indeed, doubly ironic: he thinks he *knows* that any means is appropriate to achieve victory for Israel, but he is *ignorant* of Yahweh's purposes and of Yahweh's exacting of covenantal laws. The 'knowing' reader may expect a continuation in this ironic vein, but the person of Deborah is not ironic. Nevertheless, irony is present; indeed, disparate views are introduced for varying effects in the Deborah narrative and song.

This narrative ironically juxtaposes a woman judge-deliverer and a man who follows her to battle.[15] This reversal of roles, even in light of the symbolic meaning inherent in Deborah's name, is turned to positive effect by her adherance to Yahweh. Jael is a feminine contrast to Deborah, opposing the 'mother' with the 'wife' (suggesting feminine sexuality or sterility, both derogatory).[16] Furthermore, Jael is wife of a man, Heber the Kenite, who is friendly with the enemy king (4.17).

The opening verses of the Song of Deborah (5.1-13) suggest an ironic juxtaposition of divine and human power: Yahweh and the foreign kings. While Israel celebrates *Yahweh's* victory, the enemy combattants are only men: 'Kings came, they fought; then the kings of Canaan fought' (5.19). Israel's war is 'fought from the heavens; the stars from their courses fought with Sisera' (5.20). Israel fights under divine guidance; the enemy is not only acting on its own ('kings . . . fought') but is the *object* of the divine power ('the stars fought').

Deborah's first person song (and implicitly her narrated action) is rendered ironic by the following verses (5.24-30), which laud the non-Yahwist action of Jael. Deborah, 'a mother in Israel'—esteemed in a patriarchal society which values generation—is the rallying point of the Israelite tribes, but '*Most* blessed among women is Jael' (5.24). Ironically, the Israelites honor Jael's deceptive (and brutal) acts on her own initiative more than Deborah's honorable and ethical leadership under Yahweh's guidance. Jože Krašovec comments on the irony implicit in the antitheses of the scenes depicting Jael and Sisera's mother: a simple Bedouin woman (who acts 'in a most dishonorable manner') is contrasted with the mother of a mighty warrior, waiting in her palace and consulting with the wisest of her women about the delay in her son's return (1984:33).

Through irony, the Deborah narrative recalls a motif already suggested in the exposition (2.1-3): Israel's propensity to forget the *ethics* of its covenant with Yahweh in its eagerness for land, for *substance*, a motif that will gain in significance in the subsequent narratives.

Chapter 4

COMPLICATIONS

Gideon

The pattern repeats itself: after the usual number of years of rest (forty), the people do evil, Yahweh consigns them into oppression, the people cry to him for help, and an agent of Yahweh is sent to the people. With this third narrative of a major judge, the pattern shows further variation. For the first time, the nature of the oppression is given in great detail, so that the suffering is more specific: the people of Israel are forced to seek hiding places for their harvest in 'dens' and 'caves' and 'strongholds'. They cannot even reap their own produce, for the sons of Amalak and Midian have 'destroyed the produce of the land . . . and left no . . . livestock' (6.4). In contrast to the specificity of suffering, the image of the enemy oppresssion is rendered metaphoric and thereby formidable: 'they came in like locusts in number' (6.5). Thus, even at the outset of this narrative, the oppression—Yahweh's anger against Israel's disregard of the covenant—seems to have intensified. As a result, the sons of Israel cry to Yahweh (6.6). The cry and Yahweh's response are also presented to new effect: vv. 6-8 use the poetic device of chiastic parallelism, stressing 'the sons of Israel' both as agents and as recipients:

6.6a	And Israel [was] brought very low before *Midian,*	
6.6b		and the **sons of Israel** *cried to Yahweh.*
6.7a		And it happened, when the **sons of Israel** *cried to Yahweh*
6.7b	on account of *Midian*	
6.8a	that Yahweh sent a man, a *prophet*	
6.8b		to the **sons of Israel**

The chiasm is effective: the repetition of 'cried' doubles the reader's experience of the people crying, implying they are more repentant than before (3.15). Israel is reduced to passivity, 'brought low' (in the Niphal); and the name of the oppressor *Midian* 'encloses' the activity, to *cry* to Yahweh (in the Qal), of the sons of Israel. The next passage extends the repetition of 'sons of Israel' in the B phrase, but replaces the name of oppression (*Midian*) in the A segment with an agent of Yahweh, a *prophet*.[1] This structure tersely reinforces the opposition of Midian to Israel and Israel's restricted condition under that oppression. The structure is then countered by Yahweh's 'prophet' (instead of the oppressor) against 'the sons of Israel' in the third parallel verse.

The sons of Israel are not immediately sent a deliverer, a judge; they are sent 'a man, a prophet'. This recalls 4.4, in which Deborah is introduced as 'a woman, a prophetess'. The reader is primed for high expectations. If a woman prophetess could be as effective as Deborah, what will 'a man, a prophet' be able to achieve? However, with a parallel established, variety and surprise begin to infiltrate the narrative pattern. Instead of surpassing Deborah, the prophet remains unnamed, ineffective. Gideon—a man of Israel—confirms this impression: he appears not to have heard the message of the prophet (Martin, 1975:81). The people are not ready to believe: they, like Gideon, respond only to *proof* of the power of the gods—whether Baal or Yahweh. The prophet's words go unheeded.

Yahweh's rebuke of the people reiterates that of ch. 2: the people are reminded of Yahweh's past deeds to free them from the Egyptians and other oppressors and that they should not fear[2] the foreign gods, whom they have worshipped. This expanded, ten-verse exposition is a sharp deviation from the curtailed exposition of earlier narratives and another instance of flexibility and variety within the paradigm. Following this expanded expository section, the main narrative begins with v. 11, in which an angel (messenger) of Yahweh appears.[3]

The narrative centering on Gideon is particular in several aspects. It is central to Judges by virtue of its length—ninety-two verses arranged in three chapters (only four verses shorter than the four-chapter Samson narrative)—and it is integrally connected with the subsequent chapter of Abimelech. This is the only narrative in which Yahweh speaks directly to a judge without an intermediary at least implied. Notably, the ethics of the judges first shifts decisively with

Gideon. And ironically, Gideon, singularly in the book of Judges, recalls the figure of Moses.

Gideon, like Moses, experiences a true theophany, and Gideon's call observes the 'call pattern' of the Moses narrative (Exod. 3.10-12).[4]

	Exodus (Moses)	Judges (Gideon)
call	and I will	Have I not
	send you	sent you
objection	who [am] I . . .	with what shall I . . .
	that I should bring	my family is weakest.
	the sons of Israel	I am the least in the
	from Egypt?	house of my father.
affirmation	for I will be with you	for I will be with you
sign	this [will be]	give me
	the sign	a sign

Each of these passages presents a dialogue between Yahweh and his elected servant. Both initial divine statements affirm the calls, but differently: with a promise to Moses (I will send you) and a rebuke to Gideon (Have I not sent you?). Both newly-commissioned leaders respond with protest, but there is a vast difference between Moses' humility and Gideon's pulling low rank, especially since Gideon later exaggerates the weakness of his position. The third element in the call pattern, Yahweh's assurance, uses precisely the same words in both passages. The verbal form of *'ihyeh*, 'I will be', recalls the significance of this word in Exod. 3.14, since just two verses after the call Elohim identifies himself as *'ihyeh 'ašer 'ihyeh*, 'I am (the) One who is' (Schild, 1954:302). Moses recognizes the divine nature of the speaker and 'hid his face, for he feared to look upon Elohim' (Exod. 3.7) even before the call (Exod. 3.10). In contrast, Gideon is slow to recognize the speaker and does not shield his eyes from direct vision.

That 'Yahweh turned to him' has several implications. It seems that Gideon and Yahweh (or his angel) have *not* been conversing in the usual manner among men, face-to-face. Yahweh has apparently been shielding Gideon from full vision, *expecting to be known, be recognized*, as he had been until now; but Gideon is slow. Only the 'I am' passage, which recalls Exod. 3.12, 14, changes Gideon's tone of voice from sarcasm to humility. Gideon's slowness to recognize Yahweh reiterates that of Israel, who ignored the prophet (6.7-10), and foreshadows future events. The last element, the sign, is *offered* to Moses and respectfully *requested* by Gideon. Gideon is knowledgeable about the Yahwist tradition and not only requests the completion of the call from his visitor but also is prepared to do his part, to make a sacrifice. Although the call narrative of Joshua does not correlate as fully, it nevertheless bears comparison:

Joshua

call	now, rise up...you...you	1.2
	have I not charged you?	1.9
objection	(none)	
affirmation	...I will be with you	1.5
sign	(none)	
new material	be strong and courageous	1.6
	only be strong and very courageous	1.7
	be strong and courageous	1.8a
	be not afraid nor discouraged	1.8b

Juxtaposing the Joshua and Gideon call narratives discloses that neither objection nor sign is necessary for Joshua: he has already 'known' Yahweh and needs no confirmation. The repeated stress on the need for strength and courage is not transmitted by Joshua to his people; indeed, the unity of Yahweh and Israel is so complete at this point that the *people* affirm Yahweh's message to Joshua (1.18). These variations in the call pattern contrast the *need* for strength and bravery enunciated in Joshua with Gideon's ready strength, mentioned twice by Yahweh (6.12, 14). By use of the call narrative, the author was able to extend the implications of his words, revealing through Gideon a new aspect of the relationship between Israel and Yahweh.

The deliverer, Gideon, is first shown threshing wheat in a winepress in order to remain undiscovered by his oppressors, the situation stressing the severity of this oppression as compared to that of earlier chapters.[5] That the Israelites have escalated their anti-Yahwist behavior to warrant more onerous punishment is corroborated by the words of the prophet, who, like Yahweh's angel-messengers, speaks for Yahweh in the first person and specifies the sin for which they are being punished: worship of Amorite gods (6.10). This lapse into anti-Yahwist behavior marks the intensified ethical regression which is one structural pattern of the book.

The theophany to Gideon is associated with a tree, a terebinth (turpentine tree) or possibly the 'sacred' tree. J. Alberto Soggin suggests that 'the nucleus of the sanctuary in question [was] the sacred oak and the altar called *Yhwh šalōm* (v. 24), still existing at the time of the first tradition and situated in the territory of the clan of Abiezer, near to the winepress hollowed out in the rock which traditionally belonged to Gideon' (1981:117). It was 'doubtless a sacred tree under which the oracle of Yahweh might be expected to be ascertained' (Burney, 1918:86), and recalls Deborah's presiding under another sacred tree (4.5).[6] In the next narrative (Abimelech), the terebinth is again a site of ceremony. Furthermore these three narratives develop the increasing gap between divine and human perceptions of occupation of the land.

The exchange between Yahweh and Gideon is an additional novelty; to this point, judges have been raised up (or were simply available, like Deborah) and—despite their unlikelihood—they apparently accepted the charge of leadership without hesitation. Gideon not only hesitates, he challenges: through formal address he clearly expresses doubt. 'Oh my lord, and if Yahweh is with us, why has all this happened? And where are his wonders?' (6.13) The use of *waw* conversive (*wᵉyēš*)—literally '*And* (is/exists) Yahweh with us?'—lends an ironic, even sarcastic tone. Gideon's tone betrays his sceptical regard of the stranger and his claim. His faulty discrepancy in perception is further accented: Yahweh speaks to Gideon about Gideon; the man responds in the plural, about 'us', the people. After a second imperative from Yahweh, 'Go in your strength' (6.14), Gideon narrows the range of his identity to his tribe and family (6.15). Only when Yahweh acknowledges the disparity by referring to Gideon as if he were, indeed, the singular of the people—'You will strike Midian *as one man*' (6.17)—does Gideon respond in the singular: 'If I have found grace in your eyes . . . ' This brief exchange subtly exposes Gideon's initial cautious skepticism, his lack of courage and his reluctance to even speak in his own person, and it serves as a basis for contrast with the later Gideon, full of his own power.

When Yahweh turns to him and says that Gideon, in his strength, will deliver Israel, Gideon protests the weakness of his tribe, his family, and himself in his father's house. Yahweh patiently 'reasons' that 'I will be with you'. Skeptical Gideon, however, wants not words but deeds: he wants proof. At the same time, he isn't sure whether his visitor is really who he claims to be. Suddenly polite, he requests that the visitor wait while he prepares a food offering—a great sacrifice in a period of deprivation. With prepared flesh and unleavened bread (another allusion to Moses [Exod. 23.18]), Gideon returns. The visitor commands Gideon to put them on a rock, the visitor touches them with his rod, and they are consumed. Gideon, convinced, fears because he has seen (an angel of) Yahweh face-to-face.

Convinced . . . but. When caught between Yahweh's command (to pull down the altar of Baal and its Asherah pole) and fear of the community, Gideon obeys Yahweh, but secretly, at night. Gideon is a skeptic and a coward: not even direct confrontation with Yahweh and a demonstration of divine powers eliminates either Gideon's skepticism or his fear. After Gideon's destruction of the idols, only his father's protest to the townspeople that Baal plead his own case, if he is a god, saves his son's life. The father's argument is logical, as is the son's skepticism. It is logic, not faith, that prevails. In the earlier narratives, the sons of Israel have been remiss in their faith by serving other gods. At this juncture, a new dimension arises: the doubt of reason is added to relapse from Yahwist belief, and with reason, doubt and skepticism. The conflict between Yahweh and the sons of Israel has been intensified by new forms of knowledge, new potential for irony.

Because Baal fails to defend the destruction of his temple, Gideon receives a new name, 'Jerubbaal'.[7] Leon Wood perceives the re-naming of Gideon as elevating him so that he can function as leader (1975:208-11). More typically, Martin finds 'the identification of Gideon with Jerubbaal . . . secondary' (1975:88). These readings, however, overlook the word-play suggested by the re-naming. Gideon's name is based on the verbal root *gdy*, which means 'to cut down or off' (*AHCL*, 1981:132) and is interpreted as 'hacker, hewer' by Boling (1975:130). Significantly, this form of Gideon's name is not used with reference to his cutting down the Asherah; instead, a synonym, *kh'rt*, is employed for both the command (6.25) and the discovery of the destruction (6.28). The actual deed is simply '*done*', '*āśāh*' (*w^ayā'aś*). Indeed, the appropriateness of Gideon's name is questionable at this moment. Gideon the hacker-hewer is apparently ready to contend with his visitor but is afraid to cut down the Asherah. Jerubbaal—'let Baal contend', the name given to Gideon to commemorate the deed—changes the focus of his name from one of physical destruction (hacker) to one of verbal contention (contend, strive, quarrel). With a complex ironic twist, the reluctant 'hacker' is re-named 'contender' when he secretly hews down the Asherah. And not only 'let Baal contend' is implied; Gideon has also shown himself a contender, an Israelite sophist, and he will do so again. A consortium of forces poses a great threat. This passage introduces the rare and striking phrase, 'and the spirit of Yahweh clothed Gideon'. Gideon is, in effect, surrounded by the spirit of Yahweh, as with a mantle; he 'wears' the divine spirit. The spirit that was not given to Ehud and only implicitly to Deborah *does* come upon Gideon. He receives the spirit, and in the same syntactical unit, he blows a trumpet. This action serves not only as a call to arms but as a foreshadowing of the unusual use of the trumpet in the ensuing action. Then, just when action is expected, Gideon hesitates: surrounded by Yahweh's spirit, assembling an army of the peoples, he suddenly 'becomes' Jerubbaal the contender, asking for proof of Yahweh's powers.[8] To 'prove' Yahweh's capacity to pre-determine the outcome of the battle, Gideon first asks that a fleece be wet in the morning although the ground be dry. Apparently the divine spirit is sufficient to counteract fear (Gideon assembles the men of several tribes, preparatory to doing battle), but not skepticism: Gideon tests Yahweh—not once, but twice, requesting opposite effects in the two tests. In each instance, Yahweh responds not with words but with the proof requested. When Gideon realizes that the 'wonder' he first requested proves nothing—it is perfectly natural that the fleece hold the night moisture and the earth absorb it—he cautiously (with three appeals) tests again, requesting proof *against* nature; and once more Yahweh silently acquiesces. Indeed, Yahweh shows neither impatience with nor hostility to reason. At the same time, Yahweh's silent actions of proof in response to Gideon's effusive words calls attention to the gulf between the relative knowledge/power of god and humanity.

The following passage illustrates one of the high points of the Yahweh–Israel relationship. Echoing the narratives of Joshua and Deborah, in which Yahweh took the active role and Israel the passive one, the passage shows Gideon following the word of Yahweh in assembling his forces, using his own initiative only in the spirit of Yahweh, to set the battle in motion. In an action strongly reminiscent of the Deborah–Barak episode, in which 'Yahweh routed Sisera and all his chariots and all his army before Barak' (5.15), Gideon and his men create a 'sound-and-light' show and then 'stood every man in his place ... Yahweh set every man's sword against his fellow' (7.21). The battle exemplifies the optimal Yahweh–Israel relationship in the book of Judges: human submission in faith so that Yahweh can act through his people. Should the people use their freedom to act out their destiny in a way contrary to Yahweh's precepts, as Ehud (and then Jael) does, Yahweh retreats from the scene. In this passage, the Yahweh–Israel relationship is shown to be intact despite Gideon's protracted skepticism of Yahweh's powers—and the reader's skepticism that this unpromising leader can serve Israel's cause.

The assembled forces camp beside the 'spring of Kharod', and *Kharod* is translated as 'trembling, terror, fear' (7.1). The name of the camp site recalls the fearful aspect of Gideon and anticipates the elimination of 'Whoever is fearful and trembling' in the following episode. With Yahweh's spirit and human reason, Gideon is finally ready to act. Speaking to a man of reason, Yahweh explains his purposes in reducing the size of the army: 'lest Israel glorify itself' against Yahweh and assume it has won deliverance by its own hand. Yahweh's statement reinforces the identification of the individual judge (here, Gideon) with Israel. Since 'Israel' is the particular judge just as each judge is 'Israel', the warning is clear. Gideon, the personification of Israel, should not glorify himself.

Yahweh's first tactic is to send away those who are 'fearful and trembling'. This action considerably reduces the size of the army. Then, at the water's edge, Yahweh instructs Gideon to separate those who lap water directly, as a dog laps, from those who kneel to drink (7.5). Since this first 'sorting' distinguishes those who kneel from those who lap directly, the latter suggests a posture other than kneeling, perhaps sprawling at the water's edge. This elimination suggests sorting out of those who abandon all to physical demands, like animals, to leave those who kneel to drink, whether directly or not. In the next verse, these kneelers are further reduced to those who lap water from their hands. Since some of the kneelers do *not* use their hands, they too must drink directly, 'bowing down on their knees'. Only three hundred men both kneel and use their hands, and these men will constitute the fighting force to conquer the camp of Midian.

The basis of selection has been variously conjectured since the time of Josephus, and the verse components have been reconstructed to support myriad theories, all of which assume a single test of elimination. However, careful reading of the text suggests a two-step process of selection. A further confusion which appears repeatedly in the literature—whether those who were selected were the more astute about their situation and aware of their danger (courageous men of common sense) or took water in their hands out of fear— seems irrelevant. Either way, it is a test of *attitude* (as Burney points out [1918:211]), and Yahweh chose those with the attitudes of *men* rather than those with the attitudes of *animals*.

The three stages (including the 'fear and trembling' incident) of reduction of the army occur during the day (7.1), but the final pre-battle stage, eliminating Gideon's 'fear', occurs during the night. The men who were 'fearful and trembling' are sent away from the Spring of Trembling, but Gideon's fear is sent away from *him*. In this instance the proof is *not* logical: it takes the form of a dream overheard and interpreted in the Midianite camp, a dream which portends Gideon's success as due to Yahweh's will. Gideon is convinced. He has only to enact his destiny—as he sees fit.[9]

When the dream of the Midianite and its interpretation have been overheard, Gideon appropriately worships first and then goes into action, thus setting a model of behavior for subsequent adherence or deviance. Gideon apparently devises the trumpet-torch-and-pitcher tactic, and with it the Israelites create the panic characteristic of holy war (cf. 1 Sam. 14.15). His battle cry is 'For Yahweh and for Gideon!' In deed (prayer) and word (battle cry), Gideon follows Yahweh at this point in his narrative; but, unlike Deborah, he includes his own name as a leader—suggestive of subsequent actions. The warriors, however, 'interpret' the battle cry: they shout, 'A sword for Yahweh and for Gideon!' The stress is changed from honoring the divine and human leaders of the war to its means, the sword. It is also a subtle comment on the difficulty of communication between leaders— divine or human—and their followers. Each chain in the link 'interprets' the message as he is capable of understanding it. But Yahweh is tolerant of such human error. In contrast to the active verbs applied to the enemy—'ran' (or 'awoke'), 'shouted', 'fled'—the men of Israel 'stood, each one in his place all around the camp' (7.21). Divine activity brings about the rout of the enemy.

Nevertheless, in the very next passage (7.23), Gideon calls up the reserves. Even though Yahweh has won the battle with limited forces literally standing still, Gideon proceeds logically from his point of view—which is, ironically, illogical. Forgetting the entire point of the elimination process which left him only three hundred soldiers of an army of thirty-two thousand men, 'That Israel (Gideon) may not boast ... that her own strength has saved her' (7.2), Gideon fails to give thanks for Yahweh's victory or to ask how to proceed. The coward has become confident; he directs far-flung mopping up operations which are effectively carried out. But the voice of Yahweh is stilled, not to be heard for the balance of Gideon's narrative. And the spirit of Yahweh, which brought the courage to fight a far greater military force, seems to slip from Gideon's shoulders in the process.

This juncture provides an opportunity to note a structural motif peculiar to Gideon's narrative: the time of action. The preparations for and reactions to major actions take place during the day, but commands for action and the actions themselves occur during the night.

			DAY	NIGHT
6.11-16				
	6.11-12	Yahweh appears	X	
	13-16	Gideon **contends** with Yahweh	X	
		Yahweh **reasons**	X	
6.17-32				
	6.17-18	Gideon asks for sign	X	
	19	Gideon prepares sacrifice	X	
	20	Yahweh directs sacrifice	X	
	21	Yahweh accepts sacrifice (sign)	X	
6.25-32				
	6.25-26	Yahweh *commands*		X
	27	Gideon *obeys*		X
6.28-36				
	6.28-32	People accept Gideon's deed	X	
	33	Nations prepare for war	X	
	34	Spirit clothes Gideon	X	
	35	Gideon assembles army	X	
6.36-40				
	6.36-37	Gideon **contends** with Yahweh	X	
	38	Yahweh *proves*		X
	39	Gideon **contends** with Yahweh	X	
	40	Yahweh *proves*		X
7.1-8				
	7.1	Gideon assembles people	X	
	2-8	Yahweh directs army reduction	X	

```
7.9-22
    7.9         Yahweh commands                      X
    10-14       Yahweh proves                        X
    15-19       Gideon obeys Yahweh                  X
    19-22       People obey Gideon (Yahweh)          X
7.23-25
    7.23-24     Gideon assembles army        X
    25          People obey (fight for) Gideon   X
8.1-3
    8.1         People contend with Gideon   X
    2-3         Gideon reasons;              X
                People obey                  X
```

In the three night episodes there is an alteration of contention and response until, at the last, Yahweh offers proof before it can be requested, thus dominating the action and allowing Gideon only the response of obedience. The 'night' episodes of Gideon's doubt are alternated with 'day' episodes of belief, and the entire action is framed by episodes of 'contending' and reasoning—the first between god and humanity and the second between leader and people. Failing to perceive himself as one link in a chain of command from Yahweh to the people, summarized in 7.9-22, Gideon diverts belief in Yahweh to belief in himself, acts on his own to assemble an army, and the dialectic of night and day is past. Just as Gideon contends with Yahweh and Yahweh convinces by reasoning (6.13-16), the people contend with Gideon and Gideon successfully reasons with them (8.1-3).

The narrative identifies *belief* and *courage* primarily with *day*; and *doubt* (which follows reason) and *fear* with *night*. Yahweh's initial wonder—the 'sign' requested by Gideon—is given by daylight, as evidenced by the fact that Gideon saw (the angel of) Yahweh face-to-face. The daylight wonder suggests that reason and wonder are not separate for Yahweh as they are for Gideon. Gideon reasons by day; but reason, even with wonder, is not sufficient to dispel the fear of that which he cannot subject to reason: the doubts of night. Unlike belief, which is effective day *and* night, reason is only effective during the day. Lacking the courage of belief, Gideon initially and repeatedly acts in fear by night. The episode ends as it began, with contending and reasoning. The shift in Gideon and in his relationship to Yahweh, which the entire narrative describes, is succinctly depicted in this passage.

Yahweh is consistently intolerant of Israelite worship of other gods, but in this narrative Yahweh demonstrates tolerance of *doubt*, the doubt of reason. He not only reasons with Israel, but he does so in terms humanity—Gideon-Israel—can comprehend. Although Gideon's logic rules during the day, Yahweh dispels Gideon's fear by working wonders at night, darkness defying reason. In addition, the structure of the narrative demonstrates not only the centrality of the contention-reason-proof sequence but also that Gideon subsequently 'reasons' with the people as Yahweh had reasoned with him. Through contending and reasoning, and Yahweh's tolerant proof of power beyond knowledge, Gideon gains belief and courage. The much-tested and hard-earned belief Gideon gains is, ironically, not in Yahweh but in himself, as the closing episode demonstrates. Gideon uses Yahweh's techniques for his own purposes.

These episodes utilize a natural element, the temporal aspect of night, to develop cowardice and fear as a characteristic of Gideon-Israel. Gideon destroys the Baal temple at night because he fears to do it by day, and his trumpet-torch-and-pitcher attack at night induces fear in the enemy. The miraculous central episode has the opposite effect: it assures Gideon of divine control even in the time of fear, and as a wonder it defies natural elements. It occurs during the night, the phase of the day when reason does not prevail, because that is the time when Gideon's logical fear surpasses belief in suprarational divinity.

Chapter 6 presents phases of rationality and belief, of contending for proof of a power beyond reason. With the power of Yahweh established, ch. 7 is directed to the current issue of war. The episodes expand from the cursory description of the 'tests' to detailed dramatic and narrative scenes: the limiting of the number of men, Gideon's overhearing of the Midianite's dream, and the battle-scene. In contrast with all other passages of Gideon's narrative, ch. 7 is focused on Yahweh, who dominates it with five speeches (compared to one by Gideon). The centrality of ch. 7 is further emphasized by the speeding-up of the following scenes: in ch. 8, four separate incidents are quickly narrated before the concluding elements of the judges pattern reappear. And in ch. 7, Gideon is not a man of words, a contender; but a man of action, of war—a 'hacker'.

With the close of ch. 7, the enemy is routed, the leaders' heads brought to Gideon in enemy territory, 'beyond the Jordan'. Immediately thereafter, in the first verse of ch. 8, there is strife among the Israelites: the Ephraimites complain because they had been left out of the main battle with the Midianites. With this conflict, the other side of Gideon—the Jerubbaal side—emerges. The reader knows that Yahweh had reduced the army by eliminating those less desirable for his purposes, and presumably the proud Ephraimites did not qualify. With great tact, Gideon 'reasons' with the Ephraimites, appealing to their pride, arguing that the actions of the Ephraimites, a full tribe, are inherently superior to those of Abiezer, a mere clan. Gideon 'proves' to them that Yahweh had given them the more important conquests in the war, the rulers themselves. The 'contender' humbles himself, takes no credit, and maintains peace among his people. In 7.1–8.3, Gideon exemplifies the ideal of both names, 'hacker'-Gideon and 'contender'-Jerubbaal, to the advantage of the people of Israel under Yahweh.

With 8.4, a new aspect arises. Gideon is on 'home' territory again, having crossed the Jordan with his three hundred weary men. Gideon approaches the men of Succoth requesting bread and explaining that he and his men are pursuing the enemy kings. He is refused. Not the 'mediating' but the 'contending' Jerubbaal responds: Gideon swears revenge when Yahweh has given the enemy into his power, and it is a 'Gideon' threat: to 'thresh' their flesh with wilderness thorns and briars. Succoth (and Penuel, subsequently) is not the walled city of a powerful tribe, but only a little village.[10] With the powerful, like the Ephraimites, Gideon moderates; with the weak, he over-reacts: the coward becomes the bully.

When the odds are with him, Gideon is not reluctant to take action. Formerly, reason governed Gideon's utter cowardice, but that capacity has apparently deteriorated: his reactions here are not only exaggerated, but illogical and unreasonable. With his new-found self-confidence, Gideon's relationship to Yahweh has also changed. He seems to assume Yahweh is still with him, but there is no mention of a word or a prayer in that direction. Furthermore, a disparity in goals becomes evident: whereas Yahweh's is to save his people, Gideon's is to confirm his own power, himself. Yahweh had reduced the number of Gideon's fighting forces so there would be no doubt but that *Yahweh* won the initial battle; nevertheless, Gideon is fighting on his own at this point.

Rebuffed by Succoth, Gideon makes the same request of the town of Penuel. He is answered by the men of Penuel in the same way and again threatens reprisal upon his return 'in peace'. After conquering the enemy, Gideon does return—in peace with enemy, but not with his own people. In Succoth, Gideon exacts the threatened reprisal, and in Penuel he not only breaks down the tower but kills 'the men of the city'. In Succoth, the men of the city are 'taught' by the example of their elders, but the men of Penuel as well as the tower are destroyed. In his destruction of these towns, Gideon observes the rules (Deut. 20.13) for waging holy war—putting 'all the males to the sword'—but does so against his own people. With the destruction of the tower, probably a refuge of an unwalled city, the women are without a place for protection; and without men there is no person to protect them. Gideon lays the town and the Israelite women open to ravage.[11] This judge seems to have no compunction about torturing or killing those Israelites who have doubts in *him*, which is a sharp contrast to the treatment he received from Yahweh when Gideon was in doubt.

Yet in contrast to his cold-blooded revenge on the Israelites, without commentary, Gideon seems ready to show compassion to the enemy. He passionately vows—in the name of Yahweh—that he would save the lives of the enemy leaders if they had not killed his brothers. There have been various responses to the dialogue between Gideon and the kings. Soggin understands it as 'epic chivalry' (1979:157), and Burney interprets Gideon's questioning of the Midianite kings as a rhetorical 'challenge' to produce the brothers alive to 'save their own lives' (1918:234). Neither explains Gideon's vow. Indeed, the text reveals that Gideon fails to distinguish between his people and his enemies or to see the identity of his people and his brothers. He has become the contender and hewer of his own people, and Yahweh is notably absent.

Gideon has fulfilled his original name. Under Yahweh's guidance, Gideon became a hacker and hewer of the enemy. He ceases his 'striving' for proof and acts to 'cut down' the enemy; but the 'contender' aspect of Gideon endures. Having fulfilled his names under Yahweh, Gideon goes on to fulfill them on a human level, without Yahweh.

In disposing of the enemy leaders, Gideon offers the act of retribution to his first-born, Jether; but the youth is afraid, recalling to the reader Gideon's early days. A final cursory allusion to the Moses narrative is suggested by the son's name. Jether is an abbreviated form of Jethro, the name of Moses' father-in-law (Exod. 4.18). The differences in the name bearers—the former mature and wise, the latter young and afraid—extends the earlier comparison to Moses and suggests hereditary continuation of the faithless and fearful in Israel.

The insult of being slain by a youth is unfulfilled, and so is the painful death of a bungled attempt. The warrior kings request and are given death at the hand of a man of might.[12] But though Gideon makes a show of revenge for the death of his brothers, his actions reveal other interests. As if in one swoop, Gideon kills the enemy leaders and takes booty—the moon crescents which hung on their camels' necks. This interest in booty is another indication of later developments: Gideon's increasing interest in *tangible* values. The actions of killing enemy leaders and taking booty also call attention to an unusual characteristic of Gideon. Once the first battle against the Midianites—in which Yahweh alone acts—is past, Gideon takes on a peculiar Jekyll-and-Hyde aspect. Each time he does something worthy of a judge, he immediately follows with the opposite; and the descriptions of his actions tend to become more concise, so that the opposition becomes ever more obvious. Consider:

8.1-4   And the men of Ephraim said to him ... *Then their anger was abated when he said* that

8.5-8   When *Yahweh has given Zebah and Zalunna in my hand*, I will **tear your flesh with thorns and briars.**

8.9-10   So he said to the men of Peniel, 'When **I return in triumph, I will tear down this tower.**

8.11-13   Zebah and Zalunna ... fled, *but he pursued them and capture them, routing their entire army.*

8.14-17   **He took the elders of the town** [Succoth] **and he ... taught them with thorns and briars.**

8.17   And **he broke down the tower of Peniel and killed the men of the city.**

8.21b   ... *and Gideon arose and killed Zebah and Zalunna* and he **took the crescents which [were] on the necks of their camels.**

8.23   *I will not rule over you nor shall my son rule over you; Yahweh shall rule over you*

8.24   **Let me make a request: each of you give me the rings of your spoil ...**

8.27   **And Gideon made an ephod of it ... and it became a snare to Gideon and to his house.**

Gideon's last action ironically reconstructs the initial situation and counteracts his own deed (at Yahweh's command) to destroy the idolatrous Baal temple and the Asherah. This time his family cannot save him. In fact, the opposite occurs: Gideon's ephod of gold is an evil that traps Gideon and his family. And this allusion to Gideon's family as subject to the evil he has created prepares for the story of Gideon's son, Abimelech.

In vv. 22-23, Gideon refuses the offer of leadership to himself and his sons, declaring 'Yahweh shall rule over you'. Kingship was a Canaanite practice foreign to the Israelites: v. 23 shows that the idea of a human ruler is inconsistent with the conception of theocracy, and as a member of Yahweh's people, Gideon refuses the notion of hereditary leadership. Yet in the very next passage, as if in recompense for the power refused, Gideon asks for a different power: the gold earrings of the spoil they have taken.

This passage once more recalls Moses. In Numbers 31, Moses wars with the very same people, the Midianites. Moses' warriors slay every male 'as Yahweh commanded Moses' and as required by Deuteronomic law (20.13).[13] Moses observes the laws regarding the spoils of war. They may be only taken from distant cities, and the precious metals, purified by passing them 'through the fire' and the 'water of impurity' (Num. 31.23), are to be brought before Yahweh as atonement and taken into the tabernacle of the congregation. As leader, Moses determines only the fate of human captives (Num. 31.14-20); he has nothing to do with booty. He neither takes it nor presides over its allocation. Eleazer the priest cites 'the statute of the law which Yahweh had commanded Moses' to the people and stipulates the purification rites of the spoils of war. The booty is divided between the warriors and the congregation, and a tribute to Yahweh is made from the portion of the men of war. Moses' name is in no manner associated with mundanities.

In contrast, we know Gideon kills the kings not as a sacrifice to Yahweh but for personal revenge, and he immediately 'stoops' to take spoil even if it hangs on camels' necks. Gideon does not distribute booty to the people nor does he give it as tribute to Yahweh. The weight of the gold 'that he requested' was the equivalent of seventeen hundred shekels; this weight of gold was 'made' into a ephod, which was 'set up' in Orphah, Gideon's city. The verbs used suggest that this ephod was an idol or non-eikonic symbol and that the gold involved is too heavy to denote the *ephod*, a priestly garment described in Exodus 28. This unusual use of the term calls attention to it, suggesting further implications. We recall that Gideon was clothed with Yahweh's spirit; here the term 'ephod' suggests he symbolically clothes himself with another 'value': gold. The Yahwist value, his spirit, is not truly *within* Gideon and he drops the Yahwist mantle for one of gold. Furthermore, though Gideon refuses the title of leader, the object he has made from the gold is one associated with kingship. Most telling is the reference to 'all Israel' playing the harlot after the ephod, worshipping a tangible in shape (idol) or value (gold) instead of the intangible source. Although the booty Gideon collects is passed 'through' fire (melted), the purpose is not holy purification but reshaping for human glorification. The ephod does not memorialize Yahweh or even the people of Israel: it is Gideon's ephod and an ironic realization of Yahweh's warning against self-glorification (7.2).

The ephod is a 'snare' in many ways. The Hebrew for 'snare' is *mokesh*: the fowler's bait or lure. Because the *ephod* is associated with kingship, it symbolizes the lure to power that Gideon, as an Israelite, has rejected. It remains a snare to Gideon's family, which includes his son by a Schechemite concubine. Abimelech, more Canaanite than Israelite, is familiar with the idea of kingship; and since it had been offered his father and was symbolically evident in the trappings of his father's leadership—the ephod—Abimelech went after the bait. Most significantly, the ephod is a snare, a lure to worship a *tangible* in which the *people* have invested *value* and *form*. This ephod introduces a motif which gains in significance in the remaining narratives: Israel's increasing secession from ethical Yahweh worship to worship of humanity's self-determined values, its own creations. This motif represents a shift from 'merely' worshipping the local gods with which the Israelites come into contact. Israel is no longer the innocent of the desert who is easily seduced into apostasy. Grown more confident, more worldly, more sophisticated, Israel creates its own trap, its own lure from Yahweh.

The repeated allusions to Moses in the Gideon narrative emphasize the discrepancies between a servant of Yahweh who remains humbly in contact with his god and a servant of humanity who becomes convinced of his own powers and ceases to hear the voice of Yahweh. This is in keeping with the progression of the narrative sequence: each of the preceding judges' narratives shifts from an established level of contact with Yahweh. Ehud was only 'given' to Israel and was on his own deceptive path from the beginning. Deborah, a prophetess, could interpret and relate Yahweh's will. There is no indication that this power was withdrawn from her; the story, however, shifts to the sub-plot of Jael and Sisera to show humanity's lack of reliance on Yahweh and show that humanity's victory has the last word. Though Yahweh may have remained accessible to Deborah, the story renders him silent through Jael's independent and dishonorable actions.

Gideon's story intensifies both Yahweh's involvement and his withdrawal: a first attempt to repeat the sucess of a prophet-judge like Deborah, with another prophet, falls on deaf ears: the people are not willing to hear. The next step involves an interesting reversal: Gideon is not 'raised up'; Yahweh comes (down) to him. Despite Gideon's reluctance, Yahweh is 'with' him, 'sends' him to battle, and envelops him with the divine spirit. With all the proof of Yahweh's power, Gideon nevertheless turns away from Yahweh's will—to deliver Israel—and fights an 'unholy' war against his own people. Gideon is never said to have 'judged' or even to have 'delivered' Israel. Though he ostensibly refuses to rule, Gideon arrogates to himself a worldly symbol of rule, the ephod; he thereby leads his people into a new kind of spiritual prostitution, for 'all Israel whored after it' (8.27). Of all the judges narratives, Yahweh is most evident in Gideon's. Consequently, after Gideon discovers power through belief—belief in himself and his own power, not Yahweh's divine power—Yahweh's silence is most profound.

The paradigm of the major judges is, once again, not complete in Gideon's narrative; but some of the elements are highly developed, e.g. the doubling of agents (prophet of word, Gideon of might) chosen to counsel and save Israel, the intensified nature of the oppression, and Yahweh's intensified involvement (in convincing Gideon to act as warrior on behalf of Israel). Gideon, however, is not identified as 'judge'. Among the so-called 'major' judges, only the paradigm judge, Othniel, and Deborah are credited with this activity.[14] The deviation from the pattern is characteristically significant. Instead of 'judging' and leading Israel through Yahwist law, Gideon leads Israel into a new kind of apostasy. For Gideon's belief in himself is comparable to Israel's belief in its own creation, the ephod of gold. Gideon/Israel symbolizes humankind's 'worship' of its own values above worship of Yahweh.

With reason alone, Gideon did nothing: he had no faith in himself or in Yahweh. With faith in Yahweh and human reason, he acted justly. With faith in himself and either no words or empty words for

Yahweh, Gideon acted immoderately and unreasonably, and his actions led directly to a new kind of apostasy by the people. Nevertheless, in accordance with the narrative pattern, Israel had rest as long as the judge lived, and Gideon too lived for forty years.

Irony

With Gideon's narrative, ironic oppositions increase markedly. For the first time, irony is invested in the character of the judge and the opposition between divine and human perspectives is integrated into the dynamics of the situation.[15] The most significant irony of the narrative is that Yahweh does convince Gideon of a power beyond reason—belief—and that Gideon ascribes that power to himself, to Gideon, rather than to Yahweh. Instead of judging his people according to the covenant, Gideon introduces Israel to a belief in human perceptions, human creations, leading the people yet farther from Yahweh.

The narrative is permeated with smaller ironies. There is irony in Gideon's names. Initially, 'Gideon', the 'hewer, hacker', is a hacker of wheat, and even that he does in hiding. As a result of carrying out Yahweh's command to tear down Baal's temple and destroy the Asherah, Gideon is re-named in terms of Baal—'let Baal contend'— but Gideon contends with Yahweh, not with Baal. Under Yahweh's guidance, Gideon does become a hacker of the enemy, revising his original name from ironic to literal. With belief and with confidence in himself, Gideon further becomes a hacker of Israel, Yahweh's people and his own, lending yet another ironic aspect to his name.

Relationships—between Gideon and Yahweh, between Gideon and Israel—offer several ironic aspects. Initially, Gideon presents himself as powerless, belonging to the weakest clan in Manasseh and the least in his family, but Yahweh patiently reasons with him and leads him to the power of belief. In his power, Gideon reveals himself as still cowardly: he reasons with the powerful Ephraimites but takes brutal revenge on the weak, Succoth and Peniel. Gideon 'contends' with the powerful Ephraimites and 'hacks' at the weak of Succoth and Peniel: an exact opposite to Yahweh's actions. Even though Yahweh explicitly reduces the size of the Israelite army that Israel not 'glorify itself', that is exactly what Gideon does with the ephod of gold.

Another aspect of the Yahweh–Gideon relationship is suggested in

Gideon's confrontation with the theophanic. Yahweh assures Gideon that he will not die even though he has seen (an angel/messenger of) Yahweh face-to-face, saying '*Šālōm lᵉkā*', 'Peace to you'. Gideon builds an altar which he calls 'Yahweh [is] *šālōm*'. The word *šālōm* includes 'health', 'prosperity', 'friendship', and 'peace'—the absence of war—among its meanings. The builder of this altar makes war upon Yahweh's people and leads them from Yahweh, from *šālōm* under Yahweh to worship of human constructs, implicitly the opposite of *šālōm*. Ironic use of this word recurs toward the close of the narrative, when Gideon threatens reprisal to the citizens of Peniel when he returns *in peace* (8.9). Gideon returns in peace—with the enemy, which he has conquered—but at war with his own people. Certainly the 'peace' Yahweh has granted Gideon is an ironic foil for the internecine wars he later leads. For a 'reasonable' man, Gideon does everything counter to Yahweh's wishes.

Gideon receives more from Yahweh than does any other judge, including Samson. Yahweh not only grants Gideon his spirit, but he singularly 'clothes' Gideon with his spirit; it surrounds him, envelops him. That the holy spirit is not within Gideon is revealed when he symbolically displaces the spirit of Yahweh with an ephod of gold. The priestly ephod, which belongs to the garment of a holy man, is rendered a symbol of the non-holy, the power of idolatry and gold. Gideon displaces the power of Yahwist belief with belief in himself and earthly values.

Ironically, it is Gideon of all the judges who does most harm to Israel. It is he who introduces the conflict which hitherto has only been suggested, the conflict of human values—abstract and concrete—with those of Yahweh, and this conflict dominates the rest of the book.

Chapter 5

ANTI-CLIMAX

Abimelech

With Gideon, the development of the book of Judges reaches the climax of Yahweh's participation. In the paradigm story of Othniel, Yahweh raised up a deliverer, his spirit came upon Othniel, and Othniel judged. Ehud was 'given' to Israel and he judged, but without the divine spirit. Deborah was neither explicitly raised up nor given the divine spirit (though she functioned as if both were true), and she judged; but Jael, who destroyed Sisera, acted without mention of Yahweh's name. Yahweh has dropped into the background, and then, just when the reader is unprepared, Yahweh is suddenly very much in evidence. Gideon is not 'raised up': Yahweh comes (down) and sits with him! Yahweh not only grants Gideon the divine spirit, he *clothes* and *surrounds* Gideon with it. But Gideon is never said to deliver or judge his people. The land had rest under Gideon, but he is not said to judge it. Once again, the omission is significant.

The disparity between Yahweh's considerable involvement with Gideon and the diminished outcome is provocative. In the Hebrew Bible, Yahweh is a knowing god, but not *all* knowing: humanity's self-determination takes such turns that Yahweh may repent his own actions.[1] Yahweh certainly proffers divine guidance through Gideon, but the outcome is even less than with Gideon's predecessors since Israel is farther from Yahweh by virtue of the actions of Gideon; and Gideon does not judge. Furthermore, Gideon literally 'plants the seed' for the most devastating chapter within the main narrative sequence. His many wives (and children) among the Israelite people are not enough: he must also have a woman of the Shechemites. (Gideon's foreign concubine foreshadows those of Samson, with similarly negative effects for Israel). The anti-hero of the following narrative is the son of Gideon's liaison: a fighter who exemplifies all the negative aspects of his father merged with his mother's non-Yahwist beliefs. It is strikingly ironic that Gideon, the judge who was most directly involved with Yahweh, 'delivered' the *least* positive developments for Israel.

The final verses of Gideon's narrative recapitulate the narrative paradigm (8.28-35). The link to the pattern is stressed by an additional reference to the good Yahweh had done for the people in prior times (8.34). The paradigm is familiar; surely another judge will follow. Having set up reader expectations, the narrative proceeds to shatter them completely by presenting the story of an anti-judge, an anti-hero.

As Yahweh is most in evidence in the story of Gideon, so is he least present in the following narrative, that of Gideon's son Abimelech. In Abimelech's chapters, the major judge paradigm recurs as usual in the human sphere: Israel does wrong (8.33-35), a personal detail is given (8.31), the 'non-deliverer' takes action (9.1-5), the number of years of leadership is stipulated (9.22), and the death of the protagonist is cited (9.53-54). But it is God (Elohim), not Yahweh, who appears in this chapter; and he takes part only *inversely* within the pattern. God imposes an *evil* spirit instead of the divine spirit, and the number of years of leadership under a judge, usually described as years of 'rest', or 'peace' (Hebrew *šᵉqoṭ*: 'quiet, undisturbed') are ambiguously identified only as the (three) years of Abimelech's power. Abimelech neither 'rules' over nor 'judges' Israel. The verb used to denote his tenure is *yaśar*, from the root *śûr*, which has a secondary meaning 'to be prince, to have dominion', and a primary one of 'to contend, strive' (AHCL, 1981:707). Both meanings have relevance to Abimelech, as his 'dominion' is marked by contentions between him and the peoples, Israelite and Canaanite alike. The oppressor, in this narrative, is spiritually and existentially within the people; there is no foreign enemy. The enemy is within: Abimelech is (and symbolizes) the foreign element in Israel.

The anti-hero of the book of Judges was named *Abimelech*, 'my father is king' (8.31) by Gideon, his father. The usual verb 'to name', *qaraʿ*, 'he called, he named' is not used; Gideon 'set' or 'placed', *yaśēm* (from the root *šûm*), his son's name. In this sense, Gideon not only physically created a son who was only half Israelite (and half 'enemy'), he also 'determined' or 'set' his son's future by 'putting' this name upon him. It is an age-old belief that individuals tend to fulfill their names.

The question remains: who is meant as 'father' in the name? Boling points out that the 'image of God as father is relatively scarce in the Old Testament...; the image is nonetheless ancient in Israelite material' (1975:163). For Gideon, 'Abimelech' may have referred to Yahweh as father and king, but Abimelech bases his claim to kingship on the title offered his natural father, Gideon. The ambiguity suggests irony is implicit in the name. What may have honored Yahweh becomes anti-Yahwist. That the name of Abimelech is anathema to the author is shown by its ironic over-use: after its introduction in ch. 8, it occurs thirty-seven times in ch. 9.

Ironically, although Abimelech may have aspired to become king because of the name 'put' upon him by his father, he achieves his goal through his matriarchal connections. His double-rhetorical question (9.2) implies the desired answer and compares *his* descent from Jerubbaal (using the Baal name) with that of seventy brothers, none of whom is of Shechemite stock. The massacre of the siblings is financed by the temple of the Baal of the Covenant (an ironic contradiction in terms), apparently at one piece of silver per head.[2] Funded, Abimelech hires 'worthless and reckless men'—an unusually direct introduction of authorial values. Worthless as his mercenaries may be, Abimelech is worse: it is he who kills his brothers in a perverted act of sacrifice—'on one stone'—in contempt of Yahwist covenantal restrictions, which forbid human sacrifice.

Gideon had seventy sons, a round number, to be sure. Before Gideon, only Jacob had given seed to seventy 'souls' (sons and daughters), and the people of Israel descended from those children, 'And the sons of Israel were fruitful and teeming and multiplied' (Exod. 1.15). Gideon is even more prolific since he fathers seventy sons and who knows how many daughters, but to no avail. The one 'misplaced' seed all but eliminates the potential implied in the round number 'seventy'. The single Israelite son who escapes slaughter by hiding (recalling his father's hiding from the Midianites when Yahweh visited him) is the youngest (the smallest), and though he has the courage to speak out, he is powerless to counter his half-brother.

Appropriately for an anti-judge, Abimelech is made king in an unholy, anti-holy ceremony beneath a 'planted' or 'set' tree, in contradistinction to the natural and holy trees associated with Deborah and Gideon. Deborah's palm is sacred because she spoke the word of Yahweh there, and the terebinth under which Yahweh sat and spoke to Gideon became thereby a holy site. Gideon destroyed the Asherah—a 'foreign' sacred pillar—which had been 'set up' by the temple of Baal. In Abimelech's narrative, the terebinth under which Abimelech is made king is not identified with Yahweh or even God, but with being 'set' or 'planted' there (9.6). The Hophal participle (*muṣṣāb*) stresses the human activity, thereby effectively contrasting the sacred terebinth near Shechem (Gen. 35.4-5) with this humanly planted and humanly proclaimed ceremonial tree. In these three major judge narratives, the tree as a holy site is a motif of the relationship between Yahweh and Israel—a motif which vanishes after the anti-climax story of Abimelech, 'my father is king'. The disappearance of this motif thereafter has as much significance as its inclusion in these chapters: one symbolic link is gone.

Without comment, the narrative shifts from Abimelech to Jotham, the lone remaining Yahwist son of Gideon, who climbs to a precipice and addresses the people in a parable of the trees (9.7-21)—a significant motif at this juncture. Burney observes that Jotham climbs high enough 'to make himself heard' and 'to beat a safe retreat' (1970:272). But surely Jotham could have made himself heard better in the natural amphitheater of the valley than by climbing above the people, where the sound would be dissipated. Jotham's position has another significance: he stands—literally and figuratively—*above* the people as he addresses them in a parable.

In the parable, each of the noble trees, the olive, the fig and grape vine, responds to the invitation to be ruler over the trees by a rhetorical question. This question-response alludes to the benefits of that tree (1) to God and (2) to humanity. (The fig refers only to its 'sweetness' and 'good fruit' without naming a recipient, implicitly including both God and humanity.) Finally, the lowliest of trees—without fruit or shade or long life—the buckthorn, gladly offers refuge 'under' its shade if it be truly anointed king. If not, it threatens destruction by fire. Obviously, this common, thorned and straggling bush is oblivious of its limitations, as Abimelech is, and threatens ruin if not heeded. Abimelech could not offer the people 'shelter' in his rule, as Yahweh-elected Gideon had: but he could (and did) bring disaster. The people must *look up* to Jotham; they must *look up* to the ethical ramifications of their situation.

Finally, for those listeners (readers) unable to interpret the parable, Jothan spells out the analogies. Jotham knows that the people have not dealt honorably with the family (the 'house') of his father, the man who, whatever his later transgressions, was chosen by Yahweh and had delivered them from the Midianite oppression. Jotham charges the people with rebellion against his father's 'house', with murder of 'seventy sons on one stone', with giving Abimelech, 'son of his [Gideon's] concubine', leadership over the inhabitants of Shechem—all because of blood ties, 'because he is your brother'. Jotham refers to a 'higher' morality than blood ties.

Jotham ironically suggests that if the people have acted 'in truth' and 'with integrity' toward the family of Jerubbaal, then they should rejoice in one another. If not, he predicts, they will devour each other in fire. His warning delivered, Jothan flees toward Beer. The lineage of Gideon is not eliminated, but it disappears into anonymity.

Deviating from the paradigm, which gives the details of duration of leadership and death of the leader at the closing of the narrative, the narrator emphasizes the truth of Jotham's parable by stating immediately that Abimelech ruled over Israel for three years. After the unbroken sequence of judgeships of forty years, a round number, the exact and brief limitation of Abimelech's dominion is a welcome surprise and somewhat mitigates the news of devastation predicted by the parable. Further corroboration of the narrative pattern, and an ironic inversion, is God's sending of an *evil* spirit to this evil man. Instead of the spirit of Yahweh, which may come upon a judge to inspire him to feats which will deliver Israel, an evil spirit is sent 'between Abimelech and the leaders of Shechem' (9.23). The spirit does not come *upon* Abimelech—he is evil enough—but *between* him and the leaders, punishing both sides for slaying Gideon's sons. As Abimelech dealt treacherously with his own blood, so do the leaders with him, setting their own band of 'worthless and reckless men' in the mountain passes to deploy and murder him. Like a western adventure, the tale increases in pitch as Abimelech gets wind of their plans and the highwaymen, as they wait for Abimelech, rob passersby.

Meanwhile (back at Shechem), protest is developing from the leaders and the people. The scene shifts to one Gaal,[3] son of Obed, 'servant' or 'slave'. The text does not specify the servant's master. That it is Yahweh is unlikely since Gaal appeals to the citizens of Shechem; instead, the name suggests that this unsympathetic man derives from the servant class. This is ironically implied in the use of the participial form, often used as an honorific name (e.g., 'servant-of-Yahweh') as a substantive: *ebed*, 'servant'. Gaal is 'son-of-servant', but he is 'pure' *Bene Hamor*, of the Shechemite line. One Shechem, son of Hamor, has been associated with illegal (male) sexuality (Gen. 34.2).[4] Here the town of Shechem can only oppose the mixed-blood of a concubine with its own 'genealogically pure' rabble, in whom the leaders of Shechem place trust. As Boling suggests, the Shechemites were 'scraping the bottom of the barrel' (1975:176).

The text turns to the people of Shechem. Verse 27 builds from an image of *industry* ('went forth into the fields and cut their vintage and trod it out') to one of *thanksgiving* and *festivity*, a vintage-rejoicing; moves into the temple of Baal, and closes with eating and *drinking* (presumably wine) and *cursing*—and the object of anger is Abimelech. Gaal, wielding the repeated rhetorical question form Abimelech used to gain support, also appeals to blood lines.[5] Gaal opposes the blood line of the sons of Hamor with that of the sons of Israel and asks why the former should serve the latter. Ironically, the claim of 'Gaal, son of servant' to loftier antecedents is undermined by the repetition of *ebed*, 'servant', four times in v. 28: once as a proper name and three times as the verb 'to serve'. The 'son of servant' complains about his master (his king) on the basis of genealogy! In the last question, the stressed pronoun 'we'—'And why should *we* serve him'—extends Gaal's servant status to his brothers, all of them sons-of-servants, proclaiming themselves better than the half-breed ruler. The reader recognizes the following boasts and threats to Abimelech as 'cheap talk' not to be taken seriously, uttered perhaps under the influence of drink.[6]

At this point, the narration places the reader in an unusual dilemma. Knowing that Abimelech is brutally unscrupulous in his greed for worldy power, and that he can only bring more grief to the Israelites, the reader wishes that a counter-figure appear, someone to restore order. The antidote offered in Gaal is perhaps worse than the poison, and the reader is torn between two equally undesirable resolutions.

But Zebul, Abemelech's resident deputy in Shechem, hears the boasts and threats and takes them seriously enough to get angry. He craftily ('treacherously' to those present) sends a message to Abimelech, and the message is cited verbatim so that the reader can perceive that the laughable situation has not only been given more credit than it warrants but has been blown up[7] to a massive action against Abimelech. Zebul counsels Abimelech as to tactics, advising that the king and his men arise and conceal themselves in the fields

during the night, to advance upon the city at daybreak when Gaal
and his people will go out against him. Abimelech does just that, in
four companies of men.

Inviting the reader to watch and even overhear the developments,
the narration continues in close detail as 'Gaal son of Ebed went out
and stood at the entry of the city gate'. Normally the gate of a city is a
site that comands respect: Lot was standing there when the angels
approached (Gen. 19.1), and the elders of cities frequently stand
there in an advisory capacity (Deut. 22.15; 25.7; Josh. 20.4). David
also stands there to re-affirm his leadership of the people after his
mourning over the death of his son Absalom. Gaal may be said to be
pre-tasting one of the pleasures of the power he desires, and in this
moment of 'glory' his utter weakness is exposed. Abimelech and his
'troops' arise from ambush. Gaal naively observes to Zebul that
'people are coming down' from the mountains. Zebul 'misinterprets'
the men as 'shadows', stalling for time until Gaal repeats his
observation, practically verbatim, and adds that the leader (the
'head' one) is coming by way of the soothsayer's terebinth. Lest he
feel commiseration for the exposed and naive Gaal, the reader is
reminded that the terebinth, usually a 'sacred' tree, is a 'magician's
tree' for the Shechemite. Still uncomprehending, Gaal must be
reminded of his boasts by Zebul, who challenges him to fight. Gaal
has no options: he fights until Abimelech chases him, and he flees.
Because of Gaal's idle boasting, however, 'many fell down wounded',
which once more stresses that the people suffer for having put their
faith in unworthy leaders.

All the sons of Ebed are evicted from Shechem, but the incident is
not over. Shortly thereafter, even though Zebul has already driven
out the entire clan of Gaal, Abimelech uses the exact same tactics
against the ordinary people of the city who go out to their fields.
Abimelech achieved his authority by slaughter of his (half) brothers,
and he instinctively turns to mass murder to re-assert his authority.
When these presumably unarmed people have been struck, Abimelech
and his companies rush forward and stand in the entrance gate of the
city, exactly where Gaal stood before his defeat. Abimelech,
however, continues to fight and capture and utterly destroy the city
and its inhabitants, sowing the site with salt.

To obviate any possible admiration for Abimelech, the narrator
diminishes his military leadership by showing it as largely following
Zebul's advice:

Zebul:		Abimelech:	
9.32	Rise up by night you and the people with you And lie in wait In the field.	9.34	And rose Abimelech And all the people with him by night And they hid near Shechem.
9.33a	And it shall be In the morning Just at sunrise You shall rise And charge Against the city.	9.35b	And rose Abimelech And all the people with him from hiding.

The changes in sequence and interpolations of Gaal's point of view artistically integrate and develop the key phrases, increasing reader suspense about how the dilemma will be resolved. In fact, although Abimelech 'chases' Gaal, he does not capture or kill him: Gaal escapes him. Abimelech doesn't even fight the rest of the battle; he 'remains in Arumah'. It takes Zebul to fight and drive Gaal and his brothers from Shechem.

Like his father, the hewer and hacker, Abimelech overreacts. Zebul rids Shechem of Gaal, who threatened; but Abimelech devastates the city for good measure. He overreacts again when the leading citizens of a nearby village (probably unwalled), alarmed at the fate of Shechem, withdraw into their cult stronghold. Abimelech attacks the people who have *taken refuge* for security. The author ridicules the image of Abimelech as warrior.

Though this village is called 'Tower of Shechem', the cult chamber seems to be an underground excavation or chamber, possibly indicating that the city name refers to the stronghold (tower) of Baal. In this action, Abimelech suggests another corollary with his father: Jerubbaal, in preparation for the battle and inspired by Yahweh, told his small troop of men 'to see' and 'to do' what he does. Abimelech uses the same verbs to show his followers what they are to do. The polarity of the actions of father and son, summarized below, is heightened by their both using specifically 'three companies' (7.16; 9.43) and the same form of command (7.17; 9.48):

Gideon (7.15-25)	Abimelech (9.22-49)
Theophany, belief in Yahweh Yahweh's spirit surrounds	No evidence of any belief Evil spirit intervenes

Fights superior and attacking forces, conquers	Fights non-combattants, cruelly murders
Fights to deliver Israel	Fights for personal power
Uses noise and fire to frighten	Uses fire to kill
Frees Israelites from oppression	Oppresses Israelites (and others

Abimelech's initiative in this action is merely a reversal of his father's, and the anti-hero is denied even the worthiness of an admirable tactic. And while Gideon's ploy was admirable, Abimelech's is crude and brutal. He and his men set burning boughs of trees over the underground crypt or stronghold where the people had taken refuge, thereby burning or suffocating 'about a thousand men and women [which included] all the men of the tower' (9.49). Abimelech, like Gideon, leaves a city totally without males, the protectors and progenitors. In doing so, Abimelech crowns the symbolic meaning of Jotham's parable with its literal enactment: he sets fire to the boughs of trees (*sōkot*) not bramble (*'āmad*). Abimelech himself is the brushwood, the worthless wood. He, the worthless element, uses the wood of noble trees to destroy the leaders and all the men of the city, the human 'nobility'.

Continuing his surge of destruction, Abimelech advances to the city of Tebes (twelve miles northeast of Shechem) and captures it. The details of the strategy of capture are omitted in order to focus on the following action, which is a repetition of the same tactic to effect the same goal—senseless carnage of a captured people. Once more the people flee to their stronghold for protection, but this time the tower is above ground. Abimelech fulfills Jotham's prophetic fable once more—to burn down the tower. At this point, when the narrative is resolving the dilemma in one direction (Abimelech's success against the Canaanites) and the reader is caught up in the evolution of the tale, it abruptly shifts and draws to an unexpected conclusion. Whereas the people in the underground crypt were utterly helpless, at the tower of Tebes just one woman and a millstone 'turn' the resolution to the other pole: Abimelech's demeaning demise.

His skull crushed, Abimelech asks his weapons-bearer to give him the *coup de grâce* in order to prevent the disgrace of being killed by a woman. He is oblivious of the much greater disgrace he has brought to his name, but the eternal shame he sought to avoid is nevertheless ensured: it is exactly the disgraceful aspect of his death which is affixed to the name of Abimelech, as related in Joab's messenger report to David (2 Sam. 11.21).

The story of Abimelech, 'my father is king', marks the ironic climax of the book of Judges. It serves to warn the Israelites, at this formative phase of their history, of the hazards implicit in liaisons with non-Israelites. All the good Gideon originally did for his people is more than eradicated through his co-habitation with a Shechemite, so that the promise of fulfilling the covenant is more remote than ever. Yahweh is not mentioned, and except for sending a (rare) evil spirit, God is absent from the Abimelech narrative, thus emphasizing his increased distance from the Israelites. The occupation of their land, so bright in prospect in the opening narratives, has reached its antithesis in the figure of Abimelech: instead of being a deliverer, he is an oppressor; not a leader, but murderer of the Israelites, Abimelech leads the Israelites in battle.[8]

With Abimelech's reign, the die has been cast. The last of the 'major' judge figures, an anti-judge, is followed by the so-called 'minor' judges, whose narrative pattern deviates from those of the major judges primarily by omission, but also by providing more specific information. The full significance of this climax is delayed briefly. Only after the brief narratives of the first minor judges do the people once again, as in the 'major' narrative paradigm, appeal to Yahweh; but this time Yahweh refuses them, sending them to their new gods: Yahweh is through with them. The 'territorial' relationship[9] between Yahweh and Israel has some chapters in which to be fully worked out, but the outcome is suggested, if not ultimately realized, at the climax of the book.

Irony

With the death of Gideon, the narrative initially proceeds as expected, with the first elements of the narrative pattern: 'the sons of Israel whored after the Baals ... and did not remember Yahweh' (8.33-34).[10] The next verse, however, introduces a new source of irony: the narrator. Following by only eight verses the episode of the ephod and all Israel's whoring after it and worshipping it (8.27), by seven verses the omission of Gideon as judge (8.28), and by four verses the mention of Gideon's Shechemite concubine (8.31), the comment, 'And they did not show kindness to the family of Jerubbaal–Gideon for all the good he had done with Israel' strongly suggests ironic as well as non-ironic meaning. There is no indication that *Israel* was unkind to the family of Jerubbaal–Gideon. Irony is recognized if Abimelech—born of a Shechemite mother in a socially but not cult-recognized concubine relationship—is taken as 'Israel'. If Abimelech is not Israel, there is no indication of Israel's unkindness to Gideon's family. In fact, this verse foreshadows the evil which *will* befall the house of Gideon in the narrative of Abimelech.

In the immediate context, another ironic aspect becomes apparent:

8.33　And it came to pass, when Gideon (was) dead,
　　　that returned the sons of Israel to whoring after the
　　　Baals and set up for themselves Baal-berith as a god;

8.34　and the sons of Israel *did not remember Yahweh* their
　　　god, who had delivered them out of the hand of all their
　　　enemies all around;

8.35　and they *did not show kindness* with the house of
　　　Jerubbaal-Gideon according to all the good which he
　　　did with Israel.

The first two verses offer variations on the paradigm, while the latter two ostensibly balance Gideon with Yahweh, both neglected by the sons of Israel who have forgotten Yahweh and were unkind to Gideon. Inasmuch as Yahweh, not Gideon, had 'delivered them' from the Midianites, it is only a limited 'good', *ṭōbāh*, which Gideon had done for Israel: he pursued and killed Zevah and Tsalmunna. Under Gideon, Israel set up an Ephod to worship, which led, after his death, to a new development in anti-Yahwism: introduction of a 'Baal of the covenant'—an idol that profanes the sacred covenant. Surely the 'good' Gideon introduced is to be taken with a grain of salt in this passage. The irony of Gideon's 'good' is accentuated by the verb used for the neglect by the sons of Israel: they did not show *ḥesed*, 'kindness, mercy' (*BDB*, 1983:338b) to Gideon.

Irony is implied in the names of Abimelech and Gaal. Both of these names are associated with blood-line, 'my father is king', and 'son of servant' (indeed, ironically contrasting social roles), and both individuals claim personal power based on their blood-lines. Other characters' names, e.g. Zebul, Jotham, are not ironic. These latter make no claim on their *own* behalf, and whether for bad or for good they act according to their commitments: Zebul to his king and Jotham to his god. Jotham does protest an action again his family, his blood-line, but the protest is based on mistreatment, not on blood. In conquering the Midianites, Jotham's father had benefited the

Canaanite as well as the Israelite dwellers of the area. And Jotham's protest of undeserved brutality *after* service to the people is the opposite of claiming power *before* service, merely on the basis of blood relationship. Jotham's parable is a non-ironic, 'straight' version, which creates a basis for the irony of Abimelech and Gaal.

It is irony that carries the weight of meaning in the Abimelech narrative. At this early phase of the occupation, the greatest danger facing Israel is weakening of the bond to Yahweh and the covenant through contact with other peoples. Abimelech's narrative overtly demonstrates that one seed among non-Israelites can destroy all the promise of Israel. The warning is to not assimilate, to not put faith in other peoples, even though they live peaceably. Blood will dictate morality.

Chapter 6

THE MINOR JUDGES

The Minor-Judge Paradigm

The death of Abimelech is not in any way redemptive; the Israelites who fought under his leadership can only go home. The view is black indeed. And when the reader's emotions have been so intensely involved in dilemma and brutality, the quickest way to engage them again is to ease the tension, to invoke an interlude. With a sure touch, the author follows the dark tale of anti-judge Abimelech, the last of the so-called 'major' judges,[1] with the first two of the 'minor' judges, a set of *Yin-Yang* figures, Tola and Jair. Together, these two narratives occupy only five verses (10.1-5), but they are each particularized to special effect.

The minor judges' narrative pattern deviates from that of the major judges but follows a pattern in its own right, and the narrative of Tola can be regarded as paradigm of a secondary refrain. In it, (1) tribal indentification gives way to that of the *clan*,[2] *named after the head of a large family*; (2) the judge 'rises up' or 'follows' his predecessor (he is not chosen by Yahweh); (3) specific geographical location, different from that of the tribal disposition as described in Josh. 13.7-33, is given; (4) a specific (not round) number of years as judge is stated, as is (5) identification of the place of burial. Once again, deviations, particularly *additions* to the pattern (instead of the omissions which characterized disparities with the major judge paradigm) suggest import. Notably, despite the lack of information about their specific activities on behalf of Israel and in contrast to the major judges (except Deborah), all the minor judges are recognized as having 'judged'.

Tola is particularized by the unusual details of his genealogy, his past. This is necessary because he is identified by his clan within the tribe; were only a tribe named as genealogy, further information would be unnecessary. Tola, a member of a clan derived from Issachar,[3] lives not in the Yahweh-designated Issachar territory but in Shamir, in the 'hill country of Ephraim', thus subtly introducing the motif of *gēr*, 'stranger', which takes on significance in subsequent narratives. Tola judges Israel for twenty-three years, dies, and is buried in Shamir.

Jair's narrative, observing this pattern, likewise identifies the protagonist by his blood-line, but in a variation: Jair is not designated by his forefathers, but by his descendants, his *future* generations, introduced by a round number. Furthermore, these descendants are characterized in some way that suggests power—rank or wealth. This future orientation and regard for power suggest shifting values among the Israelites, as personified by their judges. Unlike Tola, Jair lives in his own tribal territory (of Manasseh, from which half-tribe he derives [Deut.3.14; Num. 32.41]). He judges Israel for twenty-two years, just one year less than Tola, and his burial place is likewise named (Kamon). Yet even in this short sequence, diversification and particularization is achieved: the former by re-arrangement and re-sequencing of the paradigm elements and the latter by details about the family of the judge.[4]

In the individualizing reference to Jair's family, word-play with 'asses' (Hebrew *'ayārîm*) and 'towns' (Hebrew *'ayārîm*) establishes a light tone, which ironically underplays the significance of the information.

> 10.4:   He had thirty *sons*,
>   who rode on thirty *wild ass-colts*
>   and thirty *towns* [belonged] to them
>   they named (to) them the towns of Jair,
>   to this day in Gilead.

The repetition of 'thirty' seems to equalize the terms that follow: thirty sons, thirty wild ass-colts, thirty towns, all with the name of Jair. The towns and the sons are named after Jair; and the 'ass-colts' they ride, 'a badge of rank' (Burney, 1918:292), associate the family name with new conceptions of 'wealth and prosperity' (Martin, 1975:132). The contrast between Tola and Jair is even geographical: Havroth-Jair and Shamir are on opposite sides of the Jordan and in north-south opposition as well. The narratives use the similarities of the paradigm elements to *different* ends. Tola's narrative regards prior generations but Jair's, later ones. Tola is identified by clan and does not live in the appointed tribal territory, but Jair of Gilead has neither clan nor tribe—he is identified by territory. Tola's descendents and wealth are not mentioned, but Jair has both and becomes eponymous ancestor to the towns named after him. These differences contribute to the lighter tone; but, however opposite they may be, both judges succeed in administrating peaceful periods of about equal duration. And with this 'breather', the reader has relaxed sufficiently for the decline in the covenantal relationship to resume its course.

Jephthah

After the minimal minor-judge pattern of Tola and Jair, a combination major-minor pattern is introduced. Jephthah's narrative observes the paradigm of the major judges with the exception of his not being 'raised up', but it also includes the curtailed pattern of the minor judges: the specific number of years of leadership, attribution as 'judge', and the specific place of burial. The Jephthah narrative is embedded among those of the minor judges, and is generally included among the minor judges—although Jephthah 'delivers' as well as 'judges'.[5] Inclusion of Jephthah (and Samson, for the same reasons) among the minor judges reinforces the structure of the book: the rising action roughly encompasses the 'major' judges; the falling action, the 'minor' ones, with Abimelech as the crisis figure. The Gideon and Jephthah narratives, on either side of the anti-judge narrative of Abimelech, are marked by well-developed introductory elements of the pragmatic pattern. This structural device subtly isolates Abimelech and stresses the depths of his story.

Abimelech's is the most brutal narrative of the judges, but that of Jephthah the most pitiable. It is fitting that these narratives be separated only by the episodes of two minor judges (in five verses), and that the patterned introductory material of the narratives of Abimelech and Jephthah, in contrast with those of Tola and Jair, use *similar* conditions of birth and society to different ends.

	Abimelech	**Jephthah**
Similarities		
Mother	concubine, Shechemite; son legally recognized	harlot, presumably Israelite; son without legal standing, can have no Shechemite paternal inheritance

Siblings	70 sons, all but one murdered by Abimelech	several sons, who drive Jephthah away from inheritance
Associates	worthless men	worthless men
Differences		
Actions	follows tactics of others: Zebul, Gideon;	'a great warrior'
	attains power through maternal relationships, by liquidating legal opposition;	attains power by virtue of personal qualities, legal recognition
	ignores Yahweh	consecrates his agreement to leadership at Mizpah, a holy site, 'before Yahweh'

To introduce the next narrative sequence, the author once again invokes the major apostasy paradigm, this time expanded and specific with reference to the foreign gods Israel has come to worship and the extent of the oppression imposed as punishment. The evil committed by Israel is much more elaborated in this chapter than previously, particularly with reference to the various other gods served in lieu of Yahweh:

Judges:

2.11-12	served the Baals and forsook Yahweh
-13	forsook Yahweh, and served the Baals and the Ashtorot.
3.2	did what was evil in the sight of Yahweh.
3.7	did what was evil in the sight of Yahweh, forgetting Yahweh their God.
4.1	did what was evil in the sight of Yahweh.
6.1	did what was evil in the sight of Yahweh.
8.33-34	. . . and they prostituted themselves to the Baals, and they set up Baal-B'rit as their god. And the sons of Israel did not remember Yahweh their God.
10.6	And they again did evil in the sight of Yahweh and served the Baals and the Ashtorot, the gods of Syria, the gods of Sidon, the gods of Moab, the gods of the Ammonites, and the gods of the Philistines; and they forsook Yahweh and did not serve him.

The iniquity has become more specific and it has spread from a general 'evil' or 'served Baals' (with or without his female counterparts) to five additional and specific foreign gods. Yahweh's angry response (10.11-15) also involves broader physical as well as spiritual horizons. Instead of one enemy, unnamed (2.14), named (3.8; 4.2; 6.1), or with foreign assistance (3.12-13), Israel is at this point oppressed by two enemies (the Philistines and the Ammonites) on a larger landscape (both sides of the Jordan) and for a specified duration (eighteen years). Israel's occupation of the promised lands has implicitly advanced enough to invite broader prospects of confrontation, but at significant costs. A territory, the 'land of Canaan' was promised by Yahweh to his people, (Exod. 6.4 and elsewhere), but it has been occupied by a people no longer serving Yahweh. The congruity of Yahweh and Israel known by Moses and Joshua has resolved into a human-oriented expansion in which the people pragmatically adopt the gods of the lands occupied. At the outset of the book of Judges, Israel has no land but Yahweh is present. At this stage of the book, Israel has spread its extent of occupation, but has been increasingly losing contact with Yahweh: in pursuing its territorial conquest, it has lost its spiritual territory. It is ever more oppressed by the peoples whose lands it occupies; the 'evil' has spread with the occupation, and the word of Yahweh (2.3) is being realized.

But this time when Israel cries to Yahweh for relief from oppression, confessing apostasy, Yahweh will hear none of it. He quickly reviews all the enemies he has saved the people from and reminds them that *they* have forsaken *him*. Recalling Joash's remonstrance to the people when Gideon had broken down Baal's temple and Asherah, Yahweh tells the Israelites to 'Go and cry to the gods which you have chosen: let them save you'. The future of Israel looks hopeless, and the people plead 'just this once', remove the foreign gods and serve Yahweh, but 'his soul is impatient with the efforts of Israel'.[6] Robert Polzin astutely notes:

> Yahweh's annoyance [is] with an Israel who believes in the efficacy of a timely, even a desparate [sic], repentance . . . What comes through quite forcefully in this dialogue are both Israel's rather self-serving conversion as an apparent attempt once more to use Yahweh to insure their peace and tranquility, and Yahweh's argument that a slighted and rejected God will be used no longer (1980:177-78).

Inasmuch as the text does not show Yahweh in sympathy with Israel, the reader may presume that Yahweh does not intervene on behalf of the Israelites, and that the ensuing actions—up to 11.29, when the spirit of Yahweh comes upon Jephthah—are solely determined by the people.

Indeed, the narrative does not introduce a judge to enact Yahweh's will. Instead, it describes a crisis: the opposition of Ammonites and Israelites in battle encampments. The immediate problem is that the Israelites are without a leader. In desperation, the people, the elders, offer leadership over Gilead to the 'man who will begin to fight against the Ammonites' (10.18). It is not the 'military commanders' but 'the people' or 'the elders of the people' who take the initiative, and the leadership over the people is *offered* to—not bargained for— the man who will only 'begin' to lead Israel out of oppression. After eighteen years of suffering, Israel does not expect a quick triumph. (That the victory *is* quick emphasizes Yahweh's role in achieving it.)

As the narrative closes in on one figure, the future judge, it provides summarized expositional material particularizing the judge. In a brief flashback, unique among the otherwise sequentially-organized individual narratives, Jephthah the Gileadite is introduced as the son of a harlot by an unknown man named Gilead. Jephthah may well consider himself a lawful heir and regard his disinheritance as illegal, but his half-brothers have the authorities of the community on their side. This is obvious because Jephthah later accuses the elders of driving him out. They do not offer to reinstate him as heir when they offer him military and civil leadership (11.5-11).

Another possible interpretation is that Jephthah is the son of 'Gilead' by a harlot: that is, the land of his birth is personified as his nameless father.[7] In this case Jephthah has no legal claim among his fellow clansmen, and they throw Jephthah out lest he make claim to rights from their 'father', their people, their land.[8] Whether disinherited or without right of inheritance, Jephthah is unsupported by the Gileadites and, as an outlaw from Israelite territory, he flees to Tob in north-eastern Gilead where he and 'worthless fellows' go raiding, presumably caravans and travellers. Both versions support the view of Jephthah as the son of a mother of low social background, as a man whose social role is catapulted from the fringes of society to outside that society and from thence to the center of the same.

Jephthah's narrative observes the paradigmatic element of a personal characteristic of the judge, and Jephthah is as unlikely a choice as any. He is particularized in that his mother is a harlot, even lower than a socially recognized concubine. Nevertheless, he introduces no temptation to foreign customs or gods, so threatening at this phase of Israel's history; his mother is, presumably, an Israelite harlot.[9] Despite his lack of legal status, Jephthah is remembered as a 'mighty warrior', likely having developed a reputation as a successful raider; and the Gileadite leaders seek him out as a military leader. Responding to their offer, in a reversal of Yahweh's rhetorical question to Israel (10.11), Jephthah recalls what the Gileadites did to *him*:

Yahweh: (What *I* did)	*Jephthah:* (What *you* did)
Did I not deliver you from the Egyptians and from the Ammonites and from the Philistines?	Did you not hate me and drive me from my father's house?

In forthright candor, Jephthah asks the Gileadite elders, 'Why have you come to me now when you are in trouble?' and the answer he receives is just as direct: 'That is why we have turned to you now, that you may go with us and fight with the Ammonites' (11.8). The leaders promise Jephthah to be 'head' of all the Gileadites, but in his paraphrasing reply, Jephthah introduces new and relevant conditions:

Leaders of Gilead (11.8)	*Jephthah* (11.9)
. . . and you shall go with us and fight against the sons of Ammon	If you take me back to fight against the sons of Ammon *and Yahweh gives them up before me*
and you shall be our head to all the people of Gilead.	shall I be your head?

Jephthah merely repeats the offer of the elders of Gilead, in their phrasing, adding only the humble condition that Yahweh support him. He assumes no power, not even in battle; he understands that Yahweh, not man, determines whether battles are won or lost. In grounding his leadership of the people upon the success of his leadership in battle *under Yahweh*, Jephthah seeks compliance with Yahweh's will. Should he lose the battle but not his life, Jephthah would, it is implied, renounce continued leadership as not favored by

Yahweh. The elders agree that 'Yahweh will be a witness between us; we will surely do according to your word' (11.11). Accordingly, Jephthah is made civilian 'head' and military 'commander' by the people in a ceremony of consecration ('spoke his words') before Yahweh at Mizpah. Mizpah is where Jephthah had apparently settled his family (at least his daughter) on his return from Tob, and Mizpah is where the Israelites were encamped.[10]

The site of Mizpah is central to the story. Associated with it are the assembly of the army, the cult center, the vows ('words') of leadership, and Jephthah's new home among his people; it is to Mizpah that Jephthah returns from his recruitment tour (11.29), and it is at Mizpah that he 'vowed a vow' (11.30).[11] The name of this site means 'place of outlook or watch, including a watch tower', from the root *ṣafā*', 'to look out, watch'. Burney infers 'that the city was situated on some eminence or spur of the Gilead-range overlooking a wide prospect' (1970:307). This detail, however, does not explain the unusual repetition of the site-name, and repetition warrants attention. I suggest 'Mizpah' calls attention to the use of historical fact (Mizpah, 'place of outlook') for literary purposes, to underscore the narrative development ironically. For Jephthah, in one important sense, fails to 'look out, watch' both when he makes a vow and when he fulfills it; and Mizpah is *not mentioned* after the sacrifice of Jephthah's daughter.

Jephthah's first act is one of diplomacy. Although the armies are encamped and ready for battle, Jephthah inquires of the Ammonites why they plan to attack Gilead. The Ammonite king gives him answer, claiming Israel, as it came down from Egypt, took Ammonite land. In his reply, Jephthah recounts the history of the period in question, three hundred years earlier, ultimately shifting the basis for Israel's occupation of certain territories from the domain of human will to that of divine will. Israel's passage *through* the lands east of the Jordan had been refused first by Edom, then by Moab, and finally by Sihon, king of the Amorites. Only the last gathered his people and fought with Israel, 'and Yahweh, God of Israel, gave Sihon and all his people into the hand of Israel'. Jephthah repeats that Yahweh dispossessed the Amorites of the lands under question . . . 'and are you to take possession of them?' Does the Ammonite king consider himself more powerful than the god of Israel? Furthermore, these lands were Amorite, not Ammonite, and Israel won them by right of conquest. The Ammonites have no rightful claim to them whatsoever.

Suggesting that a people must accept the will of its god, Jephthah rhetorically questions whether the Ammonites will not possess what lands Chemosh, its god, gives it, and answers for Israel that it will possess all that Yahweh the god of Israel has caused (gives) it to possess. He concludes by saying that 'Yahweh the Judge shall judge between the sons of Israel and the sons of Ammon' (11.27-28). Jephthah alone among the judges declines to judge, attempting to avoid war with a foreign nation by negotiation by discussing the source of conflict; but his solution—that the Ammonites submit to the decision of the Israelite god—is understandably unheeded. (Gideon, we recall, does effectively utilize diplomacy *within* the Israelite tribes, with the Ephraimites.)

That the message of diplomacy is given verbatim attests to the importance of its contents. On the one hand, it justifies the Israelite occupation of the land in terms of non-aggression (unless in defense) and establishes Yahweh's role in determining the outcome of such provocations. Secondly, the message provides important information about Jephthah: he seeks to avoid military confrontation if possible, and he defers decisive powers to Yahweh. At this point, Jephthah seems a long-awaited exemplar, a Yahwist judge, a man who will surely avert the decline of Israel into short-ranged, merely human perspectives.

There are, however, other aspects to the message. For one thing, Jephthah has his facts all wrong. His 'logical' argument conflates Moabite, Ammonite, and Amorite historical figures and events and even transposes the national gods (Soggin, 1981:210). The conflation serves a function: it implies that Jephthah's knowledge of his people is inaccurate on a factual level. It is no wonder that the king of the Ammonites does not 'heed the message' (11.28). But most decisive is Jephthah's 'conception of Chemosh as a national deity, exercising a potency and influence in relation to this people comparable to that which Yahweh exercises over Israel' (Burney, 1970:300). For all his apparent piety, Jephthah identifies Yahwism with the *practices* of the local cults rather than the *ideals* of Yahwist faith; he does not understand belief in the *one* god, the basic tenet of Yahweh's commandments: 'Hear, O Israel, Yahweh our god, Yahweh [is] one' (Deut. 6.4).[12]

To this point, Jephthah's narrative has not identified him as a judge: the pattern of Jephthah's story, like Ehud's and Gideon's, is lacking the 'raised up' judge (or deliverer) element. However,

Jephthah, as elected leader of the Gileadites, defers to Yahweh as judge. In contrast to the Gideon narrative, where Yahweh bestows many favors on the reluctant and skeptical judge, the Jephthah narrative is remarkably meager with respect to Yahweh. The comparison is inimical to Gideon: whereas he was skeptical and repeatedly 'tested' Yahweh, Jephthah evidences no doubts, either in himself as a 'mighty warrior' or in Yahweh's powers. Jephthah immediately reveals himself as a brave and willing fighter, under Yahweh, for Israel.

Jephthah is a complex character, embodying a range of desirable qualities: strength, self-confidence, diplomacy, humility, overt piety; and one undesirable quality: basic ignorance of his belief and of his people. Because memory functions to test 'the existing cult in the light of the past historical tradition' (Childs, 1962:53), the covenant relationship between Israel and Yahweh must be reviewed by each generation. Instruction in the law is part of covenant history, and historical memory 'establishes the continuity of the new generation with the decisive events of the past' (Childs, 1962:51). Jephthah has almost every desirable quality for a judge, lacking only that one element which must be transmitted by man from one generation to another in order that the covenant be renewed and the past made present. That element is the instruction passed on from father to son, and Jephthah has no father. A condemnation of irresponsible promiscuity is implicit in Jephthah's lack of knowledge of his people's tradition. Ignorant of Israel's past, Jephthah cannot remember it, cannot participate in it, and cannot renew it.

Though he has not been 'raised up', the spirit of Yahweh does come upon Jephthah, and he commences toward confrontation with the Ammonites, presumably gathering forces at the places named. As the leader of an army and mindful of his dependence upon Yahweh's will, Jephthah makes a vow to Yahweh: if Yahweh will 'give the Ammonites' into his power, Jephthah will observe the victory with a burnt offering. Again the contrast with Gideon is exploited: whereas Gideon took his victory as proof of his own powers, Jephthah asks for victory and promises formal recognition of Yahweh's role in that victory afterwards. Gideon wanted to understand, and rationality marks his narrative. In contrast, Jephthah is not only untutored in his belief but does not recognize his own blindness. He does not know that he does not know.

Jephthah's vow has been the source of many and differing

interpretations.[13] Literally, Jephthah promises to sacrifice 'the outcoming which comes out' of the doors of his house to meet him upon his return. Although human sacrifice was not unknown, 'it was not a normal practice in Israel' (Martin, 1975:145); indeed, it seems to have been exceptional. It was not condoned and was altogether unsuitable as an offering to Yahweh, who had tested Abraham's faith with the demand of the sacrifice of his son Isaac (Gen. 22.2), only to *halt* the human sacrifice and *substitute* an animal offering. The parallel to Abraham's story is reinforced by the fact that both Abraham's son and Jephthah's daughter are sole descendants (in the narrative contexts):

Abraham (Gen. 22.2)	*Jephthah* (Judg. 11.34)
Take your son,	. . . his daughter came out . . .
your only son Isaac,	she, she alone
whom you love, and go . . .	except for her he had
	neither son nor daughter.[14]

Jephthah actually makes the human sacrifice; and the occasion is not gratitude for victory[15] but adherence to a vow, a contract. In the ancient Israelite tradition, the idea most prevalent behind 'sacrifice' is 'gift', whether sacred, burnt, or of another class. A sacrifice is not a penance but a gift to Yahweh and implies an element of communion. The best parts (especially fat) of the meat are burnt so that the odours are pleasing to Yahweh, and man sits before the altar to share the meal. Jephthah's sacrifice of his daughter scarcely accords with the character of Israelite sacrifice, in which:

> Alike the innocent mirth of the more pleasing scenes and the excess of the darker pictures strongly reflect a conception of sacrifice in which men eat before a kindly and favourable deity, not before one who needed placating . . . where *to rejoice* before Yahweh and *to eat* before Yahweh are alike synonyms for to *perform* and *to take part* in the sacrificial cultus (Gray, 1971:93; my italics).

Such a eucharistic sacrifice, offered with feelings of joy and mirth and security, is rendered grotesque with the sacrifice of a beloved daughter. Jephthah first promises a sacrifice in order to make a deal, to exert control over the god—a practice familiar to non-Yahwists.[16] The conflation of traditions eventuates in the Israelite sacrifice of a human, fully contradictory to the general tenor of biblical sacrifice.

Israelite sacrifices were freely-given gifts to Yahweh, with an increasing tendency to commute sacrifices or gifts in kind into money or to regard sacrifices and other gifts to God in the light of their monetary value. The idea of gift is expressed in the law of the first born (Exod. 22.28), in which Yahweh demands; 'The first-born of your sons you shall give to me'. In Exod. 34.19, the phrasing of the same law modifies the idea of *gift*; it implies a certain *sanctity* of the first-born: 'All that opens the womb [firstborn] is mine'. But even in the earliest laws, the first-born of humanity must be redeemed:

> nor . . . does the early law state *how* they were redeemed, whether as in the case of an unclean animal by a clean animal to which the story of the substitution of a ram for Isaac might point, or by a money payment as in the later law. But the later law and practice is clear. The first-born of man were redeemed at five shekels . . . (Num 18.16). What may, then, in early times have been something more than or other than a mere gift develops into a mere money payment, a sacred tax . . . on the first birth.
>
> The essential fact to observe is that the custom of vowing persons to Yahweh outlived the custom of sacrificing them to him; and that *in all such cases the vowed person had to be commuted for money* . . . (Lev 27.1-2) (Gray:1971:35-36; my italics. For specific commutation values, see Lev. 27.2-8).

Had Jephthah 'known' his faith, he would have known that the observance of the burnt offerings had been increasingly commuted: that Yahweh gave the best of the offerings to his priests and that, in any case, man must not be sacrificed.[17]

The Israelites were surrounded by other religious groups which practiced human sacrifice, particularly of the firstborn son. Yahweh consistently counters this unacceptable practice by demonstrating that human sacrifice is *not* agreeable to him. Yahweh is depicted as wanting the children of Israel to be 'given' to him, but in spirit, not in body.[18]

The sacrifice of Jephthah's daughter has typically been considered 'an attempt to explain, by means of a legend about the sacrifice of a virgin, an annual four-day festival in Israel' (Martin, 1975:146). The festival is alluded to, but the purpose of the narrative is not to explain a tradition; it is to forbid its recurrence. This is supported by the division of the verses: the word *ḥoq*, which may mean 'custom' *or* 'law'—and they are not necessarily the same—is the concluding object[19] (grammatically and rhetorically) of v. 39:

Daughter	*Jephthah-Israel*
39a And it was, at the end of two months that *she* returned to her *father*;	39b And *he* [Jephthah] did to her his vow which he had *vowed*;
39c And *she* never knew a *man*;	39d And *she* became a *decree* in *Israel*.

This view is supported by the *Targum of Jonathan to the Prophets*, which translates *ḥoq* not as 'custom' but as 'decree' and clarifies:

> and it became a decree in Israel, so that no man should offer up his son or his daughter as a burnt offering, as Jephthah the Gileadite without consulting Phineas the priest; for if he had consulted Phineas the priest, he would have redeemed her for money (Smolar, 1983:10).

The verse alternates its concentration between the daughter and Jephthah. Reading according to focus highlights the daughter's innocence: though she 'returned to her father', she never 'knew' a man. The sexual implication is clear; may we also understand that she never knew—understood—any man? Jephthah's daughter is not only virginal, she is unknowing, innocent; and 'innocence' is a kind of 'ignorance'. The daughter is innocent, the father is ignorant. The daughter is already a victim of her father's ignorance and that ignorance will victimize him. Jephthah loses his daughter and he loses contact with Yahweh, both through ignorance.

In Exod. 13.2, Yahweh claims 'every first-born *opening* the womb among the sons of Israel'. Such first-born are inherently sacred and belong to Yahweh. In the earliest version of sacrificial law, the first-born of clean animals are to be sacrificed to Yahweh on the *eighth* day after birth (Exod. 13.15; 22.28). The eighth day marks another significant conjunction of Yahweh and Israel, the day on which newborn male children are circumcised:

Gen. 17.12	He that is eight days old among you shall be circumcised; every male throughout your generations . . .
Gen. 21.4	And Abraham circumcised his son Isaac when he was eight days old as God had commanded him.

The original import of circumcision can only be conjectured, but among the theories which have been given some credence is the concept that circumcision was 'a form of sacrifice . . . even a substitute for human sacrifice, a part being offered up in lieu of the whole' (*IDB*, I, 1971:630). In discussion of Exod. 22.28-29, Graves and Patai interpret this law as referring 'to infant sacrifice rather than to that of youths or grown men, and could be evaded by a token sacrifice of the first-born's foreskin at circumcision' (1963:175). Circumcision may be understood as an early re-orientation of the non-Israelite cult practice of human sacrifice. 'Above all, it was an act of initiation into the covenant community' (*IDB*, I, 1971:630): circumcision serves as a sign that each man is a son of the covenant. Should the circumcision ceremony have originally also functioned to deter human sacrifice, this significance seems to have been diminished or lost by the Mosaic period, when humans were explicitly excluded from ritual sacrifice by redemption, with specific fees established for man and for woman, according to age.

Like sacrifice, the ceremony of 'shedding the blood of the covenant' must be performed on the eighth day, even if it is a Sabbath or festival, as long as the child is fit. At its inception, 'the promise that Abraham's seed should inherit the land of Canaan was bound up with this covenant'; and 'before the Israelites entered Canaan, they were circumcised by Joshua, the rite having been omitted in the wilderness owing to the hazards of the journey (Josh. 5.2 ('Circumcision', *EncJud* V, 1971:567-68).

The 'first-born', 'the [one] opening the womb' is sacred to Yahweh, claimed by him and to be redeemed. Jephthah's name means 'He (i.e. Yahweh) opens', with the likelihood that 'the womb' is implied. First-born 'Jephthah' is thus *inherently* sacred to Yahweh, and his breaking of Yahwist principles, even the covenant, is ironic in light of his own name. Jephthah's daughter is also a first-born. Yahweh has repeatedly forbidden human sacrifice, and the price of redemption has already been established, but Jephthah does not know the principles of his piety. He does not comprehend the spirit of his faith and he commits a basic offense against Yahweh.

Jephthah's reaction to his daughter's appearance suggests yet another implication in his name. In 11.35, he says 'I have opened my mouth to Yahweh', and his daughter repeats the phrase, 'You have opened your mouth to Yahweh'. This is an unusual expression for making a vow; indeed, though 'opened . . . mouth' occurs in many of the scriptural books, it is not expressly used in conjunction with making a vow except in Judg. 11.35-36. Jephthah, probably ignorantly, ironically alludes to his own sacred tie to Yahweh in making an anti-Yahwist vow.

Jephthah's act of human sacrifice misses the point of the tale of Abraham's willingness to sacrifice his son Isaac: the sacrifice was *averted, substituted* with an animal. 'Biblical history . . . stretches as a long series of demonstrations of divine power followed by tests of memory, gratitude, inference from precept and precedent, or, in short, of 'knowledge', with further demonstrations staged in reward or punishment (Sternberg, 1985:48).

This narrative, like the penultimate narrative of the book (Judges 19), re-enacts an episode from the story of Abraham, and both times the effect is devastating. The import of the Genesis narrative is not to be found in the specific events *per se*, but in the *significance* of the events. Abraham was shown that human dedication and devotion pleased Yahweh, but that human sacrifice was not pleasing to him: the substitution of an animal demonstrates Yahweh's preference. When he sacrifices his daughter, Jephthah's law- and covenant-breaking piety, based on ignorance, is implicitly disclaimed by Yahweh, who becomes silent and remains inactive during the remainder of this narrative. Subsequent to the sacrifice, Jephthah's leadership continues in pious ignorance, with less emphasis on the piety.

Jephthah's dilemma is clear: he has made a vow to Yahweh, however hastily, and the circumstances have ironically turned the vow of contract into a personal sacrifice. It is obvious Jephthah's conception of Israelite history is muddled; that the more significant spiritual level is also not comprehended should not come as a surprise. He may have been a devoted Yahwist, but—ironically to the reader—he includes aspects of heathen worship in his concept of Yahwism. In the crisis, which Jephthah initiates by his lack of caution and fails to avert by his ignorance, he reveals new aspects of his character: he never gives a thought to the person sacrificed or to her pain. Jephthah emerges as self-centered, without sympathy for his daughter. He bemoans only his own 'being brought low'. In his self-pity, Jephthah complains that his daughter has caused his dilemma, repeating that she is the cause of his grief. The daughter, whose dignity mocks her lack of a name, accepts her fate, regretting not her father's vow but her virginity, her lack of progeny. The daughter's role is as ironic as her father's. Both mean to please a higher power—father, god. As a personification of Israel, Jephthah's unwillingness to accept responsibility for his errors and his displacing them on the victim are subtle comments on the condition of Israel. The longstanding argument over whether Jephthah *intended* a human sacrifice or not is beside the point: the ambiguity is intended. Because Yahweh is not characterized as all-knowing, the ambiguity allows him to confer his spirit upon Jephthah, whose intentions are not yet clear, *before* the vow is made, so that divine knowledge of Jephthah's intentions is not involved. The point being made is that Jephthah understood the events of history only scantily and the spiritual significance of that history even less. Though Jephthah defers to Yahweh, he does so not as a believer in the *one* god, but as a believer in one of many gods. The vow that Jephthah makes may be construed as intended to please another god: just as Jephthah conflates histories and gods in his diplomatic message, he does so in this most critical moment of his life. He transposes the values of Yahweh with those of other gods, gods for whom a vow must be kept, even if it involves human sacrifice. In so doing, he implicitly acknowledges polytheism. Jephthah has not comprehended the morality which seeks the commitment of the human soul rather than the sacrifice of the human body.

The Bible

> addresses a people defined in terms of their past and commanded to keep its memory alive.... By incorporating the definition and command and observance, the narrative uniquely internalizes its own rules of communication, whereby the remembrance of the past devolves on the present and determines the future.... It was this historical memory that made Israel a people (Sternberg, 1985:31).

Jephthah's failure to know the past severs all 'communication'; it effectively separates him from his people, and his daughter's death eliminates his line of descent. Indeed, with the sacrifice, the impetus of Jephthah's career changes. The concluding verses narrate his 'victory' against his own people, the Ephraimites, which clearly contradicts Yahwism. The pride and jealousy of the Ephraimites seems to provoke the devastating war between the tribes of Gilead and Ephraim, but a closer look at the text undermines this supposition. The Ephraimites do assemble and march northward, they do threaten to destroy him (Jephthah, the Gileadites) by fire, and for the same reason they used with Gideon, i.e., that they had not been invited to fight in the battles of victory. Gideon forestalled the Ephraimites when they made exactly the same claim against him. Jephthah protests that he had 'called' them when he was fighting with the Ammonites; because they did not act to save (deliver), he had to risk his own life. Once again, Jephthah gives Yahweh credit for delivering the enemy into his power, and he questions why they have now come to fight him and his people.

Jephthah's response (12.1-3) seems a reasonable and diplomatic one to the troublesome Ephraimites, a response perhaps not as conciliatory as that of Gideon, but straightforward in stating the conditions and asking for a reasonable basis for hostilities. In 12.2, Jephthah tells the Ephraimites that he has been *'îš rîb*, a 'man of strife, war'. The word *rîb* is the root of Je-*rub*-baal—'let Baal contend'—the name given to Gideon. Jephthah identifies himself with the contending aspect of Gideon.[20]

The hope that Jephthah might yet reverse the tide is quickly dissolved in the next verse, which tells that he gathers his army and fights the Ephraimites, and why? 'Because they said, "You Gileadites [are] fugitives of Ephraim, in the midst of Ephraim, in the midst of Manasseh"' (12.4). Although Jephthah for a second time introduces diplomacy in reaction to aggression, he quickly abandons the diplomacy when a personal sore-spot is touched. Perhaps the Gileadite that was disinherited by his own people and forced to be a *fugitive* responds impulsively to name-calling, to being identified, even with his people, as *fugitive* from Ephraim. Perhaps Jephthah's unreflective habit dominates. The outcome is that one tribe of Israel decimates another and forty-two thousand of Ephraim (of Israelites) fall.

The narrative of the battle focuses on and dramatizes one incident, and that hardly demonstrates potential for great military victory. With control of the fords of Jordan, the Gileadites challenge passers to say 'shibbolet'. Apparently the territorial expansion of the Israelites had so advanced that dialects had developed and subtleties in pronunciation differentiated the peoples rather than united them. Jephthah uses this differentiation as a weapon.

A glance in a Hebrew dictionary reveals many words with the same initial consonant-vowel constellation, so that the choice suggests further significance. Jephthah chooses a word rich in potential: *šibbolet* translates as 'an ear of corn', and derives from a root which means 'to rise, grow'. Jephthah uses the pronunciation of this word to do the opposite, *to cut down* the people of Israel.[21] The choice of pass-word symbolically associates Jephthah's two anti-Yahwist actions: human sacrifice and internecine war.

It is obvious that the round number of 42,000 men struck down cannot be correlated with the one-by-one questioning at the fords. The narrative uses this large round number to heighten the implications of Jephthah's maneuver, to show how the language and other ties were beginning to give way, how the Israelites could use their own weaknesses against themselves. As a result of this action, the tribe of Ephraim was never again as powerful, and a vital force of Israel was incapacitated. This battle, like the sacrifice of Jephthah's daughter, underscores the need to learn and to understand the precepts of the covenant. Empty piety is demonstrably misleading, even destructive. The reader can share Yahweh's patience with Gideon's knowledgeable and logical questioning and his impatience with Jephthah's impetuous ignorance.

The distinction between the 'spirit' and the 'letter' of Yahweh's will renders Jephthah's sacrifice an ironic reconstruction of Abraham's non-sacrifice. Though Jephthah seems the long-awaited judge, a man who indeed will deliver Israel both from her enemies and back to Yahweh, he is revealed as lacking knowledge of who he is or of what Israel is, in 'historical memory'. And the narrative makes clear that Jephthah's error originates not in the forces external to Israel but in those within: it portrays a lack of comprehension of the basic tenants of Yahwist belief, which was in the process of substituting law for ritual.[22]

The focus is squarely on Jephthah. In Gideon's tale, minor characters are introduced and dramatized; likewise Deborah and Barak share the limelight with Jael and Sisera. Even Abimelech has Jotham, Zebul and Gaal. In Jephthah's tale, no other individual is named: neither the king of the Ammonites, nor the elders of Gilead, nor even his daughter.[23] Jephthah (Israel) alone is the source of error.

The problem concentrated in Jephthah's narrative goes beyond the lack of knowledge which directly brings ruin to Jephthah and to Israel. The hero lacks knowledge because he lacks a father, the one responsible for passing on the male bonding, the knowledge of history. In the absence of a father due to death, the nearest relatives, even the community, fulfill the father's role. But the son of a harlot, even though Israelite, has neither father nor community as 'father'. Either way, his 'disinheritance' cuts him off from his spiritual inheritance as well as his inheritance of goods, from his historical roots as well as his legal rights.

This narrative brings the problem of fatherlessness into focus: Jephthah is the single male between two generations, two women—his mother and his daughter.[24] The line of Jephthah ends, and in disgrace. It all originated in unresisted temptation: the temptation of the blood (human lust, 'whoring after' women [or gods]) which assails the covenant of the blood (the pact between Yahweh and the chosen people of Israel). The narratives of Judges repeatedly warn the Israelites to control sexual desire. Whether with foreign women (Gideon's concubine) or not (the harlot-mother of Jephthah), non-familial Israelite proliferation is shown as potentially destructive.

The minor-judge pattern already implied (Jephthah is *not chosen* by Yahweh and is identified not by tribe but by clan or territory) becomes explicit: his narrative concludes with minor judge paradigm elements: the *specific duration* of his office—six years—as *judge* of Israel and the *place of burial*. This last reference suggests an element of irony: as Jephthah's father is (the men of) 'Gilead', so is he buried in the '*cities*' of Gilead'.

More Minor Judges

The distinction between 'major' and 'minor' judges implicit in this study refers not only 'to the *length* and *style* of the literary material preserved in the case of each figure' (Hauser, 1975:190). The conventional terms 'major' and 'minor' are also used to distinguish between the protagonists of two distinct paradigms. All of the judges after Abimelech incorporate the paradigm of the minor judges, and two—Jephthah and Samson—have the mixed-bag of both major and minor patterns, albeit differently composed. Jephthah's narrative is uniquely surrounded by those of the minor judges—two before and three after. Ibzan, Elon and Abdon observe the five-part minor judge paradigm elaborated above (p. 81), and these brief narratives are also particularized.

The scantiest minor-judge report is that of Elon the Zebulunite. In contrast to the negative information—shifts from covenantal, tribal values—about the other minor judges, Elon is singularly free from disparaging comment and he is described in terms of his tribe. This judge is known to be the eponymous ancestor of a clan (Num. 26.26), but the Judges text neglects to mention those descendants. Elon judges ten years, the longest office of the minor judges. That he is buried in a city which bears his own name, Elon (Aijalon), in the land of his fathers, the land of Zebulun, suggests that Elon represents a link between covenantal and earthly ethics.

The last of the minor judges, Abdon, bears the name of his father, Hillel, but the father had already lost tribal identification: he is 'the Pirathonite', member of a clan named after a geographical area. The blood-ties have become so short-lived that political and geographical formulations have assumed greater importance. Abdon has continuity only one generation preceding him and two generations into the future. The significance of the 'forty sons' and 'thirty grandsons' is implied both in the surprisingly *diminishing* numbers of descendants and in the importance attached to wealth: the significance accorded to the prestige of riding 'ass-colts'. Abdon, like his predecessors, has a brief and specific number of years as judge. Round numbers, which seem to carry more significance, have been shifted from the duration of judgeship to number of progeny—in this instance, ironically diminishing. The report of Abdon's death repeats the *full* name, ironically almost empty of meaning.[25] He is buried in Pirathon, situated in Ephraimite territory.

The focus of the minor-judge paradigm contributes significantly to the impetus of the entire book. The early narratives of the book of Judges advance the concept of Israel as a people composed of tribes and focus on the spiritual rewards of Yahwist belief. Tribal designations, on the one hand, and success in the cause of Israel, on the other, may be seen as linked elements which reflect the state of the conquest as realized by Yahweh's covenant people. At the outset of the book of Judges, the tribes of Israel sought to occupy the promised land. Yahweh promised the land to the *tribes* which were *sons of Israel*, the name Yahweh had given Jacob, reinforcing the link between Yahweh and his people; the land was not promised to *clans* which honor *themselves* or their *geographical areas* in their designations. With the re-focusing from Yahweh-designations to those of the people, the book of Judges calls attention to changes taking place in the concept of success: from that of Yahweh's Israel to those of worldly, often tangible values.

Othniel, the first judge named, and model for the subsequent major judge narratives, is indirectly designated, through his father and uncle, as a member of the tribe of Judah;[26] and Ehud is said to be of the tribe of Benjamin. There is no mention in either narrative of personal reward.[27] Shamgar, probably a non-Israelite, is identified by his delivery of Israel. No other glorification or reward is recorded, and Shamgar, whose values accord with those of the other judges of the early chapters, is passed over quickly; but Deborah, of the tribe of Issachar, is favorably juxtaposed with the mother of Sisera, who seeks pleasure in the plunder her son will bring home: Deborah's reward is success in the cause of Israel. The rewards of Ehud and Deborah (and implicitly Shamgar, Barak of Naphthali, and even Jael) are not individual and personal; they are the rewards of the people of Israel.[28] With the Gideon narrative, the book of Judges introduces distinct changes in both group designations and leadership values, changes which may be considered as linked. 'Clearly something new begins with Gideon' (Feldman, 1963:96).

Gideon is the first of the judges to not be specifically identified by tribe: his father is 'Joash the Abiezrite', and Gideon is 'son of him'. He is of the tribe of Manasseh because the clan of Abiezrites derives from that tribe (Josh. 17.2), but the narrative does not specify the tribe; it identifies Gideon only by his clan. For the first time, in this narrative, tribal names, which are held to by synonymous with 'Israel', give way to clan names, which only secondarily serve that function. 'Tribe' need not demonstrate Yahwist values, but is not associated with the individual and his personal success; 'clan' may intermittently evidence Yahwist values, but is consistently associated with power and wealth. With this shift of designation, interest turns from Israel's Yahwist and ethical *raison d'être* to other forms of motives: wealth, power. Unlike the earlier, tribal-designated judges, whose rewards may be understood as their victories over the enemies of Israel, Gideon seeks personal glory and collects plunder, worldly wealth. Though the *ephod* he builds with this gold is identified with temple worship, it becomes an idol and is associated with Gideon's town and Gideon's name. It is an object that is anti-Yahwist and intended to serve for personal glorification.

Abimelech, the anti-hero of the book, cannot be included among the saviors of Israel since neither his tribal designation nor his values come into question. The minor judges, however, may be compared to the early tribal judges in these respects.

In the post-Abimelech period, several minor judges are mentioned. Tola is a minor judge whose tribal origin is given (10.1-2). A member of a small remnant of Issachar in the hill country of Ephraim, Tola is not noted for any values: he neither delivers Israel nor is he marked by

personal wealth. Like all of the minor judges, he 'judges' Israel. Tola
is mentioned as a clan designation elsewhere (Num. 26.23; 1 Chron.
7.1ff.), and the name has been regarded as a 'possible confusion of
personal and clan names' (Boling, 1975:186).[29] The text, however,
identifies Tola, through his immediate forefathers, as 'a man of
Issachar'. One of the two minor judges identifed by tribe, Tola is not,
like the minor 'clan' judges, associated with worldly values. This
observation is supported by the narrative of Elon (12.11-12). Like
Tola of Issachar, Elon is identified by tribe, Zebulon; and Elon, like
Tola, is not associated with anti-Yahwist values. Elon becomes the
eponymous ancestor of a clan, the Elonites (Gen. 46.14), but he is not
associated with the clan in this text. Neither of these 'tribal' minor
judges is noted for his wealth or power.

Tola's follower, Jair, is a Gileadite, a designation which may refer
to the tribe of Gad or to a clan of the tribe of Manasseh, but here
refers to a third possibility, the geographical *area* called Gilead
(10.5). Tribal Gilead (Gad) is mentioned in a sequence (5.17) which
names the tribes in respect of their participation in the war against
Sisera. Jephthah the Gileadite, however, is a member of the Gilead
clan, one named after his 'father' (11.1). In the Jair narrative, 'Gilead'
is specifically identified as a geographical 'land', that 'fathered' or
'begat' by Gilead the son of Machir, of the line of Manesseh (Num.
26.29). The original tribal name of the Gileadites, 'Manasseh', has
probably localized as a clan named after Gilead, and the name
shifted from the ancestor to the territory. Thus two 'Gileads' are
cited: one tribal (Gad) and one clan, though the clan may represent
either an eponymous ancestor or a geographical territory. In any
case, the land of Gilead is distinguished from the tribal designation.

In the Jair episode, the tribal designation is vague at best, and
Jair's offspring are known by their wealth (ass-colts) and the cities
they found, which bear the name of their clan. If 'numerous
"progeny"' signifies 'large administrative responsibility' rather than
wealth, as Boling contends (1975:216), we may nevertheless assume
that the ass-colts represent power, and with power goes a comfortable
living standard. Shammai Feldman maintains that 'riding on mules
is a symbol of princely rank' (1963:96). To summarize, Jair's
judgeship not only attains but furthers mundane values—personal
glory in name, power and wealth—and an accompanying withdrawal
from Yahwist values.

After Jephthah, another minor judge, Ibzan, is not—even implicitly—identified by his tribe. Ibzan is typically not called up; he simply appears 'after' his predecessor. He is not identified by his tribe, but neither is he associated with his clan. In a move away from bloodlines toward identification with the land itself, this judge is distinguished as a man of a city, of Bethlehem. Ibzan bears comparison with Jair: like Jair, Ibzan is linked to a place, and the name of the place has no ties whatever to a tribal designation. Ibzan is from Bethlehem, and he makes his mark solely by the number of sons and daughters—thirty of each—he fathers. Those descendants offer a further point of comparison: both Jair and Ibzan are individualized by their descendants, specifically in the same round number, thirty. Ibzan does manage to 'improve' the situation: he has not only thirty sons but also thirty daughters. The number 'thirty' is held to have political significance, which is supported by Ibzan's marrying his progeny outside 'his clan', thereby forming political alliances which emphasize the importance of the clan; and whereas Jair could establish thirty towns in the clan name, Ibzan can make further political alliances by sending his thirty daughters abroad and by bringing in thirty 'daughters' for his sons. Nevertheless, Ibzan judges only seven years. He is buried in Bethlehem. No allusion is made to tribal designations.

The last minor judge, Abdon, is member of a geographically named clan, the Pirathonites; and like Ibzan, he prolifically fathers sons and grandsons, all of whom ride ass-colts. Burney infers that Ibzan's and Abdon's descendants' names, like those of Jair, represent village sesttlements (1970:289). The clans are thus shown to be spawning ever more clans, geographical areas linked by clan, sub-clan and geographical names without reference to tribe of origin.

In none of the minor judges' narratives is there mention of Yahweh. Shamgar simply 'delivered' Israel; the later minor judges not only 'judged' Israel, but founded wealthy clans which bore their names, an aspect that introduces an element of irony into their 'judge'-ment. These judges of family-clans or geographically named clans, or of cities without reference to clan, represent the weakening bond with Yahweh, the bond which makes Israel a unity.[30]

The Minor Judges

	Citation		Orientation	
Judge	Tribe	Clan	Israel	Individual
Shamgar	–	–	xx	–
Tola	Issachar	–	–	–
Jair	–	Gilead	–	xx
Ibzan	–	Bethlehem	–	xx
Elon	Zebulun	–	–	–
Abdon	–	Pirathon	–	xx

Robert Alter called attention to the 'most rigorous economy of means' through which biblical texts convey information (1981:22). Through such means, the narratives suggest a correspondence between the association of clan-names with mundane, non-Yahwist values, and a shift in this direction can be discerned.

The pattern is consistent for the major judges as well. I have already discussed Gideon, the first clan-designated judge, and shown why Abimelech is outside the entire scheme. Jephthah, the next 'clan' judge, is a Gileadite. 'Gilead was the father of Jephthah' (11.1), but 'Jephthah the Gileadite died, and was buried in his cities in Gilead' (12.7). The text does not enable us to determine whether in this instance 'Gilead' refers to the eponymous ancestor of the line of Manasseh or to the tribe of Gad which occupied the territory, but either way, Jephthah is identified not by tribe but by ancestor or territory, not by the Yahweh-blessed (through Jacob–Israel) designations of his people but by Israelite, human ones.

It may be objected that the spirit of Yahweh descends upon Jephthah, a 'clan' judge. Actually, as Israel has been supplanting Yahwist values with her own, Yahweh has been accepting the increasingly short-sighted Israelites available to him to accomplish his goals. But note the exception with Abimelech. Though half-Israelite (by his father, not the determining mother), his values are fully foreign, and the only divine involvement is God's sending the opposite of the divine spirit, and evil spirit (9.23). And after Gideon's initial reluctance and subsequent apostasy, Jephthah seems to do everything right. He credits Yahweh with his anticipated success and takes his vow before Yahweh at a holy sanctuary. When Jephthah, a clan-member, *behaves* like a tribal Israelite and appeals to Yahweh, divine grace is bestowed. In gracing Jephthah with his spirit, Yahweh demonstrates willingness to help a Yahwist Israel. But Jephthah proves to be a clan descendant with all that that implies, and Yahweh withdraws his support from Jephthah as he had from Gideon and will from Samson.

Jephthah, associated with a territory, is banned from the territory which gave him a name until needed by the very men who had banned him. This is the only judge narrative in which a judge is chosen by the people and subsequently empowered by (given the spirit of) Yahweh to fight for the cause of Israel. However, after Jephthah betrays his ignorance of Yahwist belief and his people's history, he fights against a true tribe, the Ephraimites.

Despite a long introduction to this episode, a narration which describes the Ephraimite confrontation of Jephthah and Jephthah's reasonable response (12.1-3), the internecine war does not arise from the grounds for complaint given in the expository section. The men of Ephraim want to avenge themselves for having been denied part in Jephthah's victory, and Jephthah could answer that charge, presumably to their satisfaction. What Jephthah could not 'answer' is the Ephraimite charge of 12.4; he attacks the Ephraimites because they call the Gileadites 'fugitives' of Ephraim 'in the midst of Ephraim [and] Manasseh'. Ephraim and Manasseh were sons of Joseph and counted among the original twelve tribes. In this sense, any group that identifies itself by ancestor or territory instead of its tribal name *is* fugitive: it has left, indeed 'escaped' membership in the tribal groups of the covenant people, Israel; it has established (under an eponymous ancestor) a name-oriented group or become part of a geographically designated one.

The point of Gideon's successful diplomacy (8.2) also becomes clear: 'Are not the gleanings of [the tribe of] Ephraim better than the vintage of [the clan of] Abiezer?' Gideon humbles the military successes of the clan before those of the tribe; he is intelligent and knows the significance of the tribes of the Israelite covenant, even if he does succumb to the temptations of earthly 'glory'. Jephthah, less knowledgeable, possibly confuses his personal phase as fugitive with the more profound accusation of the Ephraimites. The son of a clan compounds his errors against Yahweh by initiating an 'unholy' internecine war, a clan war against a tribe, a 'Yahweh' group.

The last judge, Samson, is a Danite. His father, Manoah, has been held to be the eponymous ancestor of a clan division of the Danites inhabiting Zorah, and other interpretations of the relationship between Manoah and the Manahites are noted.[31] In a designation that would be curious except for the pattern demonstrated, that of shift from tribe-of-Israel to clan-of-people or -area, the Danites are referred to in this narrative *not* as tribe, but as clan or family (*mišpaḥāh*). Though one of the original tribes, Dan is specifically identified in 13.2 as a clan. This otherwise inexplicable naming of a tribe as clan does function to direct the reader's attention to the configuration proposed. Consistent with clan values, Samson's interests, despite his 'calling', are never the cause of Israel; and they are decidedly 'earthy'. Once more, but for the last time in this book, Yahweh extends his grace to his chosen agent.

The Major and Minor Judges

Judge	Citation		Orientation	
	Tribe	Clan	Israel	Individual
Othniel	(Judah)	–	xx	–
Shamgar	–	–	xx	–
Ehud	Benjamin	–	xx	–
Deborah	Issachar	–	xx	–
Gideon	–	Abiezite	xx	xx
Abimelech	–	–	–	–
Tola	Issachar	–	–	–
Jair	–	Gilead	–	xx
Jephthah	–	Gilead	xx	xx
Ibzan	–	Bethleham	–	xx
Elon	Zebulon	–	–	–
Abdon	–	Pirathon	–	xx
Samson	–	'Dan'	–	xx

Thus most of the post-Deborah judges are identified by clan rather than by tribe, and the 'clan' judges, even after initial forays on behalf of Israel (e.g. Gideon and Jephthah) are shown to be concerned with values other than the cause of the people of Israel: 'the meaning of earlier data is progressively, even systematically, revealed or enriched by the addition of subsequent data' (Alter, 1981:11). By having the clan designations of the judges conform to the orientation of their actions, the author subtly suggests that the Israelite cohesion is fragmenting from within. The external conflict, necessary for realization of Yahweh's promise of occupation of the land, is undermined by an increasing tendency toward splintered eponymous groups in place of the unified, Yahweh-centered tribes of Israel; and by a shift in values from those of Israel to those of the individual, material and worldly.[32]

Irony

The paradigm of the minor judges is inherently ironic and is ironic in relation to the paradigm of the major judges. The covenantal attributes of the major judges are replaced by the time-, place- and value-limited ones of people who cannot 'judge' themselves but are said to 'judge' Israel. Accordingly, irony is both structural and integral to the major-minor narrative of Jephthah. Yahweh has refused to honor Israel's pleas or sudden devotion (10.15-16) and Israel must act without Yahweh to save itself. Israel's behavior and that of its leader-judge, Jephthah, is exemplary, and Yahweh does bestow his spirit upon Jephthah shortly before war against the oppressor is begun (11.29). Ironically, *immediately* (11.30), Jephthah makes his profoundly anti-Yahwist vow.

When called to serve Israel, a social outcast unexpectedly reveals himself to be Yahwist and ready to lead the people, and at this pinnacle his actions reverse the reader's expectations once again. 'Mizpah', the *look-out* point where Yahweh takes his vow, symbolizes what Jephthah does *not* do. Jephthah's very name—'He opened'—alludes to his being a first-born, one *sacred* rather than sacrificed to Yahweh; and this irony is emphasized by Jephthah's own words to his daughter: 'I have opened my mouth to Yahweh'. Jephthah's narrative brings the ironic counterpart of Yahweh's knowledge to new depths of ironic ignorance.

Of all the 'variation[s] on the theme of the incongruous deliverer' (Sternberg, 1985:273), Jephthah initially seems the *least* likely to save Israel: he is not even chosen, let alone 'raised up', by Yahweh. He is the son of a harlot, and by the main action of the narrative, he has been disinherited by his family, has become a fugitive from society, and engages in highway robbery. Ironically, Jephthah responds to the call of the Israelites with the *most* Yahwist behavior; Yahweh accepts Jephthah, granting him the divine spirit. The narrative then reverses itself once again, and a newly most-promising judge commits the *greatest sin* against Yahweh. Ironic reversals structure the main narrative of Jephthah.

The high point of the narrative, the sacrifice of Jephthah's daughter, is ironic on several levels. The sacrifice of a human, a daughter, as a 'gift of gratitude', a festivity shared with Yahweh, is grotesquely ironic. Jephthah's ignorance, which permits him to make the sacrifice to Yahweh, is underscored by the innocence-ignorance of his daughter who demonstrates 'honor' in heroically acceding to her father's vow.

This narrative also alludes to other narratives—both in earlier biblical books and in Judges—to effect contrast. Jephthah's sacrifice of his daughter alludes to the non-sacrifice of Abraham's son; Jephthah's ignorance recalls Gideon's knowledge (though ignorant compared to Yahweh). Even comparisons are used for ironic effect. Both Abimelech and Jephthah are sons of sexual relationships outside the marital vows. Granted, a concubine had the status of a 'second wife', and the children of such a union were legally recognized. In these narratives, however, both sons of non-familial wives effect serious damage to Israel in opposite ways: Abimelech as anti-Israelite, as enemy; Jephthah as Yahwist, Israelite, friend. And the Yahwist is the more destructive; as a consequence of failing to recognize the *oneness* of Yahweh, he sacrifices a human to Yahweh, and he leads an internecine war against one of Yahweh's tribes, a definitive blow in the history of that tribe.

Chapter 7

THE LAST JUDGE

Samson

Samson's narrative not only integrates disparate elements, but it also involves an unusually complex structure. On one level, an episode of promise-and-fulfillment is encapsulated within a larger framework of reversal of expectations. J. Cheryl Exum (1980:43-59) has demonstrated that Judges 13 constitutes an independent story in a 'ring composition' which fulfills the promise of birth, thus effecting closure. She distinguishes three major divisions within this structure: the first is an inclusio involving 'appearance', the second is a series of questions and answers, and the third is, like the first, an inclusio—in this instance involving 'watching'. The analysis shows the first section anticipating 'the structure' of the whole in miniature' (Exum, 1980:58). Manoah is at the center, as Samson is in subsequent chapters, but the male figures are 'led' by women.

The structure of ch. 13 creates more than a 'literary bridge' to the adventures of Samson in the succeeding chapters: it creates a pattern of promise and fulfillment, of anticipations to be further realized. In effect, the development of ch. 13 establishes expectations, but these expectations are consistently reversed so that the initial structure also serves as a ploy to lure the reader into renewed optimism and leads to the crux of Israel's apostasy under the judges.

The narrative of Samson, the last of the judges, is both an anomaly in the sequence and, paradoxically, epitomizes the judges of the prior narratives. And it clearly has its own unique qualities: it is vividly earthy and humorous, and it allows the reader to share the hero's actions—and his thoughts and feelings as well.[1] As a result, the Samson narrative seems (but only seems) to offer the reader more information. Despite the concrete presentation, the reader soon discovers that Samson cannot evaluate information according to the desired standard, that his perspective is 'unreliable', and that his information may be misleading. He is full of high spirits and low ethics. Four chapters long, Samson's narrative effectively combines disparate elements of the sacred and the secular: traditional biblical motifs, allusions to other Judges' narratives and other biblical books. It is not surprising that this, the most complex of all the narratives of this book, has generated more commentary, and more conflicting interpretations, than any other.

Indeed, because of this complexity I have deviated somewhat from the sequential exposition of earlier narratives. In addition to narrative sequence, I direct the reader's attention to the extensive allusions of the Samson narrative to earlier major-judge narratives and to earlier biblical books, using these allusions as a secondary expository framework. This discussion, then, will trace both intimations of past narratives and books, and progression of the Samson narrative.

The first verse complies with the pattern of the major judges' narratives: Israel does evil and is oppressed by foreign (here Philistine) powers for a standard round number of years (forty), but neither the nature of the evil nor of the oppression is dwelt upon. These elements have been progressively developed in prior narratives: this narrative surprises, and perhaps prepares for further unexpected turns, by rushing through the necessary 'formalities'. This time Israel does not even cry to Yahweh for relief from oppression. The story begins abruptly, *without any background in time and place.* This lack symbolically foreshadows the developing emphasis of this story and the ones that follow.

With the progression of the narratives, Yahweh has tended to be ever less present, less verbal, less participating. In Deborah's narrative, in which Yahweh does not directly speak or take action, his involvement is suggested through her words in his name and is corroborated by his deeds. By contrast, in each of the post-Deborah narratives, whatever contact is initially present is notably withdrawn as the judge deviates from the covenant.

In the pre-Samson narratives, Yahweh's presence and participation is most notable in Gideon's, prior to and including his Yahweh-led battle. Gideon's narrative serves as a transition, his doubt an ironic echo of the unquestioning belief of Othniel, Ehud and Deborah, and his later self-aggrandisement an anticipation of the half-heathen power-lust (of Abimelech) and ignorance (of Jephthah) which follow.

And in the second phase of Gideon's narrative, Yahweh is notably less in evidence, less in contact with his people. Gideon's first battle is 'fought' by Yahweh, who 'set every man's sword against his companion' in the enemy camp (7.22). Subsequently, Gideon fights his own battles without comment or assistance from Yahweh. Abimelech's 'leadership', for he did not 'judge' Israel, is anti-Yahwist, and records only a single, negative involvement of God (an evil spirit). Jephthah's judgeship is only seconded by Yahweh's granting of the divine spirit; and man's choice, based on battle experience (brigandage), proves no better than Yahweh's (whose basis of selection is unknowable). In each of these narratives, as the judge proves himself unworthy, Yahweh becomes 'silent' and takes no further part in the action.

The reader, then, is quite unprepared for another visit from (an angel of) Yahweh and is probably as surprised as the barren wife at the message he brings. This time Yahweh does not appoint or inspire a judge; he announces the birth of a son. The divine visitor dictates specific prohibitions for the woman, reiterates her fruitfulness— indeed, she is already pregnant!—and explains that the son shall be a *nazîr* to Elohim from the womb and shall initiate delivery of Israel from the Philistines (13.5). This leader-to-be is twice sacred to Yahweh in being a first-born and in his consecration to Yahweh at conception.

The reader anticipates that a hero will be forthcoming. Delineating 'four heroic origins', James Nohrnberg (1981:36) notes that these may color one another, so that 'the more complete the cycle, the more something larger than the advent of the individual hero is betokened'. The birth of Samson observes three of the four 'heroic origins': it is heralded by an 'annunciation', the hero is 'called from the womb', and he is a *nazîr*. If 'the hero's life is determined by the principle of heroic singularity' (1981:36), then I suggest the principle is used ironically in the Samson narrative.[2]

The annunciation is a recurrent motif in biblical narratives, and textual allusions suggest that this annunciation is intended to specifically recall that of Sarah (Gen. 21.1-3). True, there is no reference to Manoah's wife's desire for a child, her importuning Yahweh or her giving her handmaid to her husband in order to 'have' a child. In the Samson narrative, the desire and all other details of the woman's childlessness are presumed. But something curious does occur, and only to Sarah and the nameless wife of Manoah: both women become pregnant *during* the visit of Yahweh (or his messenger).

Genesis 21	Judges 13
1 And Yahweh visited Sarah and he had said; and Yahweh did to Sarah as he had promised	2 ... and his wife [was] barren and had not borne.
2 And Sarah conceived and bore to Abraham a son in his old age at the appointed time that Elohim had spoken of with him.	3 And the Angel of Yahweh appeared to the woman and he said to her Behold now you [are] barren and have not borne, but you shall conceive and bear a son.
3 And Abraham called the name of the son who was born to him, whom Sarah had borne to him, Isaac.	4 ... 5 For behold you [are] pregnant and bearing a son ...

Implicit in both narratives of theophany, explicitly annunciations, is a transaction between the divine male figure and the human woman. In the Genesis annunciation, there are signals of the nature of the visit. The first verb which suggests a sexual component is 'to do'; 'and [he] did Yahweh to Sarah' (Gen. 21.1). The nature of the deed is unknown, but the result is pregnancy. A second hint that the divine visitor brought about Sarah's pregnancy is alluded to by the *waw* consecutive particle attached to the verb: 'and conceived' (*wattahar*). Whether translated as 'and' or 'for', the effect is the same: the pregnancy follows the theophanic visit and may be interpreted as a consequence.

Sarah's theophanic visit warrants further exploration. The verb 'visited', *pāqad* (Qal, perf., 3rd pers. sing. masc.) is a relatively infrequent expression, occurring only a score of times in the Bible in this form. *BDB* translates this verb as 'attend to, visit, muster, appoint'. The use of the verb in Judg. 15.1 is defined as 'visit, c[um] acc[usative], for *different* purposes', but 'esp[ecially] of Yahweh, *visit graciously'* (*BDB* italics, my emphasis; 1979:823). The term which may connote human sexual desire is, when assigned to Yahweh, interpreted as 'gracious', or 'in a kind sense' (Wilson, n.d.:469). Among the biblical instances of this verb, three involve meetings between the sexes, and in these there is ambiguity between sexuality and graciousness.

Gen.	21.1	And Yahweh *visited* Sarah as he had said . . .
Judg.	15.1b	And Samson *visited* his wife with a kid of the goats and said: I will go to into my wife, into the inner room.
1 Sam.	2.21	And Yahweh *visited* Hannah, and she conceived and bore three sons and two daughters.[3]

The verb 'visited' functions in all three instances to signal human sexual desire or divine graciousness.

In the Genesis annunciation, an intercourse—a wonderworking deed, a graciousness—between divinity and man seems implicit. It is important to note an active, if non-specific verb, *as'* 'to do', enacts a wonder that renders a barren woman pregnant, and that the verb 'visited' is associated with generative wonder in this passage. That Samson's *visit* to his wife, after his anger has cooled, has sexual connotations is strongly supported by the emphasis given expressions of entering:

15.1	And visited Samson his wife and he said I will come *to into* my wife *to* the inner room.

The use of the old accusative ending to denote 'direction of motion towards' a place (Weingreen, 1959:67) alleviates the awkwardness of the repetition in the Hebrew to some extent. The overuse of the preposition underscores the implications of the verb 'to come': when describing a meeting between male and female it connotes—then as now—sexual intercourse.[4]

While the annunciation to Sarah is alluded to by the nature of the *conception*, divine intercession, another annunciation is alluded to by the nature of the hero. Judg. 13.5a also recalls Yahweh's annunciation to Hagar. Hagar had conceived when Sarah could not, and the handmaid has run away from Sarah's harshness. Yahweh sends her back, saying 'Behold you [have] conceived and [are] bearing [a] son'. Hagar's son 'will be a wild ass of a man, his hand against all [men] and the hand of all against him; and he shall dwell before [in the sense of "against"] all his kinsmen' (Gen. 16.12). The annunciation event in the Samson narrative has no verbal expression as explicit as 'Yahweh did to Sarah', but a suggestion of sexual transaction between the divine messenger and the wife of Manoah is implied in the woman's report to her husband: 'A man of God *came unto* me' (13.6). In response to his wife's account of the meeting, Manoah asks that the man of Elohim come to *them*. Instead he 'came again' to the woman, explicitly alone:

> 13.9   ... and came the angel of Elohim again unto the woman
> and she [was] sitting in the field and Manoah her husband
> was not with her.

Overtly, it is assumed that the woman is sterile since the failure to conceive is always ascribed to the woman in biblical narrative. In the Genesis text, Abraham's feritility has been proven with Hagar, but time has passed and Abraham is presumably beyond the age of conception. Though it is clear that Sarah too is old, her age is not even alluded to: she rejoices that she has 'borne a son to *his* old age'— a hundred years at the birth of his first son by Sarah (Gen. 21.2, 5). There is a hint that part of the problem could lie with Abraham, at least at this phase of his life. Yahweh makes the old man fertile, the old and sterile wife fruitful.

In the Judges text, Manoah is depicted as a weak, 'unmanly' character, and it is not too far-fetched to interpret him as 'unmanned' as well. Initially, the suggestion of theophanic conception has been displaced from a narrator report (Yahweh did to Sarah) in the Genesis text, to a potentially less-reliable character report ('A man of God came to me') in the first Judges report of the visitor. However, the reliability of the character report is reinforced when the second visit is described in a narrator report ('and came the angel of Elohim again unto the woman'). In the annunciation of the Samson narrative, the deed is, like the other details of this narrative, subsumed; during the conversation the woman who *is barren* is told that she *will conceive* and bear. After a single expression of caution against wine, strong drink and unclean food, the woman is told she *is pregnant*: 'behold you conceived and [are] bearing [a] son'. The perfect aspect (completed action) of her barrenness, and imperfect aspect due to a prefixed waw-consecutive (incompleted action) of her 'bearing' are emphasized in 13.3-4 by repetitive stress on the particle 'now': 'behold now' (*hinnēh nā'*), 'and now' (*weattāh*), 'now' (*nā'*).[5] The theophany *cum* conception of Manoah's wife alludes to that of Sarah and the birth which followed: the birth of Isaac, one of the Patriarchs and the father of Jacob-Israel. The similarity between the annunciations and impregnations of Sarah and the wife of Manoah foretells another great patriarchal figure in the established tradition, a later judge worthy of his calling. The reader's association of the passages encourages the hope for a son worthy of the annunciation, a son like Isaac—or even better, since this son is also *nazîr* to Yahweh from conception. Only as Samson fails to live up to these expectations is the allusion to Sarah's theophany recognized as an ironic parody.

The expectations in the book of Judges generated by allusions to past narratives have remained unfulfilled due to one or another human failing, and Israel has fallen farther and farther from the promise at the opening of the book. In this narrative, it seems, Yahweh will take no chances: he will create the kind of judge necessary to lead Israel. Indeed, with the appearance of the angel, the reader's hopes are raised to a level of certainty, tempered perhaps by the caution of the angel's statement that Samson will *initiate* delivery of Israel from the power of the Philistines (13.5). This and the allusion to the theophany of Hagar subtly mitigate high expectations and foreshadow a less-than-hoped-for consequence of the annunciation. As Hagar's annunciation makes clear, not all divinely-announced births are *intended* to produce just and worthy men. Despite the foreshadowing, reader expectations of a worthy judge remain high.

Another aspect of the singularity of this narrative among the judge narratives is the position of the judge in his family and his society. All of the prior judges whose stories are fully told are marked by a weakness or a social disadvantage. Ehud's left-handedness was considered in the same light as a crippling or deformity ('*îṭṭēr*: 'bound, lame'); Deborah, a woman, is at an obvious disadvantage in the literature of a patriarchal society; Gideon, the last and cowardly son of an insignificant family in an insignificant clan, even protests to Yahweh that he is in a weak position (6.15); and Jephthah is not only a social outcast but is, in *deed*, cast out. In direct contrast, Samson is born to an Israelite married couple, pious parents of the tribal clan of Dan, and the birth involves some degree of wonder—if only in the intention of Yahweh. Unlike the other judges, who begin disadvantaged, Samson begins with every advantage.

This final tale of a judge culminates the series.[6] Chapter 13 raises the highest level of expectation by virtue of the theophanic visit, which not only promises the wonder of birth to a barren women, but a 'chosen' son, dedicated to Yahweh before his very conception and emergence into life. Samson's tale also uniquely symbolizes Israel. Each of the judges represents Israel and verifies a particular aspect of Israel's apostasy, but the correspondence of Israel with the figure of Samson is not merely in the form of apostasy. The comparison is implicitly more extended. Like Samson, Israel was pre-conceived (in the period represented by the narratives of the Patriarchs) and finally 'gestated' (in the extended isolation of the wanderings) before it entered the reality of life in Canaan. Israel, Yahweh's people, is symbolically re-born in a single human form in this narrative. Yahweh's high expectations for Israel, and her subsequent short-comings are dramatically embodied in the figure of Samson (Greenstein, 1981:244ff). The irony is telling.

With the opening three verses of Samson's activities (14.1-3), the reader's expectations of a hero are immediately mitigated, if only slightly. Samson's going down to Timnat denotes leaving Israelite territory; it connotes leaving its traditions as well. Samson is shown to be influenced by appearance (superficial values) when he sees, and consequently desires, one of the daughters of the Philistines, and to lack honor for his father and mother when he ignores his parents' counsel.

Current with these suggestions about Samson's character, this passage is one of few to disclose the narrator's understanding of Yahweh's *modus operandi*. Samson's desire for the Timnite woman is not justified *by* Yahweh; it is *attributed to* Yahweh by the reliable narrator: 'he [was] *seeking* an occasion against the Philistines' (14.4).[7] The narrator is reliable—within human limitations of knowledge. Significantly, he does not present Yahweh as a divinity of magical or unlimited powers, for Yahweh seeks to stir man to enact the divine will. In the covenant relationship binding both man and god, Yahweh does not effect his will by divine *fiat*, and man's free will is stressed.[8] Yahweh's *seeking* does not imply that Yahweh incited Samson's desire for the Timnite woman. Rather, it suggests that Samson's irregular actions nevertheless accord with Yahweh's will.

The hero is not, as McKenzie would have it, 'morally neutral . . . neither better nor worse than other men [but] simply the instrument through which Yahweh works deliverance' (1967:158). As leader, the hero must demonstrate ethical standards. Without such standards, the leader is not a hero. Sometimes, as in the Samson narrative, man accomplishes Yahweh's will unwittingly, and the divine purpose is realized as a consequence of man's unethical actions.[9] In the book of Judges, Yahweh has repeatedly recalled Israel to the covenant. Not morally neutral but morally unfaithful to Yahweh and his commandments, each protagonist is Israel, each is an image of the covenant relationship of the people with its god; and as a result, the book records the degeneration of the people. Samson-Israel, the realization of Yahweh's annunciation, dramatically synthesizes the recurring dilemma of Israel in the book of Judges. Yahweh would help his people, but the people must be agents of his will. As he turns from Yahweh, each of the Israelite judges abuses the covenant, which in turn incites divine frustration, anger. Finally, in this last, all-out effort, Yahweh pre-conceives a judge; but man is so perverse, the narrative implies, that Yahweh's will is not realized in a judge, in his people: even the sacred generation fails to produce a worthy leader.[10] Yahweh's will is fulfilled despite—even through—human inadequacies.

In prior narratives, the judges were implicitly judged by Yahweh as he withdrew in word and in deed, and the reader was put in the position of an observer. In this narrative, Samson's behavior— after all the expectations generated by the annunciation, the allusion to Sarah (and Hagar), and the consecration as a *nazirite*—is so contradictory to expectations that the reader must recognize the irony that Samson is blind to. The reader is drawn into the role of ironist. As Yahweh is knowledgeable and Israel is victim, the reader is knowledgeable about Samson—and Samson is victim. The reader is, in effect, put in the position of Yahweh as Samson betrays the anticipations generated by the annunciation, the birth and the *nazirite* dedication. Israel is reflected in Samson's foolish ways, and the reader must judge Samson as Yahweh has judged Israel. Thus the original title of the book, simply *šōfetîm* (Judges), is more profound than a mere reference to the series of judges of the narratives (Driver, 1913:160).[11] The sequence of narratives leads the reader to a position of knowledge with regard to these narratives and to recognize the irony is to partake of Yahweh's knowledge and vision—his judgment.

Certainly Samson betrays this highest level of expectation on most demeaning grounds. Each of the judges has a basic weakness, but

Samson's 'surpasses' them all. This last judge is not conniving, like Ehud; not a 'weak' female, like Deborah; not self-serving, like Gideon; not an unscrupulous enemy, like anti-judge Abimelech, not unknowledgeable, like Jephthah. Ironically, Samson, the strong-man of the book, reveals himself as essentially the weakest, weaker than any of his predecessor judges, for Samson is *subject*, a *slave* to physical passion—the lowest kind of subjugation. And because his passions demand woman, Samson is at the mercy of womankind, a deplorable situation from the point-of-view of a patriarchal society. The last hope of Israel in the book of Judges is, then, a judge who chases women instead of enemies and who avenges only personal grievances.

That Samson, like Israel, has been dedicated to Yahweh from his conception makes his—and Israel's—blithe obliviousness to ethical values all the more poignant. Both Israel and Samson are *nazirites* in that they are dedicated to Yahweh from 'conception', and both seem more concerned with personal gratification (including the pleasures of worldly values) than with the less tangible covenant.

Samson's lack of interest in Israel is ironically turned to a momentary advantage of the people, and Yahweh's will *is* done, even through man's 'free will'. In the final verses of his narrative, Samson does 'begin' to save Israel from the Philistines. And though the reader is forced to 'see' and to judge, Samson remains blind both physically and spiritually. He does not pray for Israel; he prays for revenge. He finds strength in the renewal of his *nazirite* vow: his hair, *growing*, but not yet fully grown, is symbolic of his bond to Yahweh—his faith—but Samson is still blind to his role as Yahweh's chosen. In finding the strength to enact his personal revenge, however, Samson ironically enacts Yahweh's ethical will.

The Samson story is notable in that women take varying and interesting roles in this story.[12] In fact, whether for good or for evil, women lead the way both literally (13.11) and figuratively (14.15-17; 16.6-19). Samson's mother is not accorded a personal name at all and is sometimes not even given the designation of 'Manoah's wife'. In 13.3, 6, 9 and 10 she is 'the woman', and even Manoah refers to her as such (3.11). Nevertheless, the nameless woman understands more than her husband, who is named 'Manoah'.[13] The woman immediately senses the 'wonderful' aspect of the visitor, calling him a 'man of Elohim ... in [the] appearance of an angel of Elohim, very awful'

(13.6). She unquestioningly believes the announcement of her prospective delivery of a son, and she sensibly stills her husband's fear of death because 'we have seen Elohim' (13.22).

Other women in the narrative also influence the plot development. Samson's wife cajoles him into disclosing the solution of his riddle, but the woman who 'leads' him is Delilah. Samson, whose name alludes to the *sun*, become subject to Delilah, *night*.[14] As a result, Samson loses his 'light', his sight, and becomes both physically and figuratively captive of night in blindness. That only these two names (and that of Manoah, the father) are given in the text focuses on the polarity of day and night, which is here symbolized by man and woman: Samson, the son/sun of Israel, and Delilah, the night of foreign womankind.

Delilah is identified not by the name of her home town, but only by a region, the *nakhal sorek*. This is particularly noteworthy in a cycle that includes far more proper names of settlements than any other narrative in the book, e.g. *Zorah, Eshtaol, Timnath, Ashkelon, Lehji, Hebron* and *Gaza*. The only places left unspecific are the 'Camp of Dan', which apparently was not a permanent settlement with a proper name, and the 'Rock of Etam', a geological feature. That Delilah is not provided with a genealogy is not surprising since her actions associate her with the Philistines.[15] Indeed, Delilah is associated with a rather large territory: the *nahal śorēq*, now called *wadi-es-Sarar*, is one of many *wadis* or flood beds that carry water down from the higher regions, in this case from the hills of Judah. The *nahal śorēq* describes a geographic area that cuts through the harsh Judean hills on the one hand, to the fertile coastal range, on the other.

The first term in Delilah's area of identification, *nahal*, refers to the sort of desert run-off channel now called *wadi*. With the rains, these become virtual torrents, and the word 'torrent' is a more appropriate translation than 'valley', which suggests a stable landscape: or 'creek', a tranquil water-route. The second term, *śorēq*, a reference to 'choice wine', serves to recall one of the two *nazirite* vows Samson has already broken: that which prohibits eating or drinking of the fruit of the vine.

The Shephelah is an area of vines, and in the region of the *nahal śorēq* the choice wine grape called *śorēq* gave this torrent-valley its name. In a literal sense, however, the name is contrary to reason. The combination of flood bed and wine cultivation is impossible.

Obviously, the flooding waters would wash away the vines. The impossibility symbolized by the area identified with Delilah is relevant to her relationship to Samson. Delilah represents an uncontrollable element of nature (torrent) and one of the *nazirite* prohibitions (wine). These polarities cannot be reconciled. One aspect—either the torrent or the prohibition—must give way.

The Samson cycle begins with Manoah's wife as a model of Israelite womanhood and an ideal receptacle for a wondrous conception, while the other women of the narrative proceed undeviatingly from this nameless apogee to its opposite. The Timnite woman, also unnamed, can perhaps be forgiven if not justified in her betrayal of her husband in light of her countrymen's threats. But her action reveals that she has more allegiance to her people than to her husband. Unlike Manoah's wife, she does not tell her husband whom she encounters or what was said.[17]

The Timnite woman, a legal wife who betrays, is yet not as condemnable as a prostitute, the passive female figure of the next episode involving Samson with a woman. The cause of the fall from the initial promise of the book is symbolized by prostitution. Israel has 'sold' its soul to other gods for transitory pleasures just as a woman 'sells' her body for man's momentary pleasures, and Yahweh has already complained of Israel's 'whoring' (2.17; 8.27, 33) in the book of Judges.

Worst of all is the third woman, the only named female figure, Delilah, whom Samson 'loved' (16.4). Comparison of Jacob's love for Rachel with that of Samson for/of Delilah is suggestive:

Gen.	29.18	And-he-loved Jacob Rachel
Judg.	16.4	And-he-loved [a] woman in the torrent-bed of Sorek and her name [was] Delilah.

Unlike Jacob, Samson is *not* named: it is an unspecified subject, a verb with a pronominal ending who loves, and this love is for 'a woman'. In Samson's love, the sexual is given prominence: there is no description of the woman or her qualities or her family, as in the Genesis passage (Gen. 29.12). The connotations of Delilah's dwelling place—literally a 'torrent bed', a place where water (a symbol of fertility) sporadically rushes through—further qualifies the character of this love and of this woman: both are rootless in time and place, transient.[18] Although Delilah is not specifically identified as a prostitute, she is obviously a woman available to men. John B.

Vickery, in claiming that both the woman of Gaza and Delilah are prostitutes, makes a valuable point:

> the difference is that the former is an honest one explicitly plying her trade in exchange for money and restricting her involvement to physical functions. Delilah is, as it were, a whore at heart aware of the hero's love for her and how his emotions may be manipulated to serve her greed and lust for power (1981:69).

That she betrays, for a price, the man who loves her renders Delilah a compound of the Timnite woman and the prostitute: a prostitute betrayer. Delilah represents a lack of ethics and morality, an ironic opposite of Achsah, the bride.

Samson, the central character of the narrative, proves to be the antithesis of the hero augured by the annunciation, thus making the ironic element integral to this narrative. And though Samson is dramatically presented in a range of situations from conception to death, his character remains ambiguous.

Samson's identity is the subject of a perceptive analysis by Edward Greenstein, who explores it through information given and withheld by the narration. 'The central character of the birth episode', Samson's mother, is not given a name. The father is named and further 'identified by town and tribe. But he is the only important male leader or begetter of a male leader in the books of Judges and First Samuel . . . who is not represented together with his paternal affiliation' (1981:240).[19] Manoah's name even lacks genealogical roots. The messenger of God is not exactly nameless: his name is 'wondrous', beyond man's knowledge. Manoah's wife knows better than to ask his name, for he has the appearance of divinity.

But Samson's name 'verges on anonymity'. Samson's name, unexplained in the text, may well be derived from the word for 'name': two-thirds of Samson's name is 'name', *shem*. 'Samson is virtually cut loose from any specific lineage'. 'Samson', Greenstein suggests, signifies the 'generic designation "Name"', somewhat analogous to . . . the biblical character "Adam" ("Man")' (1981:241). Unlike 'Man', who has descendants to call upon his name and to keep his name and spirit alive, 'name' has neither genealogy nor descendants. The text calls our attention to the significance of naming, and it does so by not once properly naming. Samson–Israel has been cut off from 'named' tradition by the apostasies of his forefathers; and by his own deeds he effectively cuts off his own name, for he is left childless, without descendants to invoke his name.

The one meaningful name given to Samson is that of *'Nazir* to God'. In the Niphil, the verb *nazar* means 'to withdraw oneself; to restrict oneself; to abstain from; to consecrate oneself' (*AHCL*, 1981:542). The noun implies all of these, and it is obvious that 'Name' (Samson) does not live up to his name, *'Nazîr* to God'. Israel, of whom Samson—like the other judges—is a symbolic and dramatic embodiment, has failed to live up to its names of 'wrestler with God' and 'prince with God'. Israel has ceased struggling with its god and has fallen into the 'easy' ways of the Philistines. Samson–Israel squanders its 'names' in ethical prostitution.

Manoah is one of the three characters named in the entire cycle, but remarkably little other information is given about Samson's father: no genealogy, and his tribe is curiously called a 'clan'. This narrative, abounding in word-play, invites scrutiny of the few names provided, but 'Manoah' does not imply any further significance.[20] Manoah is an unimposing figure in the Samson narrative, one who is led by his wife and cannot guide his own son from temptation. If anything, 'Manoah's dullness . . . brings into relief the special merit' of his wife (Simon, 1969:227). Manoah's distinction as man (and as father-to-be) is first displaced by the divine response to his prayer: the angel does re-appear, not to *him* or to *them*, but once more only to Manoah's wife. The question Manoah puts to the angel is not even acknowledged, and the angel's answer to Manoah is directed to Manoah's wife. Finally, only the ascension of the visitor in the flames of the sacrifice convinces Manoah, a man apparently removed from simple belief. Manoah's character is brought into question by his reaction to the 'wonder': fear of their deaths; his reponse is knowledgeable but automatic—and illogical, as his wife shortly discloses.[21] Significantly, Manoah does not honor the occasion and the site with a Yahweh-honoring altar name,[22] which sets a precedent for Samson's more flagrant violations of Yahweh's grace. Jephthah has no father; Samson, the narrative implies, has a father in 'name' only.

The nameless wife is shown to have more faith than her husband and to be an unquestioning and presumably responsible carrier of Yahweh's champion. A woman who conceives wondrously and brings the promise of Yahweh into life and history, Manoah's wife nevertheless remains ironically anonymous, her ineffectual, perhaps impotent husband ironically named. The pattern of naming is symptomatic of a world with inverted values. Manoah is said to be a 'man of *Zorah*' (13.11), but Samson is not of *Zorah*. Manoah must have left the stable settlement of *Zorah*, a Danite town in Judah, and gone to live in a less-settled 'camp'.[23] Such a move from an urban area, no matter how small, to a 'camp'— from a settled social pattern to a semi-nomadic one—is provocatively contrary to expectations. Furthermore, because the final reference elides mention of the camp of Dan, it effectively stresses *between* *Zorah* and *Eshta'ol*. The text first places Samson in the camp of Dan, between *Zorah* and *Eshtaol* (13.25), and it concludes by burying him there, in the grave of his father (16.31). *Zorah* (*ṣorāh*) is translated as 'smiting, defeat' (*AHCL*, 1981:651). The other pole, *Eshtaol*, means 'petition, request', from the root *ša'al*, 'to ask'.[24]

Literally, Samson first felt the spirit of Yahweh *between* 'defeat' and 'petition', and he was buried in the same place. 'Petition, request' is the duty of a *šōfet*, a judge, in order to avoid 'defeat'; and Manoah's move, early in the narrative, was in the right direction, toward *Eshtaol*, 'petition', in the land given to the tribe of Dan. The very meaning of 'judging Israel' has been interpreted as 'asking the will of God . . . by a charistmatic person' (Thomson, 1961-62:78). *Dan*, from the root *dûn* (or *dîn*),[25] 'to rule; judge; defend; punish' (*AHCL*, 1981:147) and *Eshta'ol* 'to ask, inquire of, consult' (*AHCL*, 1981:694) seem the proper goal of Samson-Israel. That goal is not realized in the narrative. Samson does not *ask* or *request* of Yahweh except under personal duress, and even then 'Samson's speech to Yahweh [is] more an impudent harangue' (Boling: 1975:239).

Manoah, though the masculine figure and named, has to follow his nameless wife (13.11) to come to the angel. After Manoah has been assured that this is indeed the man who spoke to the woman, he asks about the son to be born:

13.12b   . . . what will be the judgment (*mišpaṭ*)
                of the boy and his work?

One can discern the sense of the noun *mišpaṭ* (it is usually 'rule [of life]', 'custom', 'manner'), but that is not the point. This word is a variant of the key word of the book: the Hebrew title of the book, *šōfᵉtîm* is implicit in the noun. The words share the same consonants, *šft* (*p* and *f* are exchangeable in the biblical Hebrew).[26] For—perhaps because—dull as Manoah may be, he asks a crucial question.

Literally, Manoah asks, 'What will be the judgment of the boy and of his work?' English speakers are tempted to phrase the question, 'What will be the judgment and the work of the boy?' but the separation of 'judgment' and 'work' by the noun 'boy' permits ambiguity of emphasis: 'the boy' can be subject or object of the verb 'judgment'. Manoah's question is usually understood to ask:

> What will be the boy's judgment
>   (attribute, manner)
> and what can he be expected to do?
>   (judgment inherent *in* the boy)

I suggest a shift of emphasis:

> How will the boy be judged
>   (judgment *of* the boy)
> and how will his work be judged?
>   (judgment *of* his work)[27]

The ambiguity invites the reader to consider the multiple aspects of judgment in this narrative: the use of *mišpaṭ* foreshadows the judgment of Samson-Israel to be made *by the reader* by the end of the narrative. Manoah's question also calls attention to the fact that his wife omitted information from the angel in her report to her husband, so that 'the dissonance of a single phrase subtly [sets] the scene for a powerful but spiritually dubious savior of Israel who will end up sowing as much destruction as salvation' (Alter, 1981:101). The angel does not answer Manoah's question; he reiterates the abstentions the woman must observe. He does not charge Manoah with the duty of watching over his wife, but says she should watch herself:

> 13.13   And said [the] angel of Yahweh unto Manoah from all that I
>   told to the wife she must take heed.

Manoah explicitly 'did not know' the angel of Yahweh and asks his name to honor him—not immediately, but when his 'words come to pass' (13.17). Manoah's cautious skepticism may be noted; at any rate, the angel answers the question with a rather ironic counter-question which presumes Manoah knows better than to ask. The ascension of the visitor in the flames of the sacrifice offered to Yahweh convinces Manoah—and evokes his fear. Once again, Manoah's wife has understanding through belief, and she allays his fears.

The nameless wife is presumed by the reader to be a responsible carrier of Yahweh's champion, a woman who has faith in Yahweh. Not so with the foreign women, the pleasing but unnamed Timnite woman and the treacherous Delilah. Samson never has the sense to choose a wife like his mother; he only follows the instincts of his senses, and the foreign women are more intriguing than those of Israel. Their ties are to the easier and more civilized life of the Plain; Samson's are to the harsh ruggedness of the Judean hills. That Samson is overwhelmed by his appetites is made clear by his twice falling for the same ruse; any *thinking* man would know better. In restrospect, Samson's behavior suggests a configuration in the principle forces behind the three great warrior-heroes of the book: Gideon is ruled by logic, Jephthah by uninformed belief and Samson by lust, which can overrule all reason, all sense, all faith.

Samson has been dedicated to Yahweh from conception, is blessed by him in his youth (13.24), and receives his spirit. Of the earlier judges, Ehud is merely 'given' the spirit and Deborah has received it only implicitly, but it 'was upon' Othniel (3.10) and Jephthah (11.29), and dramatically 'clothed with itself' Gideon (6.34); in its negative form, it was sent as an 'evil spirit' between Abimelech and the Shechemite leaders (9.23). Samson, in contrast, receives the spirit of Yahwh in four separate actions, and three times with unusual vigor.

13.25	And she began, the spirit	
	of Yahweh, to *impel* (urge) him	l^efa'amô
14.6	And she *descended* (rushed) upon	wattiṣ^elakh
	him the spirit of Yahweh	
14.19	And she *descended* (rushed) upon	wattiṣ^elakh
	him the spirit of Yahweh	
15.14	And she *descended* (rushed) upon	wattiṣ^elakh
	him the spirit of Yahweh	

Furthermore, Yahweh responds when Samson, thirsty after battle, calls to him. True, Samson acknowledges himself as a mere agent of Yahweh's act of salvation, at which Yahweh obligingly opens a rock to provide water for the man 'dying of thirst', but Samson's hyperbole diminishes his image. Although Yahweh pulls Samson out of his scrapes through his 'spirit' or by active intervention, Samson does not once acknowledge Yahweh's saving grace. Samson celebrates only himself, naming the sites of Yahweh's victory and Yahweh's fountain after himself: 'The Hill of the Jawbone' and 'The Caller's Spring'. These are not etiological tales; they reveal the protagonist's character and ironically distinguish Samson's egocentricity from the humility before Yahweh demonstrated by earlier judges (2.5; 6.24; 11.30) and even by his own father. Manoah's fear of Yahweh serves as a foil for Samson's lack of it: the latter treats his god like a powerful buddy rather than an awesome divinity. In fact, Samson takes his consecration to Yahweh as if it were the opposite: Yahweh's consecration to him. Samson–Israel take Yahweh for granted and honors not his god but himself.

When Samson calls on Yahweh to relieve his thirst, the words are 'right' but the tone is not. Yahweh is given credit for the victory, and Samson calls himself Yahweh's servant, but there is no reverence or *fear*. Even the nature of Samson's request seems inappropriate; one doesn't call upon god for a drink of water. In effect, Yahweh does for one man immediately after a brief battle what he did for the entire people of Israel after they had wandered for an untold period through the desert wilderness of Sin. The names Moses gives this source of water (*Massah*, 'fear' and *Meribah*, 'find fault') memorialize Israel's awe of Yahweh and her own faithlessness; Samson's name for the spring which restores him does not even acknowledge Yahweh's participation. 'The divine awfulness pervades the whole of the Old Testament' (Pederson, 1940:625), and this fear serves to unite the community of Israelites in love of her god. Yahweh is not pleased by arrogance; he attacks those who will not humble themselves, but he exalts the humble (Pederson, 1940:628). Although Samson's mother, Manoah's wife, recognizes the 'aw(e)ful' aspect of the man of god who comes to her in the field (13.6), Samson is oblivious of the awesomeness of Yahweh. If the reader is not surprised at Yahweh's 'humble' response to Samson's importunate request, he may be by Samson's repeated and arrogant honoring of himself in naming the site, the event.

In light of Yahweh's unusual participation in this narrative, it is striking that there is no specific divine response in the concluding segment of the story. A humbled Samson does not 'call' to Yahweh', he 'prays', repeating the word, begging 'only this time'. This time the tone is right. Samson has lost the power he assumed was his, and he knows that Yahweh honors the just vows that man honors. But Samson has not learned. He asks not for his people but for himself, not to avenge his people but to revenge himself. He wants personal revenge: one vengeance on the Philistines for his two eyes. And there is no act of Yahweh, no spirit, in response. Yahweh has bestowed his spirit upon Samson more than upon any other judge, but no grace is bestowed at this juncture. Samson does find the strength to bring down the roof because 'the hair of his head began to grow, as he had been shaven' (16.22). The symbol of Samson's *nazirite* consecration 'began to grow again'; and that dedication, finally acknowledged, provides Samson with the strength to enact his will (vengeance) and that of Yahweh (to initiate delivery of the Israelites from Philistine oppression). Exum finds prayer the key to the theology of Samson's narrative, and the destruction of the temple of Dagon Yahweh's answer to Samson's prayer (1983:422-45), but does not address the question of the narrator's failure to record both spirit and act of Yahweh at his critical juncture—in a narrative otherwise notable for their explicit dominance.

In disclosing his secret to Delilah, Samson innocently (and ironically) encloses the sacred vow—the single bond of strength—within two references to being unshaven, which 'encompass', even protect the vow. Samson's unshorn hair is the last vestige of his *nazirite* bond to Yahweh and symbolizes the strength of that bond. The verse is completed with reiteration of the consequences of 'cutting' Samson from his vow:

16.17   A **razor has not come** upon my head
          for a *Nazirite to God* am I
          from the *womb* of my mother
       If I were **shaved**,
          my strength would depart from me
          and I would be weak and be like any man.

The structure of the verse contradicts Samson's purport: in revealing he 'conceals'. The central, prenatal *nazirite* vow is surrounded by verbs of hair-cutting, and the final two phrases of the verse counter the chiastic parallelism of the first four with augmenting parallelism. The structure of three parallel but opposing terms suggests an identification of the central terms, 'Nazirite to God' and 'strength'. Should the uncut hair, the last remnant of Samson's *nazirite* relationship to Yahweh be taken from (around) the *nazirite* vow, Samson would no longer be special in strength.[28] The reader is invited to recognize the uncut hair as symbolic of Samson's bond to his consecration, while the Philistines perhaps regard his uncut hair as a magical power.

Samson's new hair growth represents returning strength: a new 'growth' of belief. I suggest that with the shaving of his hair Samson finally learns the significance of his *nazirite* vow; it is his dedication as a *nazir* to Yahweh that has grown—symbolized by his hair and evidenced by the tone of his prayer. The lack of a clear divine response to Samson's prayer and the demonstration of Samson's returning strength imply that 'strength' may come from belief and humility.

In his arrogance, Samson needs Yahweh's spirit to accomplish his incredible feats of might. With humble prayer and a renewal of dedication to Yahweh, Samson finds strength within himself. Indeed, Samson—as Israel—must find strength within: Yahweh has significantly withdrawn from the sphere of humanity and neither speaks nor acts until the concluding chapters of the book (ch. 20). And Yahweh's words and deeds in the concluding section, the resolution of the book, have a different function and effect than those of the main narratives.[29]

The motifs of this last story provide a link to each of the prior major judges and even some of the minor ones. The first, the Othniel-Achsah narrative (1.13-15, prior to the paradigm Othniel narrative), presents a model relationship between man and woman; that of Samson, the opposite. Achsah seeks land and water for her husband's seed to grow; Samson 'plants' his seed in foreign 'fields'.[30] Despite his parents' objections, Samson disdains Israelite women and seeks to marry a Philistine. Foreign women, if not preferred wives, are assimilated and even celebrated in the Bible (e.g. Miriam, Ruth, Tamar), but not in the book of Judges. In like vein, harlotry may be justified in other texts (e.g. Tamar), but not in the book of Judges. In this book, foreign women and harlotry are implicitly but repeatedly condemned; and Samson's adventures are not in the battlefield against the Philistines but in the bed, expressly with foreign women: an unfaithful wife,[31] a harlot and a woman whose name suggests as much.[32] That Delilah is not a true lover in the sense of a loving woman is made clear by her ready acceptance of a fee for betrayal of her lover.[33] Achsah, the bride of Israel to her god, has been forsaken for Delilah, the traitor to love for pieces of silver as Samson-Israel whores after foreign cultures. These two narratives provide the framing for all the others; they represent the initial hopes of Israel—and the depths to which the people (still an entity) fall.

Ehud and Samson share an interest in word-play. Ehud dissembles when he tells Eglon, the Moabite kings, that he has a 'secret word', a 'mesage from Elohim' (3.19). Ehud builds up Eglon's expectations, which Ehud then reverses on behalf of Israel. Samson's riddles are a much more self-conscious form of word-play than Ehud's, and Samson's word-play, falsely entrusted, leads to a reversal of *his* expectations (and the reader's) when the Philistines respond in an answering riddle. The initial reversals based on word play in the Ehud narrative foreshadow and are intrinsic to the larger pattern of reversals in the Samson narrative sequence. Ehud uses the deceit inherent in word play to Israel's advantage, but the Samson narrative shows that deceit (word-play) can be turned against Samson–Israel.

Links betwen Shamgar and Samson have been frequently noted.[34] Superficially, the names bear a certain resemblance; also striking is the similarity between Shamgar's smiting six hundred Philistines with an ox-goad and Samson's elimination of a thousand Philistines with the jawbone of an ass—unclean food forbidden a *nazirite*, even to touch. The comparison also serves to contrast the acceptable if unusual weapon used by Shamgar with the non-acceptable, indeed expressly forbidden, but likewise unusual weapon used by Samson. The allusion to Shamgar (3.31) makes Samson vulnerable by comparison: at the end of his battle Samson is 'dying of thirst', but Shamgar's brief tale describes no difficulties. Incidentally, the narratives of Shamgar and Samson, at the beginning and end of the main narrative sequence, are the only ones which direct action against the Philistines.[35]

Deborah's narrative shares with Samson's a rare biblical reference to bees, and in both instances the reference carries dubious innuendoes.[36] Samson openly defies the *nazîr* restriction against eating unclean food (13.4) when he scoops honey out of the carcass of a lion he has killed; the bees, represented as building their hives in dead flesh, are thereby asociated with a forbidden deed, a broken vow.[37] In scooping the honey, Samson acts in a premeditated manner, so that the first *nazirite* restriction is willfully broken in this verse.

14.9   And he scraped it out *into his hands*, and went on, walking and eating; and he went to his father and to his mother and *gave* [some] *to them*; and they ate, but *he did not tell them* that he had scraped the honey from the carcass of a lion.

Samson's killing the lion and his later taking and eating honey from the carcass function primarily in the riddle episode, but that he explicitly does not tell his parents implies that he knows he is involving them in his breaking his vow.[38]

The narratives of Deborah and Samson bear other points of contact, ones which bring female figures into juxtaposition. The very similarity of the sounds of 'Deborah' and 'Delilah' reverberates to contrast the women who bear the names: 'Deborah . . . a mother in Israel' (5.7) is replaced by Delilah, a non-Israelite seductress and betraying lover. The 'episode involving Delilah exploits a classic paradigm of deception: a wily woman overpowers a mighty warrior' (Greenstein, 1981:245). This paradigm also appears, with a reversal of allegiance-roles, in the Deborah narrative, as Israelite Jael lures a foreign warrior-adversary, only to betray the code of the host-guest relationship. In both instances (4.15; 16.15), a male's 'turning aside' to the enticements of a woman are disastrous; but only in the Samson narrative are they disastrous for Israel.[39] (True, the outcome is disastrous for the Philistines, but only after a series of intervening and determining events. Samson's love of Delilah is in itself adversative for Israel and beneficial to the Philistines.) Men may follow women in other respects when they, like Deborah, lead the people in the ways of Yahweh or when they, like Manoah's wife, lead the way to faith. Samson's narrative actualizes the negative implications of feminine potential which were introduced in chs. 4–5.

Shared episodes of theophany and sacrifice in the narratives of Gideon and Samson have often been remarked. Gideon's doubt of the divine presence marks Israel's skepticism at that phase, but Manoah seems innocent of any thought of a divine presence, as the narrator takes care to point out (13.16), even though his wife has described her visitor as 'awesome'. In a sequence which ironically recalls Moses' humble but 'knowing' question—but not Yahweh's answer (Exod. 3.13-14)—Manoah blithely and foolishly asks his visitor's name. The divine reply presumes Manoah does '*know*' his visitor: 'Why [do] you ask, since it [is] wonderful?'[40] The theophanies of Moses and Gideon serve as foils for that of Manoah, and the latter's want of traditional Israelite knowledge and faith undermines the pattern of promise and fulfillment which seems to mark ch. 13.

Of all the judges, Gideon and Samson are singularly marked by unusual verbal expressions attributed to Yahweh's spirit. In other narratives, Yahweh's spirit 'comes upon' the judge, but it 'clothes with itself' Gideon (6.34) and it impels (or urges) (13.25) or descends (or rushes) upon Samson (14.6, 19; 15.14). The verbs used to describe the action of the spirit of Yahweh curiously suit Samson's dominant character trait—lust, which may also be said to 'impel', 'urge', or 'rush upon' the individual. These two judges receive more support from Yahweh than the others, and both their narratives are followed by periods of marked misfortune in which lack of Yahwist values is accompanied by Yahweh's relative silence and inaction. More than any other, Gideon's narrative anticipates Samson's, and Abimelech's tale prefigures the denouement.

Except by contrast or polarity, Abimelech's narrative lacks ties with Samson's. The former protagonist is brutal and grim; the latter 'earthy', his crudeness mitigated by playfulness and humor, even wit. Although it is an outgrowth of Gideon's narrative, Abimelech's has few links with the rest of the book[41] and lacks the interwoven motives characterstic of the others. In contrast, Samson's narrative has links throughout the book of Judges. Contrast of these two narratives attests to their differentiated functions in the book. The Abimelech story is that of an anti-hero; Samson is a non-hero. The former, a half-Israelite, allies himself with the foreign element against Israel; the latter, a 'blessing' from Yahweh to an Israelite couple, betrays the Israelite covenant. Abimelech's tale is brutal, but Samson's despite the wit, is even more devastating.[42]

Jephthah and Samson are comparable both directly and in contrast. These are the boldest, likely the strongest warriors, and each suffers from a related lack: Jephthah is uninformed and Samson is unthinking. That Samson's parents have fulfilled their responsibility to their son's *nazirite* consecration is implied in the 'short prayers' Samson twice employs (15.18; 16.28). Such condensed prayers abstract 'the basic contents of a prayer' relative to the demands of the story (Reventlow, unp. abstr.). That Samson is portrayed as abstracting from the form of a fully developed psalm of lament attests to his familiarity with the Israelite heritage and sufficient intelligence to use that knowledge. Because he calls/prays to Yahweh, Samson cannot be unbelieving; but he never seems to take his responsibility as an Israelite, let alone Nazirite, seriously. Greenstein observes that 'Samson differs from Jephthah in a crucial way: Jephthah famously keeps a vow, Samson breaks three' (1981:240). Jephthah the outcast is piously ignorant; Samson the elect takes

Yahweh for granted. Notably, Jephthah and Samson are the only judges explicitly without heirs, and in each instance this is due to lack of judgment of the judge.

Significantly, both Gideon and Samson have liaisons with foreign women. The earlier judge has seventy Israelite sons and one son by a Shechemite concubine: moreover, that one destroys all the potential of the seventy. Samson has no Israelite women, no Israelite children. His marriage to the Timnite woman is not consummated, so there are no legal half-Israelite progeny. Propagation is a significant issue for Israel in the book of Judges. Although Othniel's possible progeny are only alluded to (1.15), and those of Ehud not mentioned, Deborah is celebrated as a 'mother' in Israel (5.7). Each judge, major or minor, from Deborah to Samson (excluding Abimelech, the 'anti-judge') begets children, even grandchildren.[43] Samson's lack of heirs is marked.

Whereas the focus of the earlier narratives is on conquering Israel's oppressors, in the last it is on Samson's passion for Philistine women. His battles are clearly secondary, consequential to his overriding lust for three different non-Israelite women. Even so, despite the sexual focus, Samson ironically leaves no heirs.

The narratives of the preceding judges call attention to Samson as a 'dead end'. The narratives of the major judges make mention of the parentage of each judge, and those of the succinctly drawn minor judges focus pointedly on the number of children and grandchildren. Jephthah has only one child, a daughter, and through his ignorance he cuts off his own line. Samson, son of a man without a genealogy, does not attain fatherhood of an Israelite child or even of a child of marriage with a non-Israelite. Samson disdains the field Othniel and Achsah cultivate, and Israel has no harvest at all.

Samson's courtship of his wife bears some notice. The first well-scene which leads to a betrothal—the seeking of a bride for Abraham's son Isaac (Gen. 24.10-61)—is the 'type-scene' or model for subsequent betrothals at a well, such as the encounter of Jacob and Rachel. Samson's courtship suppresses all the traditional elements of the well-scene: there is no symbolic water, no invitation to the woman's home, and no recognition of their common background and heritage. The bride-to-be doesn't hurry home; in a reversal that anticipates the turn from tradition of the entire marriage episode, Samson goes to *his* home, and he doesn't hurry excitedly either. He simply 'goes' or 'comes up' to his parents to tell

them of his wishes, to demand that they 'get her for him as a wife'.
The son doesn't even acknowledge his parents' protests; neither is
the sharing of food, a ceremonial observation of a betrothal,
mentioned in this episode. The shared meal which brings blessing to
the family in the form of betrothal, marriage, and new generations is
ironically turned into a completely informal and unsocial event:
Samson scoops honey into his hands and goes on, 'eating as he went'
(14.9) without the traditional aspect of a shared meal. Indeed, he only
'shares' his transgression. Instead of bringing blessing to his family,
Samson does the opposite, for he entangles his parents in his sin of
eating impure food, taken from the carcass of a dead animal.

The lack of a betrothal type-scene is only the first instance of a
pattern in the Samson stories. Robert Alter identifies six 'commonly
repeated biblical type scenes' (1981:51).[44] Whereas earlier narratives
in the Judges' sequence have been structured around the major or
minor Judges' paradigms and have interspersed non-paradigmatic
allusions, the Samson narrative barely invokes the paradigm motif.
The shift from the paradigm of the Judges subtly suggests the erosion
of the validity of that paradigm as a standard of behavior for Israel.
Instead, this narrative alludes in unusual plenty to the type-scenes
established in earlier biblical books. In fact, all six type-scenes
identified by Alter are either employed or pointedly suppressed in the
Samson cycle, and all are invoked for ironic effect.

The Samson narrative begins with an 'annunciation . . . of the
birth of the hero to his barren mother' (Alter, *loc. cit.*). Annunciation
narratives typically develop the personal aspects of the barren
woman's plight. These elements, elaborated in earlier annunciation
type-scenes, are absent as regards Manoah's wife. This annunciation
observes the common parameters of the barren woman, a divine
apparition which announces the birth of a son, and the realization of
that prophecy; it also bears specific allusion to the original
annunciation event, that of Sarah (Gen. 21.1). In the event of
barrenness, divine response to prayer, with or without annunciation,
has consistently led to the appearance of a great leader: Sarah
delivered Isaac (Gen. 25.1-2), Rebecca gave birth to Jacob and Esau
(Gen. 24.21-26), and Rachel had Joseph (Gen. 30.22-24).[45] The
implication is that Yahweh's intervention brings the birth not just of
a son, but of a potentially great man. In Samson's narrative, the
annunciation to a childless woman naturally arouses expectations of
type-scene consequences, a great man. Expectant, the reader

discovers the opposite: insted of a deliverer and judge, this product of wonder behaves like an over-sexed muscle-man, clever enough to compose victory ditties and to pose riddles and rejoinders—at best a hero of common values, a folk hero. In effect, the annunciation type-scene arouses expectations which are diametrically opposed to the reality. The reader is set up for incongruity, for irony.

The 'encounter with the future betrothed at a well' is subsumed in simply 'seeing' the Timnite woman (Alter, 1981:61-62). This type-scene requires that a future bridgroom (or his envoy) travel to a foreign land where at a well he encounters a girl (*na'arāh*) or someone's daughter. Water is drawn, the girl *runs* or *hurries* to her home, usually a meal is offered the guest, and a betrothal is concluded. Samson has gone down to Timnah, a foreign land, but no well-scene, symbolic of fertility, is described. In contrast with the type-scene, the Timnite woman is a woman, *'iššāh*, not a girl, and there is no genealogy of her family. There is no ceremony (drawing water, sharing a meal) leading up to Samson's betrothal: he sees, he wants, he demands. The 'running, hurrying' is in the opposite direction, for instead of the girl running to her parents, the bridegroom simply 'goes' or 'comes up' to his. Once again, the type-scene is alluded to for ironic effects. The reader is invited to perceive thereby that the marriage will not be fruitful.

The 'epiphany in the field' type-scene occurs with the second epiphany of this story, after that of the annunciation. Instead of revelation, Manoah and his wife receive *diminishing* information; their hospitality is refused, and only *after* the divine visitor has been carried aloft in the smoke of the burnt offering is there 'revelation'. An epiphany signals the presence of the divine power and normally one can expect that it implies great events to follow. This type-scene serves, like the others in this narrative, to contradict the convention. Samson–Israel does not prove to be a heroic figure worthy of annunciation and epiphany. These three type-scenes provide fanfare for an anti-climactic if entertaining figure. They also serve to provide momentum for another episode in Israel's struggle, even if the deviations from the type-scene paradigms imply a divergent outcome.

The remaining three type-scenes function differently. Instead of flourish and display for later reversal, the scenes themselves effect reversal of narrative expectations. The type-scene of initiatory trial— the first time Samson acts not only as an individual but also as an

Israelite—overturns the anticipations of military success: instead of establishing his heroism by saving his jeopardized people, Samson is handed over to the enemy by his own people, bound fast. Inversion of the type-scene creates an ironic impression of the tribe: this is surely not an intrepid people, a resolute leader. The irony is enhanced in that antipathetic elements, the spirit of Yahweh and a fresh jawbone, the divine and the forbidden, are joined in force to slay the captors. Nor does Samson's victory constitute even a beginning of Israel's delivery from Philistine power. It is, finally, merely a personal event.

Perhaps the most ironic use of the type-scene in the Samson-cycle is that of 'danger in the desert and the discovery of a well or other source of sustenance'. Samson's 'danger' is of 'dying of thirst' after a one-man victory over a thousand Philistines (a round number), and Yahweh graciously provides a well to revive the 'hero'. As mentioned earlier, Yahweh does for Samson what he had done for the entire nation of Israel during their hardship years in the desert. The recipient of Yahweh's assistance has, however, degenerated from a covenant-people to a self-indulgent egocentric.

Even the last allusion to type-scene, that of the 'testament of the dying hero', is ironic. In dying, Samson seeks personal revenge, not freedom from oppression for his people. Samson fails to fight for Israel—not because he *is* Israel, but because Samson–Israel is 'courting' the Philistines and their way of life.[46] Even blind, he gains minimal insight. He humbly turns to the god of his fathers, but only to revenge personal afflictions. Finally, Samson's 'blindness' to the greater significance of Israel's plight forces the reader to 'vision', to judgment.

Of three passages of particular intensity in the Samson narrative, two involve women—the riddle episode and the famous exchange between Samson and Delilah—and both employ ironic effects.[47] Whereas the irony of the type-scene allusions involves 'irony of situation', in which the discrepancy is between appearance and reality, in these passages 'dramatic irony' creates a contrast between what Samson says and the reader knows to be true.

Samson's famous riddle has, perhaps, attracted interest away from more subtle elements in the Samson cycle. On the other hand, the variety and intensity of critical attention afforded the riddle has clarified many of the ambiguities so that the inherent word play has become more evident. One of the greatest problems has been the opinion that Samson poses a riddle that is inherently unanswerable without special knowledge. In other words, the riddle is not subject to logical or linguistic processes: it is a *Halsrätsel*, a 'Neck Riddle', the kind often found in folk tales when 'one's life [one's neck] hangs in the balance'. James L. Crenshaw defends the Neck Riddle as a traditional variety of verbal witticism and as precisely what Samson's narrative 'demands' (1978:113).

Another approach to the impenetrability of Samson's riddle, one which also seeks to resolve the ambiguous relationship between Samson's riddle and the Philistine's answer, has been offered by J.R. Porter, drawing on research by H. Bauer (1962:107). Porter suggests that substitution of a current word for one which had become archaic rendered the riddle unsolvable to its readers, who lacked that etymological information. Demonstrating that biblical Hebrew (and Arabic) had a word for 'honey', *'arî*, which formed a pun with the word for 'lion' based on the same consonant cluster, Porter suggests that the Philistines recognized Samson's riddle as 'an example of popular etymology', with the first line of the distich a 'kind of clue' to the answer and the second line the riddle proper:

14.14a   Out of the eater came forth eats
    14b   And out of the strong came forth sweets.

The Philistines answer only 14.14b:

14.18   What is sweeter than (*'arî*) honey?
    What is stronger than (*'arî*) lion?

As an etymological riddle, the answer implies 'the word (*arî*) "honey" was derived from the word (*arî*) "lion"'. These identifications, Porter grants, are 'not being made on the basis of accurate linguistic knowledge', but 'by means of a play on words such as is frequent in the Old Testament' (1962:108-109).

Othniel Margalith develops this potential: using the *Sitz im Leben* of the Danites to confirm the intermingling of foreign cultures with that of Yahweh's people of the covenant, he finds that both Samson and the Philistines share the tales and traditions which would allow the Philistines to answer the riddle (even though contrary to the facts of nature) (1986:228). Samson attempts to mislead them, but the Philistines do not fall prey to the false clues of crude sexuality—'appropriate' to a wedding—which would have snared them had they taken these clues at face value. Crenshaw elaborates:

A veiled allusion to the sex act, the riddle uses the ciphers 'eater' and 'strong one' for the groom. Similarly 'food' and 'sweetness' signify semen, which is sweet to the bride who 'eats' the sperm. From man proceeds sperm which nourish woman; from a strong man goes semen that is pleasant to a wife (1978:115).

As wary as Samson is overconfident, the Philistines demand, and get, from Samson's bride, the knowledge necessary to get their necks out of the linguistic noose. They answer word-play with word-play and their answer signifies the formidable powers with which Samson–Israel is 'playing'. Samson's first encounter with the enemy of Israel, the contest of Samson's 'neck riddle' versus the Philistines' duplicity, leads to their victory, one that may seem ameliorated by Samson's slaughter of other Philistines to pay off his debt but only leads to a power see-saw in a chain reaction of events.[48]

Nor does Samson's riddle function solely as an initiator of a power play. The riddle, Greenstein submits, suggests a 'formative pattern' for the entire Samson cycle (1981:247). The 'riddle' Greenstein poses is the identity of Samson, and 'What appears to be Samson is the people Israel; what appears as the Naziriteship of Samson is the Israelite covenant' (*loc. cit.*). This symbolic function is not true only of Samson. Each of the protagonists is a symbol of Israel. Samson, as the epitome of them all, epitomizes Israel.

Clever as Samson tries to be with the Philistine men, he cannot resist the wiles of women, be they communicated by tears or by words, and he behaves with Delilah just as he had with his Timnite wife. Like Jael and the Timnite women, both of whom demonstrate stronger ties to their people than to their husbands, Delilah's ties are to her people (and her profit) in preference to her lover. Jael proves herself Israelite; Delilah proves herself Philistine. In all three instances the action is condemnable . . . perhaps least with Delilah since Samson is merely her lover, not her husband.

The dramatic exchange between the 'hero' and the foreign seductress also draws notably on linguistic devices to achieve its effects. Samson's riddle involves word play and the Samson–Delilah dialogue uses repetitive devices to structure the 'deliberately irregular' recurrent elements which create pattern (Licht, 1978:60). Building upon Licht's basic scheme of 'key terms' to include the speech elements of the Philistine leaders reveals a progression of these elements in the sequence of speeches: one element is retained in each new formulation.

Philistines	16.5	*strength*	**bind**	maltreat
First speech	16.6	*strength*	**binding**	maltreatment
Second speech	16.10	ridicule	lies	**binding**
Third speech	16.13	ridicule	lies	**binding**
Fourth speech	16.15	love	ridicule	*strength*

In this scheme, verses are paired by repetition of the three key elements, and one element from each pair of lines shifts one position in the subsequent formulation. 'Bind/binding' shifts from second to third element, and 'ridicule' shifts from first to second. The last element, 'strength', frames a closure with the first. When the key elements are grouped according to recurrence, a pattern emerges:

binding	4	
ridicule	3	strength
maltreat	2	lies
	1	love

The most repeated element in the Philistine verbal attack is 'binding': that which the Philistine leaders primarily desire is repeated by their accomplice to a total of four times. 'Strength' and 'ridicule', each iterated three times (twice as the first element in a verse), contrasts Samson's *divine* resource and Delilah's very *human* perception of his evasiveness—both important to Delilah. Likewise, 'lies' and 'maltreatment' contrast the efforts of Samson and Delilah (Israel/Philistine) on a somewhat more earthy and less intense level, twice each. The least important element on Delilah's tongue, mentioned only once, is that which makes Samson 'weak' to her, 'love'. Knowing that these are all Philistine–Delilah's words, the reader recognizes that Samson's position is hopeless. Delilah wants only to bind Samson; love is literally one of the last things that occurs to her. Samson, like many another lover, hears only what he wants to hear; thus the reader judges the lover who should be judge. The art of the writer has created a dialogue of dramatic irony in which the reader knows more than the protagonist.

Irony

The Samson narrative compacts an unusually wide range of literary techniques and forms—type-scene, allusion, riddle—and they are all used to one effect: irony. The type-scenes anticipate the birth and activities of a major figure, a 'hero'. Against such expectations, Samson is laughable—but painfully so. In like fashion, allusions to each of the former judges and to pre-judge patriarchs and leaders provide standards for 'measurement' of Samson's non-commitment to covenant precepts. Even the riddle ironically serves the conditions Crenshaw carefully elaborates:

> Riddles establish worth or identity rather than native intelligence
> ... Riddles provided an excellent means of assuring a group's integrity (1978:100).

Instead of assuring group integrity, Samson's 'playful' riddle polarizes the bond of marriage and the bond of peoplehood. It functions in the narrative to define the 'group' to which the Timnite woman primarily belongs: husband or folk. This is particularly ironic since riddles in folk narrative normally function to *win* the bride.[49]

It is significant that the narrative of the last judge is permeated by irony, since it culminates the series of narratives which began with tribal unity and covenant faith.

Chapter 8

RESOLUTION I

Micah and the Danites

With Samson, the period of the judges is over, and the concluding chapters remind us repeatedly that 'in those days there was no king in Israel' (17.6; 18.1; 19.1; 21.25). The significance of this phrase has been subject to conjecture, most often with regard to the period of its composition—monarchic, exilic or post-exilic—and the consequences of the phrase.[1] S. Talmon has approached the significance of this phrase differently: he proposes that the term *melek* 'does not carry the connotation of king' in this text. Talmon's analysis of passages where *melek* and *šōfet* are used in parallel structure and interchangeably, and their like employment in other ancient Semitic languages, leads him to suggest that *melek* 'should be equated with *šōfet*, which is the typical designation of the hero and political leader in the Book of Judges'.[2]

The focus of the phrase, then, is not on the advantage of the monarchy, 'but rather a negative appreciation of the interims in the pre-monarchic period in which no ruler maintained . . . public or cultic order in Israel' (Talmon, 1969:243). According to this interpretation, the resolution of the book does not reflect regret of the absence of what is yet to come but recognition of the failure of the original goals.

Talmon's equation of *šōfet* and *melek* underscores the fact that Yahweh formerly chose leaders for his people; the judges are all either Yahweh-elected or Yahweh-accepted to leadership. Monarchy appears in response to popular demand: it represents a shift in the relationship between Yahweh and Israel.

After Samson, Yahweh no longer sends judges to save the Israelites, a permutation emphasized by this phrase, which is recognized as part of a coda paradigm. The unity of Yahweh's people, the tribes, has been dismantled: 'each man did what was right in his own eyes'. This phrase is paradoxically true even when the tribes act in unity (21.19-23).

The preceding chapters have predicated that the tribal- and clan-named judges are symbols of Israel, each representing an aspect of Israelite apostasy. This symbolic function applies to the central figures of the two post-judge narratives as well. Personifications of Israel without being divinely appointed judges, these protagonists lose significations as well. They are concrete in their actions but lack the genealogical and tribal ties characteristic of the early judges, ties that symbolize covenantal ties with Yahweh. Minor judges have already substituted clan and geographical designations; the non-judges lack either a befitting name or any name at all.

The protagonist of the first narrative sequence is named, albeit ironically, *Micaihu* ('Who is like Yahweh'), but the last narrative of the book does not name the Levite whose actions generate the events of the story, or his concubine, or their host in Gibeah. The other Levite, the priest introduced in 17.7, remains anonymous until 18.30, where he is identified with regard to his past and his future: in retrospect as Micah's former priest and in anticipation as founder of a priestly line to Micah's graven image made of stolen silver. The dialogues between nameless characters and the descriptions of their actions are in notable contrast to the presentation of 'Phinehas, the son of Eleazar, the son of Aaron' (20.27). Named and provided with a genealogy as well, Phinehas, 'standing before the ark of the covenant', only asks Yahweh whether the united tribes should fight Benjamin. The man of the covenant, who asks a valid question of Yahweh, has a place in time and tradition; the individuals who act on their own essentially lose their names.

The gradual disappearance of naming correlates roughly with an increase in worldly values and clan identification, so that the characters become less individual and more emblematic even as their values become more worldly and less abstract. They *seem* to be more individualistic ('Each man did what was right in his own eyes') but are shown to actually be less so: they are inappropriately and ironically named, or even nameless, and full of talk and action which unfold with diminishing reference to time (tradition, history) and, in a certain sense, place (city, geography). The resolution of the book of Judges, then, projects the utter namelessness of the individual cut off from the tradition of the covenant. It suggests that worldly values of power and wealth ironically isolate man from his world and that ethical values give man a name, a place in time and in space, a world. And these men, the individuals of the resolution who do not comprehend the covenant with Yahweh, are Israel after the period of the judges.

The narratives of the resolution are loosely linked with the prior judge narratives, especially the first and the last (1-2 and 13-17), and within themselves. The most obvious element of internal articulation is the paradigm, which appears in two versions:

17.6	In those days there was no king in Israel; man did [what was] right in his own eyes.
18.1	In those days there was no king in Israel.
19.1	In those days there was no king in Israel.
21.25	In those days there was no king in Israel; man did [what was] right in his own eyes.

The complete statements are given first and last in the series, and effect an inclusio.

This patterned expression in the resolution is the third paradigm-with-variations sequence in the book of Judges. The paradigm of the major judges is enunciated in the exposition, in a narrated version (2.16-19) which anticipates the full paradigm statement (of the major judges) first dramatized in the Othniel narrative (3.7-11). After the Abimelech narrative, the minor judge paradigm is introduced; later the major and minor paradigms are variously merged. All of the paradigms—major, minor and resolution—are modulated in varying degrees, linking the sequences of exposition, central action and resolution internally and sequentially.

The sum of eleven hundred pieces of silver is a tangible link to the foregoing Judges narrative. Delilah takes just this amount of silver as bribe money from each of the Philistine lords, and by so doing demonstrates her personal values. In the Micah-mother episode, the negative implications are even intensified. The high price of betrayal—perhaps warranted by personal values and/or danger from Delilah's perspective—remains the same, but bribe money becomes stolen money. In the Micah narrative, the money is stolen, not exchanged between consenting parties. Worse, Micah betrays the trust of blood-tie, of the mother-son kinship. The former exchange was between Philistines, not Israelites, on a 'business basis': a set fee for a specific service. There is no call for Micah, as there is for Delilah, to protect his people from a threatening force, and there is no financial need. The silver (a material entity) is esteemed for its own sake, and that value apparently overrides all others. Delilah, the gauge of evil—foreigner, seductress, betrayer—is surpassed by Micah, Israelite betrayer of Israelite values without reason. The commandment of Exod. 20.15 is broken among *Israelites*, and it is broken within the most intimate sphere, the family. When family members covet and appropriate each other's goods, Yahweh has no family, no chosen people. This is the crux of the action of the book of Judges, and it is manifested in these concluding chapters with ever widening and deepening ramifications.

A further link between the Samson cycle and the following chapters is the site called Kiriath-Jearim in Judah, expressly identified with a 'Camp of Dan'. Samson first experiences the spirit of Yahweh in 'the Camp of Dan, between *Zorah* and Eshta'ol' (13.25). That Manoah is introduced as '*from Zorah*' (with pre-fixed preposition, *mi*, 'from' instead of the customary construct form, which implies 'of') does not suggest any particular significance. The 'Camp of Dan', when first named, is likewise associated with the tribe, and there is no reason to suspect that it represents a movement away from Yahweh-designated territory at this point in the text. Even the burial of Samson, 'between *Zorah* and *Eshtaol*, in the burying place of his father, Manoah' (13.31) only alludes to the Camp of Dan. Samson never reached *Eshtaol* (from 'to ask, enquire'); indeed, he moved away from it.

In ch. 18, the majority of Danites, dissatisfied with their allotted portion, migrate northwards to a territory of their own choosing. These Danites disobey Yahweh's distribution of the land and assume their perception of the situation more relevant than Yahweh's, who specified the site which history and tradition accorded them. As they prepare to move on, they establish a temporary 'Camp of Dan'. Thus the equivalence of the 'Camp of Dan' in the Samson narrative with Kiriath-Jearim in Judah only becomes clear in ch. 18. The delayed release of information 'alters' the reader's understanding of the past and the circumstances of Samson's narrative thus assume a new significance. Samson, born of a father *from* the Danite territory of *Zorah*, is recognized as not having lived in Danite territory and as being a *gēr*, or 'stranger' in the territory of another tribe all his life. His 'wanderings' from the Israelite covenant may be seen as grounded in his *gēr* status. *Gēr*, subtly introduced in the Samson narrative, becomes a key word and an important motif in the chapters of the resolution. Each allusion to the Samson cycle links the 'post-judge' narratives with the 'judge' narratives, thereby contributing to the unification of the book. The allusions also illustrate new depths of apostasy in the deeds of the Israelites.

Several motifs pervade these closing narratives, motifs that have been prepared for in the main action and here reach their logical completion. One such motif is that of the *gēr*. In the text of the exposition and main narrative, the protagonists—whether 'major' or 'minor'—have been shown to be decreasingly identified with Yahwist tribal affiliations and increasingly associated with man-oriented clan groups. Their values have shifted from abstract, Yahwist, and righteous to concrete, human and practical: from ethics to power. In chs. 17–21, this shift is completed; the protagonists are described either without any genealogy, tribe, or clan, or as tribal members who are *gērîm*, 'strangers' in the territory of another tribe. Micah belongs to the first category; all the succeeding figures lack names, lack genealogy, and are 'strangers'. The Levite priest remains one of the nameless *gēr* figures until the conclusion of the narrative, when his identity is revealed for heavily ironic effects. Even though they profess belief in Yahweh, these 'strangers' have left Yahwist territory ethically and physically.[3] Consistent with this pattern, the Levite of the second narrative is another nameless *gēr*: 'a man, a Levite . . . *gēr*' (19.1).

The motif of guest-host relationships is also dominant in these final narratives. The Levite priest initially approaches the house of Micah as a guest, hoping to do unspecified work. Micah offers him the honorable position of priest, pays him well, 'and the young man was to him as one of his sons'. On their way to search for a more satisfactory 'inheritance [for itself] to inhabit' (18.1), the Danites are also guests at the house of Micah (18.2). The details of their stay are not given, but Micah apparently hosts the five Danites appropriately, for 'they lodged there'. The text specifies that they were no longer under Micah's roof—technically, no longer his guests—when they recognized the voice of the Levite priest, approached him, and learned of the 'treasures' in Micah's 'house of gods'. Later in this narrative, the Danite spies rob their former host. The crisis of the last narrative arises through another abuse of the guest-host relationship.

The final chapters fall into two narratives, each composed of several episodes. The first narrative (chs. 17–18) begins *in medias res* with a minimum of presentation: place and name. The missing information is provided in the ensuing dialogue, but sparsely, with no circumstances, no initial causality. Then, just as the reader begins to piece the logic of the sequence together, the narrative shifts in scene and *dramatis personae*, so that the reader must continue to reconstruct; and the narrative seems fragmented. This 'unedifying reading' (Cundall, 1968:182) has been generally attributed to multiple sources and/or editors.[4]

I suggest that the effect is intentional and that the abrupt beginning and disjointed manner serve to promote the impact of the narrative. When a story begins with expository information, the reader has a chance to enter the scene and to follow the sequential thread of events, comfortably holding information in abeyance during intervening flashback and resuming the main thrust when the gap is closed. The reader, unthreatened by the causal structure, feels comfortable even if the story deals with unpleasant circumstances. The reader can sit down to enjoy a murder mystery or a war story, secure in a predictably structured, if horrifying, situation.

This narrative denies the reader that comfort. The first six verses shift abruptly: the man is identified and he tells of his deed; his mother responds and takes consequent actions, the man reacts to the mother's deeds; suddenly a commentary intrudes: 'In those days there was no king [leader, judge] in Israel; every man did what was right in his own eyes'. Somewhat parallel with 17.1, v. 7 begins abruptly once again, with another man, another place. The reader's perspectives are jolted about in quick succession, and even though the two men are brought into contact, the focus of the narrative is not discernible until 18.4 and only becomes clear in the concluding verses of that chapter. The discontinuous form of these verses serves to reinforce the content and to enforce the experience of the narratives. The reader, denied the security of narrative progression, is made insecure and uncomfortable by the disjunctions. Because the reader cannot 'enjoy' the sins of the early Israelites; he or she must 'suffer' them.

To enhance this effect, the narrator of these chapters continues to abstain from registering any feelings. I cannot agree with Moore that 'The author's sympathies, so far as he shows them, are on the side of the spoilers; he makes them not only rob Micah, but mock him' (1895:370). Cundall's observations are closer to the point: 'The original editor may well have included them [the incidents of the "appendices"] without comment, allowing them to speak for themselves (cf. the Samson narratives, which have a minimum of editorial comment)' (1968:182). The reader is forced to experience the events, to weigh them. As in the Samson narrative, the reader is judge.

Like the earlier narratives, the resolution begins with dramatic presentation of a character or two. This time there is neither an exposition or a statement of the condition of the people, and the characters have no genealogy, no clan, no tribe; in fact, most of them have no name.[5] The final five chapters admit only two names of major characters, those of Micaihu (Micah) and Jonathan, and both are used for heavily ironic effect. Micaihu, 'Who is like Yahweh', is the formal name of introduction (17.1) and appears only once more, in the narration which describes the location of the image (17.4): 'and it was in the house of "Who is like Yahweh". The ironic point is literally spelled out. Otherwise, the abbreviated version, Micah (with like meaning) is used.

Micah's first statement thrusts the reader in the midst of a family crisis. Micah reminds his mother of the eleven hundred shekels of silver taken from her, about which she uttered an oath, *'alāh*; he admits that he has the silver and that he had taken it. The redundancy of the verbs 'taking' and 'giving back' in 17.2-5 have been taken to indicate a disrupted text.[6] Though these two verbs dominate the initial passages, these verses actually emphasize *three* verbs, all concerned with handling the silver.

The first verb is *lāqat*, 'to take', which Micah uses twice in his first statement (17.2). The repetition intensifies the fact of taking (actually stealing) and, by contrast, makes his mother's response seem admirable. In 17.3, the silver is *yāšeb*, 'restored' twice,[7] and the verb *'āśāh*, 'to make', is introduced. In this passage, the mother's initially admirable response is notably tarnished: her words of 'blessing' are shown to be insincere by her retention of the greater part of the silver and non-Yahwist by her intent to make idols of the returned silver. In the following verse, the full range of these verbs— 'to take', 'to restore', 'to make'—is used, once each. Finally, the last verse of the narrative has only 'made'. The force of the verbs shifts. It is balanced in 17.4, but in 17.5, a final 'made' is decisive. Each of these verbs is used three times, but there is only one action of 'taking' and one of 'restoring'. Only the last verb, 'making' actually describes three actions: making an 'image', and an 'idol', and an 'ephod'. The tripled repetition suggests ethical equivalence in the verbs.

17.2	taken,		
	taken		
17.3		restored	
		will restore	make
17.4	took	restored	made
17.5			made[8]

The verb for 'take' is used to mean 'steal' as well as 'take'. Similarly, 'restore' denotes 'returning of confiscated goods' and a free 'giving back' that is not 'restoring'. The verb *'āśāh*, 'to make', is here identified with the making of an idol or graven image. The two verbs associated with condemnable actions, 'to take' (steal) and 'to make' (an idol or an image) surround the apparently redeeming verb of 'restore', or 'to give back'. The 'restoring' is revealed to be not only empty words (nine hundred of the silver pieces are *not* given back) but worse: the silver, contaminated by theft, is *restored* to be *re-formed* into a non-holy, anti-Yahwist, forbidden image. In this context, then, all three verbs have negative connotations. The verbs, each used three times, range from taking (from within the family) to making (images as idols), from sacrilege within the family to sacrilege before Yahweh. The pattern of these verbs also anticipates the widening significance of the following narratives—from family sin to community idolatry to tribal apostasy.

As if the invidious comparison implicit in his name and the pernicious behavior described in the first five verses were not enough to vilify Micah, the concluding verses of ch. 17 add scorn. After assuming the prerogative to name his own son (or anyone else) to priesthood, Micah puts his son out of this honorable position in his household and invites a vagabond Levite to fill that post, and he explains his actions: 'Now I know that Yahweh will do good to me because the Levite is priest to me' (17.13). Micah believes that he can manipulate things (silver), people (his mother, his son, the Levite priest), and even Yahweh to his advantage. Instead of being a servant to Yahweh, Micah tries to control events so that Yahweh will serve him. Micah tries to exploit everyone, even his god.

Micaihu-Micah, one of the few characters named in the final chapters, is introduced by name and location, but both terms are vague. Micah has neither tribe nor patronym, and the 'hills of Ephraim' is an unusually vague description of place. Nevertheless, biblical characters are not 'flat', and Micah is no exception.[9] He has enough fear of Yahweh that he returns the silver under threat of his mother's (blasphemous) oath, he observes the ritual of consecration when he takes it upon himself to install his son as priest, and he not only remunerates the Levite for his services but treats him 'as one of his sons'. He is a complex character, with positive as well as negative attributes. The negative ones are, however, significant and preponderant.

Not named although dramatically presented, Micah's mother recalls Samson's unnamed mother, which invites comparison of the women. The judge's mother is presented as a good Israelite who follows Yahweh, but Micah's mother falls far short of this standard.[10] According to her son, who reports the incident, his mother's response to her silver being stolen is to utter an oath . . . and what an oath.[11] The noun used, *'ālāh*, means 'to invoke God': the primary meaning of *'ālāh* is 'oath, especially a covenant made by an oath' (*AHCL*, 1981:26). The import here rests not with the contents of the oath, but that the woman took it upon herself to make an oath *with this word*.

The use of *'ālāh* is selective and infrequent in the preceding books of the Bible. Abraham had caused his servant to swear, *šāba'*, to bring back a bride for Isaac only from Abraham's family, but in his recounting of the event the servant elevated the occasion to a covenantal oath, *'ālāh* (Gen. 24.41). The term is used by Abimelech in his recognition of Yahweh when he asks Isaac for a covenant of peace (Gen. 26.28). Finally, at the threshold of the promised land, Moses calls the entire people to him that they may enter into the covenant and the oath with Yahweh, to establish them on that day as Yahweh's people (Deut. 29.12, 14). Clearly the word is used with special reverence. Yet this is the word used by Micah's mother. She has apparently invoked a covenant with Yahweh without benefit of a priest, and for mundane rather than ethical purposes: to regain her silver. A few verses later, the woman blesses the thief, her son, by Yahweh because he has returned the stolen goods. Micah's mother apparently uses Yahweh's name much as Micah seeks to use Yahweh, for her own convenience: she assumes the right to make oaths and invoke blessings, and to do these on behalf of a worldly tangible— silver. Her consecration of the silver further maligns her ties to the Israelite tradition, for she withholds the far greater sum (900 pieces) and the two hundred she does expend are used to make an image, expressly forbidden by Yahweh. Micah's mother, therefore, is ironic compared with Samson's mother. Micah has learned his mother's values (as Samson did not), and he has already involved the third generation, his son, in the practice of anti-Yahwist 'Yahwism'. The deterioration from the ethical covenant which once marked Yahweh's people—a deterioration which was cyclical rather than constant—is shown being passed from generation to generation and becoming entrenched and established.

With the economy typical of biblical style and with narrative objectivity that does not judge the events described, the first three verses relate the desecration of as many commandments.[12] The circumstance of the concluding narratives is secured: the high standards established by Yahweh for his people have degenerated to the point—at the opening of the final chapters—that members of an Israelite family break holy commandments among themselves.

Whether one image or two was made of the silver is irrelevant: the various kinds of idol serve to encompass the practices of idol-worship. The mother contributes a *pesel* (a molded image) and a *maṣṣēbā* (an idol, set upright). Both of these words for image stress that they are fabricated. Micah contributes two more artifacts, *ephod* and *terraphim*, probably also in human form but distinguished from the others in that the latter serve as media for oracles. These doubled terms are more than hendiadys.[13] The terms constitute an inventory of idols to be found in a shrine (house of gods). In a succinct fashion, most of the words for household god have been named. *Pesel* and *masseba* emphasize the *fabricated* aspect of the image; *ephod* and *terraphim* the oracular.[14] The terms as used in the Judges narrative stress humanity's part in either *making* the idol or in *using* it:

ephod	robe of approach to God; image representing deity, *used* in consulting deity.
maṣṣēbā	idol, image; *hewn* of stone or wood
pesel	metal image; *made* of molten metal
terraphim	a kind of idol, object of reverence; *means* of divination.

The text specifically includes and implicitly censures a range of forms of idol or image for worship: those made by people, whether carved or graven, those 'set up' to serve that function, and those used as oracles. Notably, one word for an image that is *made* and has not been condemned is *ṣelem*, the word used by Elohim when he created man: 'And Elohim created man in his own (*ṣelem*), image' (Gen.

1.27). The omission of *ṣelem* contrasts 'human-made' with divine creation. Elohim may create man, but people cannot 'create' gods.[15] Humankind is reminded that it may not make images of gods—or man, since man is in the 'image' of his god. Similarly, Yahweh may speak to his chosen priests through a medium, but the medium (ephod, terraphim) may not be used at convenience to summon Yahweh. Prohibition takes precedence over logic, and Micah's mother gives him an image that is both 'graven' and 'molded'. Micah adds the other two. He has a full house of forbidden icons.

The Micah narrative provides a detailed scenic background for the final sequence of the book, making the point that nothing good can come of immoral means. The oath invoked by Micah's mother does not put an enduring curse *on* the silver; it is the *immorality* of the theft that cannot be undone except by giving to Yahweh. Making a (forbidden) image from the returned silver does not 'restore' the silver, already associated with the immorality of theft, and it certainly does not fulfill the mother's promised consecration to Yahweh. The silver is consecrated but retained and perverted to personal, anti-Yahwist purposes—paradoxically, in the name of Yahweh. The mother's blessing cannot undo the oath: neither has been made at a sanctuary by a priest of Yahweh. Leviticus 6.1-6 prescribes the ritual necessary for the expiation of a sin which has generated an oath. Micah has confessed and repaid the principal, as required, but he has failed to acknowledge his sin before Yahweh. The sinner has not brought his guilt offering to Yahweh before the priest so that the latter can make atonement for Micah before Yahweh (Lev. 6.7), and he has not paid the prescribed fine : 'a fifth [of the principal involved] he shall give to him to whom it belongs, on the day of his guilt offering'.

Mother and son have literally done nothing right. As types of Israel, Micah and his mother symbolize how far from Yahweh the people have come. Micah's stealing silver from his mother (inter-family theft) anticipates broadening covenant-breaking, the tribal theft of the same silver after it has been re-formed into an image. The mother's responses—oath, blessing, without benefit of sin-offering or priest, and indeed, without relinquishing *any part* of the silver she has consecrated to Yahweh—correspond to those of the Levite hired as priest: independence of Yahwist principles and ritual. Not all Levites were priests, and the Levite-priest away from his assigned city-territory was no longer capable of Yahwist service: he too had disobeyed. Neither Micah's mother nor the priest are capable of fulfilling priestly functions. Finally, when Micah installs his own priests, 'upgrading' from son to Levite as opportunity presents itself, he is presuming to usurp Yahwist authority,[16] just as the tribe of Dan does in deciding to re-locate in territory other than that assigned to it by Yahweh. Micah, his mother, the Levite priest and the tribe of Dan are figures of expanding Israelite *ḥuṣpāh*, presumption of human knowledge and will above that of Yahweh and his covenant.

The second phase of the Micah story introduces the Levite, a 'sojourning' *gēr* figure—an individual of an tribe alien to that of residence. The alien quality is stressed in the complex description:

17.7   And there was a young man
         from Bethlehem in Judah,   (territory: city)
         of the family of Judah,   (tribal association)
         and he [was] a Levite;   (tribal office)
         and he *ger* [sojourned] there.

Joshua 21.4 delineates the assignment of Levite clans to the various tribes, which tribes were to allot Levitical cities and surrounding fields to their Levite residents. Because all Levites are assigned residence in the tribal territories of other sons of Jacob, they have two affiliations: the inherited (Levite) and the assigned (tribal territory, fixed by Yahweh). They cannot be considered *ger* in the assigned tribal territories because they, like the tribe, have been assigned there by Yahweh.

In the resolution narratives, the *gēr* motif is reinforced by a subtle syntactical shift. Until ch. 12, no judge is described as *from* a tribe/ clan or locality, though Barak is 'son of *Abinoam*, from *Kedesh Naphtali*' (4.6). Immediately after the Jephthah narrative, Ibzan *from* Bethlehem (without genealogy or tribe) judges Israel seven years (12.8). His successors, Elon and Abdon, have clan affiliations and are not described as being *from* a place (12.11, 13). Use of the prepositional particle 'from' as a means of identification is first pronounced in the introduction of Manoah:

13.2   And there was one man *from* Zorah,
         from the clan of the Danites
         and his name [was] Manoah.

Samson is son of a *gēr*. Significantly, he is never referred to as 'son of'. He is only 'named' by his mother.

The Levite is initially identified as a *gēr*; only later (18.30) does the reader learn he really is Jonathan, a Levite of the sons of Gershom, in the direct line of Moses. At the birth of his son, Moses

Exod. 2.22 called his name Gershom; for he said
I have become a *gēr* in a foreign land.

To be a stranger is not necessarily blameworthy. Moses is a *gēr* that he may know being a stranger and can lead the people, under Yahweh, to their own land; but the Levite runs from his divinely appointed place in Israel. The identification of the Levite with his ancestor deprecatingly contrasts with Moses' flight from oppression. The Levite abandons the land, the opportunity, and the responsibility won in the intervening years of hardship. The Gershom–Levites were assigned to cities in the territories of Issachar, Asher, Nephthah and Manasseh (Josh. 21.6). Like Micah, the young Levite has already deviated from Yahwist land distribution; he has chosen a different tribe (Judah) and territory (Bethlehem–Judah) to live in and serve than that assigned to the Gershomites, and he has even given up his first choice of residence:

17.8 And the man went from the city of Bethlehem in Judah,
to live where he could find a place.

The Levite can justly be called a vagabond.

With one notable exception, the protagonists of the post-judge narratives are provided no genealogical background. Their tribal designations may be indicated, but they are *from* or live elsewhere than in their tribal territories. Even Micah, whose tribe is not given, is *from* the territory he occupies.

17.1 And there was a man *from* the hill country of
Ephraim and his name [was] Micaihu.
17.7 . . . a young man *from* Bethlehem-Judah *from*
[a] family of Judah and he [was] a Levite.
17.8 . . . and went the man *from* the city *from*
Bethlehem-Judah . . .[17]

The author uses restraint for telling effect: at the completion of this narrative, the Levite priest is exposed with name and genealogy, both of which have ironic significance:

name: Jonathan: 'whom Yahweh has given'.
genealogy: (past and future): 'son of Gershom, son of Manasseh,
he and his sons were priests to the tribe of the
Danites until . . . ' (18.30).

The shift from genealogical and tribal descriptions in the construct state (denoting 'of') to geographical and clan descriptions prefixed with the prepositional *mi* ('from') subtly underscores the movement from Yahwist belief, the erosion of the whole, the disintegration of Yahwist Israel. Attrition from obedience and the spread of naive individualism is conveyed symbolically, ironically and syntactically. These figures observe cult and use ritual for their own purposes; they epitomize religion without ethics and ritual without faith. They are far fallen from the 'chosen' people.

Chapter 18 begins, as noted earlier, with an abbreviated refrain and an abrupt shift of place and character, the latter involving an expansion to the clan/tribal level.[18] Although not all the Danites migrated northward, the text is specifically inclusive (18.2): the five men who are chosen to spy out new territory have come from the entire tribe, from 'the whole of them'; there is a decided impression of unified action. Pointedly, the five men come from the same Danite towns, Zorah and Eshtaol, which furnish the background (literally) to the Samson narrative. In neither narrative does any action take place in Yahweh-designated Danite territory.

The two narrative threads begin to merge when the Danite spies come into the neighborhood of (close to) Micah's house and receive his hospitality. Once outside again, no longer under Micah's roof and technically no longer guests, the Danites recognize the 'voice', the accent, of the Levite priest. What the Levite was saying or to whom is irrelevant; it is his accent that makes him known as a stranger, a *gēr*, in these parts.[19] The Danites 'turn aside' to the Levite. The spies are not said to have turned from the road when they come to the house of Micah:

18.2   and they came [to] hill [country]
         of Ephraim, to house of Micah,
         and they lodged there.

But when they hear the unfamiliar accents of the Levite they recognize another *ger* and they *turned there*. Normally, 'to turn aside/depart from a way', especially to turn aside to any person, is written with *'al*, 'to, unto'. The preposition, however, is missing in this text: *weyasuru šām*, 'and they turned there'. The omission calls attention to word-play: in depicting the men as 'turning aside' from their path to go to the Levite, the language foreshadows departure from an ethical 'way of life'.

The recent guests of Micah pose a series of questions to the Levite priest:

18.3   Who has brought you here?
        What are you doing in this [place]?
        And what [is] for you here?

The Levite priest ignores the first question completely. Unlike the priest, the Danites have not left their Yahweh-assigned territory independently, but on behalf of their tribe. The Danites unwittingly acknowledge the seriousness of their own breach when they assume someone has *brought* the Levite priest away from his Levitical city. Apparently they cannot think that the young man has simply taken it upon himself to relocate according to his own pleasures.

The Levite priest answers the second question, but initially focuses his answer not upon himself, as demanded by the question, but upon Micah:

18.4   And all this has Micah done to/for me
        And he hired me
        And I am priest to him.

Only in conclusion does the Levite priest answer the second question directly. The third question, like the first, goes unanswered. The Danites seem not to recognize the Levite's evasive responses, nor do they pay any attention to what Micah has done for the priest. They are interested only in their own prospects. The multi-layered irony of this exchange is remarkable: the Danites (who are leaving Yahwist-designated territory) ask a Levite priest (who has left his Levitical city and the first alien city of his own choice) to inquire of the household gods made of stolen silver to determine if the 'way', *derek*, they are going is in accord with God's will.[20]

The Levite priest represents the ritual element *sans* the God whom it serves, empty cult. Like Micah and the Danites, even the priestly caste is symbolized as substituting obedience to Yahweh and Yahwist principles with meaningless cultic practices. Certainly not every individual, not each tribe, not all Levite priests are included in these symbolic figures, as the later text makes clear. It is evident that each of the symbolic levels—individual, tribal, priestly caste—is shown to profess belief in Yahweh: Micah returns the stolen silver because of his mother's curse in the name of Yahweh, the Danites ask the priest whether God is with them, and the Levite serves as priest to the tribe of Dan, however blasphemously. Nevertheless, all have shown by their actions that they are, in their *deeds*, utterly separated from Yahweh. The priest's exchange with the Danites (18.6) is especially ironic. The Levite priest, who has himself disobeyed Yahweh, tells the Danites (who have done the same) to 'Go in peace: the way you go is before Yahweh'. That the disobedient priest cannot interpret Yahweh's will is evident on many levels; and his priestly benediction adds an ironic element to his earlier actions.

The goal of the Danites is a city called Laish. The description of Laish and its people suggests an important difference between the peoples and territories Yahweh has designated for conquest and occupation and those the Israelites—here represented by the Danites—choose to call their own. Yahweh has specified the peoples with whom the Israelites should do battle:

3.3   five lords of the Philistines,
        and all the Canaanites,
        and the Sidonians,
        and the Hivites that lived in Mount Lebanon . . . .

Yahweh included the Sidonians among the peoples/lands to be conquered, but Laish is not Sidonian. Although these people lived 'like Sidonians', they were situated far from them and not under Yahweh's directive. Furthermore, k^e*mišpaṭ*, the word used to express the idea that the people were living according to the 'custom, manner' of Sidon is based on the root *šōfat*, 'right, judgment'. Other words that could express this idea are:

ôrāh:	'a way or mode of living',
	based on root meaning 'way, path'.
derek:	'way, road, manner'.
hō:	'custom, privilege', based on root
	meaning 'fixed, appointed'.

The people of Laish are not living according to the *way* of life or 'fixed' customs, but according to *right* or *judgment*.[21] They are living 'within' their city, their customs—not wandering from them as the Israelites are wont to do. Their 'custom' both emphasizes their contentment and the unethical, anti-Yahwist action of the Israelites, who destroy 'right' living. The Laishites are described as *'am boṭēḥa'*, 'a people secure', with implications of 'trusting'. They are also said to live far from the Sidonians and to have no *dābar*, 'words', 'connections' with others. The people of Laish apparently are content without conquest of or power over other peoples.[22] Implicitly, these are the qualities Yahweh upholds and would not have destroyed: certainly not by the hand of the Israelites, the chosen people whom Yahweh had repeatedly rescued from slavery and oppression, the chosen people who should further righteous and peaceful living. When the spies report at Zorah and Eshtaol, they tell the Danites of a people 'secure, and the land large of both hands; for God gave it in your power—a place without lack in the land' (18.10). The people of Laish live *secure* and *content* lives; that destruction of this contentment is considered 'God-given' augments the irony of the Israelite action. Yahweh had delivered the Israelites from oppression in Egypt and from other oppressors. How pointed that the Israelites oppress a peaceful people in the name of Yahweh, who is against this oppression.

Even the name of Laish contributes to the irony. This very city was named in Josh. 19.47, but there it was spelled *Leshem*, which translates as 'ligure', a precious stone, possibly a yellow jacinth. In this tale, 'Leshem' is called 'Laish'; the precious jewel becomes a 'lion', certainly an ironic name for the situation and behavior described.

As the warriors of Dan—six hundred men with weapons of war—travel on their way to Laish, they set up camp at the very place where the spirit of Yahweh had first begun to move Samson, in the Camp of Dan behind Kiriath-Jearim. The text confirms that the site was named 'Camp of Dan' from that day. Although it may seem illogical that Samson's experience is placed in a future-named site, this lack of logic serves the significant purpose of linking the beginning of Samson's exploits with those of his people, the Danites. This passage also provides additional information about Samson. In the earlier chapter,

13.25   And the spirit of Yahweh began to move him
         in the Camp of Dan, between Zorah and Eshtaol.

The named towns belong to Danite territory, and in this context, the camp of Dan seems to be part of the Danite complex. It is only in the next verse (14.1) that Samson obviously leaves Danite territory. The detail provided in 18.12 illuminates Samson's character retrospectively: the man elected *in utero* to enact Yahweh's will was even prenatally away from his assigned tribal territory and was a *gēr*, however passively, in the land of Judah, in Kiriath-Jearim. Although each of the judges has seemed an unlikely choice, Samson, *ger* from birth, is literally the 'strangest'. Like all the other judges, each a symbol of an aspect of Israel, Samson represents the human material available to Yahweh, at that phase, to effect the divine will.

Samson was blessed with Yahweh's spirit; nevertheless, he neglected not only his calling as judge but also his responsibilities to the covenant. In the present context, the Danites have *chosen* to leave Yahweh's territory—literally and figuratively—and to go their own way. They camp where Samson first felt the stirrings of Yahweh's spirit, but that spirit remains significantly absent for them. Once again, the logic of the sequence is waived in favor of more significant connotations implicit in the presence or absence of Yahweh. The retrocessive information also reminds the reader of the limitations of human knowledge: that one may be ironically ignorant even in the security of apparent knowledge.

The fighting men seem to take the same route as their scouts had taken, and they too come upon Micah's house. The five spies, who were guests of Micah, either remind the troops of information given earlier, as a rhetorical question, or perhaps transmit the information at this junction in question form. Nothing is said of Micah's hospitality; only the 'treasures' in his houses are enumerated: 'an ephod and terraphim, and a graven image and a molten image'. Knowledge of the treasures implies a consequent action: 'And now you know what you are to do'. It is not clear (or important) which group initiates the action, for the verse could be spoken by either party, spies to men or vice versa. They all turn from the path toward Laish and come to the house of the Levite—one of the houses of Micah, the text stresses.

This brings the 600 men right up to the house, where the priest remains standing as the spies go inside, taking the household idols after they have greeted him in peace, 'shalom'. The irony of the greeting is emphasized by the following verse, which describes the 600 armed men standing at the door-gate to (the place of) justice (*petaḥ haššāʿar*).[23] The term *šāʿar*—which includes the space inside the gates where elders or judges sat officially, the place where justice was administered—modifies *petaḥ*, a courtyard opening/gate.

Metaphorically, 'gate of justice', the place where justice is administered, is introduced into a scene where the opposite occurs. The irony is emphasized in the repetition of the phrase, stressing that while (waw consecutive) the men 'went up'[24] and entered and took the household gods, the priest and the girded warriors were standing in the door-gate, the place of justice. The six hundred men have come right up to the house, where the priest remains standing in the door-gate as the five spies go inside and take the household idols.[25] The tripled verbal repetition (took, restored, made) of the opening passage of this narrative (17.2-5) is alluded to in these verses (18.14-20). As in 17.2-5, the silver (now idols) is 'taken' three times (18.17, 18, 20); and, consistent with the non-committal style of the book, the implications of Micah's deed are merely intimated by the explicit designation of the entire sequence of idols: ephod and terraphim and graven image and molten image. The consequence of Micah's *taking* is made ironically clear as the idols (and the priest) are *taken* from him. That which began in taking (stealing) ends in taking (stealing); the verbal repetition serves as an inclusio which marks the completion of the major aspect of the tale, even though the narrative continues with two short epilogues.

This narrative of resolution of the book has its own elements of resolution. the first (18.21-26) depicts the confrontation between the thief (Micah) and those who rob him, which escalates the level of theft. Micah's 'taking' from his own mother was covenant-breaking, but the 'taking' of idols (to say nothing of the Levite priest) as 'believers' in Yahweh is nothing less than bizarre. Micah, who cherishes tangibles more than Yahwist ethics, goes home empty-handed and, presumably, empty-spirited.

The second epilogue (18.27-30) describes the conquest of Laish and its re-naming as 'Dan' in honor of the tribal founding father. Jacob's death wish (Gen. 49.16-17) was that 'Dan shall judge his people as one of the tribes of Israel', for 'Dan' means 'judge'. The tribe of Dan, which should be

Gen.   ... a serpent on the way, a horned snake
49.17   on the path that bites the heels of the horse, and its rider falls
            backwards ...

is itself *gēr* from Yahweh's territory, has oppressed a peaceful people and destroyed its town, and has established a sanctuary with idols (stolen, at that) and a *gēr* Levite priest. This is Dan, judge in the book of Judges.

Chapter 9

RESOLUTION II

The Levite and his Concubine

The last narrative sequence of the book, in which the initially projected conquest is depicted in ethical collapse, encompasses the final three chapters of the book of Judges. In this second narrative of the resolution, the shortened refrain once more introduces an abrupt transition in character and location and, in the following chapter, an enlarged social milieu. Once more the protagonist is a Levite living in Ephraim territory, once more a *gēr*—even more estranged, in the remote parts of the hill country—and once more unnamed. Unlike the Levite priest, a Gershomite, this Levite is not associated either with an eponymous ancestor or with a Levitical city. This Levite came from nowhere in time and in space. The Levite priest travels in a consistent direction, from Bethlehem–Judah to Ephraim territory (where he resides with Micah), to new territories. But this Levite travels in a circle: from Ephraim territory to Bethlehem–Judah, and back via Gibeah to the remote hills of Ephraim.[1] Both of the narratives of resolution sustain the figure implied by the protagonist's travels: the Levite priest fathers a *line* of priests to the Danite temple, but the Levite's round trip involves an ever-widening circle of Israelites in a devastating war.

That the Levite lives in the *remotest* hills of Ephraim is suggestive. 'Ephraim' means 'fertility', and 'remotest, on the far side' is derived from the root *'rk*, 'descendants, comers out of the thigh; hinder part; recesses; remotest parts' (*AHCL*, 1891:348). Both words are at least implicitly concerned with generation. The phrase suggests that the Levite lives on the far side of the hills, remote from the heights of Ephraim, fertility. Indeed, there is no mention of generation occurring within the entire tale.

Another curious aspect is that the Levite has 'a wife, a concubine' but no primary wife is mentioned. Biblical Hebrew distinguishes clearly between 'wife', *'iššāh*; 'second wife' ('female adversary, rival') *ṣôrāh*; and 'concubine' (a non-semitic loan word), *pilgeš*.[2] Sometimes the patriarchal concubines were the slave girls of their wives, offered to the husbands when the wife failed to conceive. Although the descendants of a concubine had the same rights as those of a wife, she may not have had the right to name her child; for instance, Gideon named the son born to his Shechemite concubine. Some wives did not name their sons (Moses', Joseph's), but these wives were not Israelite and could not name their sons properly. Nevertheless, concubines must have had a special place in the household; often they are named in the narratives when wives are not. Finally, 'womanhood, being a wife' may be a metaphor for being a bride to Yahweh, but concubinage is never used in this sense.

Raphael Patai discusses the marital customs of the Middle East, which he maintains have remained virtually unchanged.[3] Marriage usually involves union within a relatively narrow circle, preferably between the children of two brothers, although children of other near relatives or of families belonging to the same local or tribal group are acceptable substitutes. In this patrilocal social structure, a daughter leaves her own extended family with marriage and becomes incorporated into the extended family of her husband.[4] Nevertheless, the daughter's consanguineal family remains responsible for her moral conduct and represents her interests in case of improprieties on the part of her husband. Because the families are patriarchal as well as patrilocal,[5] difficulties might arise when the daughter-wife belongs to another group. The proximity of the daughter's family provides support for her should her husband not treat her properly; with distance, the daughter is virtually unprotected. The close blood ties and physical proximity of the bride's family effectively reduce the threats on both sides.

The *gēr* Levite living in the hill country of Ephraim has taken a concubine-wife from Bethlehem–Judah: another location (and implicitly, tribe). As a *gēr*, he is far removed from his patrilocal society. The Levite appears not to have acquired the slave-girl or concubine to counteract his wife's infertility; no mention is made of another woman as wife. Given these conditions, the Levite seems to have bought the girl for purposes of sexual gratification or housekeeping (or both), possibly because he could not afford the bride price of a wife. The narrative supports this conjecture: the Levite pretends to be more affluent than he really is; and although he pursues his concubine to bring her back, he ignores her in every respect but one: in presenting her to the Gibeaites for abuse, he acknowledges her as a sexual object.

The reliable narrator tells that the concubine was *tizneh*,[6] 'unfaithful to, like a harlot' to her husband, but the Levite does not punish his wife's infidelity according to the precepts of Deut. 22.21. A woman who behaves like a harlot should be stoned to death, but this would leave the Levite without a woman for whatever purposes he had acquired her. The narrative leads one to believe that the Levite's needs are more important to him than Yahweh's moral strictures. The concubine's taking the initiative in leaving her husband is the only instance of a woman assuming the male prerogative of repudiation of a partner; her husband's pursuit of her is likewise an anomalous reaction to an unfaithful wife. Boling suggests the woman is unfaithful by virtue of leaving her husband, for which there were no legal provisions (1975:273-74). 'Prostitution' seems too strong a term for such a case were not the figurative meaning, 'spiritual whoredom' or 'idolatry' not also implicit. The woman's unfaithfulness, either by sexual infidelity or by leaving her husband to return to her family, is one more instance of 'doing what is right in [her] own eyes'. Her husband's behavior is another. Neither the concubine nor the Levite have lived within the tradition of the covenant. The consequences of her actions are an implicit judgment of her as well as of her husband.

For that matter, the concubine's father, who remains responsible for his daughter's behavior, is also remiss in not punishing her for her immoral action. The father-in-law of the Levite is apparently willing to patch things up without worrying about the prescribed penalties and is extremely hospitable to his son-in-law. The three days customarily accorded a guest are observed: 'The first day is supposed to be spent with greeting and inquiries about each other's health and family. The second day is supposed to be devoted to feasting, and only on the third day is the guest supposed to state his errand or the purpose of his visit' (Patai, 1959:54). The three-day hospitality is assumed, and the narrative only goes into the details of the encouraged prolongation of the visit beginning with the fourth night and repeats the description for the fifth night and the invitation to the sixth.

The prolonged hospitality is particularly relevant. That the concubine is a purchased slave-girl suggests her family is poor. Since they live in a house, not a tent, the family of the girl (or young woman) is presumably engaged in a settled (like farming) rather than nomadic (herding) way of life. The young concubine's family also lives in a city, 'Bethlehem in Judah', rather than out in the hills. The Levite lives in a tent, not a house, as his father-in-law remarks (19.9). The girl, then, has been sold from a stable, urban household to a rootless man and a nomadic, isolated life. If the girl has not been sexually unfaithful, her rejection of these conditions to return to the house of her father is 'prostitution'. And she is a girl, at most a young woman, *na'ārāh*, not a woman, *'iššāh*. On the other hand, if she has been sexually unfaithful, the men have been remiss: her father and her husband in their separate failures to punish her, and her husband in taking her back. On this point, the narrative is ambiguous.

When he arrives at the home of his concubine, 'she took him into her father's house' and her father 'was glad to welcome him'. There is no suggestion of the concubine's response; she simply observed the code of the guest-host relationship and brought the Levite into the house, where the two men virtually ignore the daughter-concubine, the reason for the Levite's visit. The concubine returns with the Levite, but just as she was ignored by the Levite and her father, she remains ignored during the trip to the Levite's home. The Levite and his 'boy' discuss where they will spend the night, but the woman is not included in the conversation. The person for whom the Levite made the trip is apparently not worthy of conversation. Indeed, the girl is never addressed and never utters a word during the entire narrative for which she provides the motivation.

Under the circumstances, the fact that the Levite stays beyond the conventional three days certainly imposes hardship upon the economics of the host family. The character of the Levite—that he is selfish and inconsiderate of others—emerges from his overstay.

As he travels back to his home, the Levite rejects the suggestion of sojourning in Jebus, a non-Israelite city. Davidson suggests 'Jebus' (literally, 'place trodden down') is derived from a conjectural verb, *bûs*, 'to trample upon, tread under foot' (*AHCL*, 1981:71). Another verb with the same consonant cluster has a contradictory meaning: 'to be high'; with the implication of '*religious worship*, true or false', including the 'high places' of Baal worship, (*AHCL*, 1981:71).

Jebus: root *b's*, 'to trample... tread under foot'
           'place trodden down... ancient name of
           Jerusalem'.
           root *b's*, 'to be high'; high place, usually
           dedicated to religious worship, true or
           false' (*AHCL*, 1981:71)

The Levite suggests Israelite cities, both of which have implications
of 'high, lofty'.

Gibeah: root *gb'*, 'to be high; hill' (*AHCL*, 1981:128);
           'especially as place of illicit worship'
           (*BDB*, 1979:149).
Ramah: root *r'm* 'to be high, lofty' (*AHCL*, 1981:678-79);
           'term. techn. for *shrine* (for illicit
           worship)' (*BDB*, 1979:928).

Although the primary meaning of the non-Israelite city is negative
(down-trodden) and that of the Israelite cities is ethically and
spatially the opposite and positive (high), all three have secondary
meanings which include 'illicit worship'. There seems to be no real
choice, and this foreshadowing is substantiated in the subsequent
action. The Levite prefers the apparent heights to the apparent
depths. He prefers to sojourn in an Israelite city, presuming its
residents will observe the guest tradition he has just abused at his
father-in-law's house. Gibeah was a Levitical city in the tribe of
Benjamin, but the Levite apparently found no members of his tribe
in the city. Presumably they were, like the Levite, *gēr* somewhere
else.

With the arrival of the Levite, his concubine and his boy in
Gibeah, the narrative begins an extended parallel with the story of
Lot in Sodom (Genesis 19). Burney set out the verbatim repetition of
words and phrases in a side-by-side comparison of the texts
(1970:443-45). The divergences between the two narratives, however,
are more revealing. The parallels function to highlight the deviations,
each of which recalls and inverts a detail of the Genesis narrative.
Meaning is once more created through ironic opposition.

Both episodes begin with seated figures, both in the proximity of
the city gate:

Gen.   19.1   ... and Lot sat at the gate of Sodom
Judg. 19.15   ... and he sat in the plaza (*reḥōb*) of the city.[7]

The parallel is supported in a subsequent verse: in response to Lot's invitation, the angels say they will

Gen. 19.2   . . . stay in the plaza (*reḥōb*).

and the old man counsels the Levite:

Judg. 19.20   . . . do not spend the night in the plaza (*reḥōb*).

The gates of the city provided an open place where markets and courts of judgment were held and where the idle assembled. Judges 18.16-17 makes symbolic and ironic reference to the gates of the city. The present allusion draws on the motif of the gate, and once more injustice begins in the place of justice.

The similarities of the Genesis and Judges narratives suggest that the old man *from* the hills of Ephraim[8] is in the host position of Lot and his guests; the Levite with his concubine, servant, and asses in that of the angels.[9] The very juxtaposition conveys ironic meaning. In the Genesis episode, Lot was seated at the gate when the angels came to Sodom, and 'When Lot saw them, he rose to meet them, and bowed his face to the earth' (Gen. 19.1). In the Judges version, the guests, the Levite and his group, sat unwelcomed: 'there [is] no man that [takes] them into his house to spend the night' (Judg. 19.15b). Lot does not ask any questions of this guests; he offers hospitality because they are there. The old man is more cautious: he asks 'Where are you going, and where do you come from?' The Levite answers both questions directly. He then adds that he is going to 'a house of Yahweh', intimating that he is a priest: and he adds that he has straw and food and bread and wine, thereby giving the impression that he is well off. He does not mention that his home is a tent in a remote area, which would reveal him as other than a priest. Apparently the Levite's pretensions have the desired effect, for the old man offers his hospitality and fodders the Levite's asses. This hospitality is not freely offered, like that of Lot; it is given to someone who is deemed worthy of it, even if that opinion is based on pretension.

Lot prepared *mišteh*, a feast, he baked unleavened cakes, and they ate. The verb and its object, *ya'as mišteh*, 'to give a feast', is used in the Genesis narrative but not in Judges, where the verbs 'they *ate* and they *drank*' receive no embellishment to signify gracious hospitality. The noun 'feast' is derived from the verb root *šth*, 'to drink', but it came only late to convey the noun 'drink' (*BDB*, 1970:1059). The primary meaning of *mišteh* is 'feast, banquet' (occasion for drinking), and the word certainly has this implication in the description of Samson's wedding feast (Judg. 14.12, 17). In the Genesis narrative, however, there is no allusion to drink.

> Gen. 19.3b-4 And he made them a feast, he baked unleavened cakes; and they ate. They had not yet lain down. . . .

The old host, by comparison, doesn't prepare for his guests.

> Judg. 19.21b . . . and they washed their feet and they ate and drank.

The last word of the verse highlights the discrepancy, and the first phrase of the next verse develops this image,

> Judg. 19.22 As they were making their hearts merry. . . .

and perhaps provides a basis for their differentiated reactions to the proposals of the town's ruffians. The angels were 'not yet in bed', but the old man and the Levite 'were making their hearts merry'. The deportment of the host and his guest contributes to their reactions to the Benjaminites since their reason—and piety—are clouded by alcohol.

The Gibeahite host, true to the Genesis pattern of the allusion, offers two women to the men: his own virgin daughter and the guest's concubine. The old man observes a motif (two [virgin] females) in the Genesis narrative but in so doing disregards the substance of the guest-host tradition—the protection of the guest, including his party—when he offers his *guest's concubine* to the men with his own daughter. When the men will not listen to the host's offer, the Levite acts. The angel visitors to Lot were protected from the men because Lot closed the door after him when he went out to them, and the men of Sodom protested that the visitors should judge. The Levite's host goes outside to the men but does not shut the door, and the Levite *does* make a judgment: he takes his concubine and brings her to out to the men. (Lot's visitors also made judgment, but their judgment condemned the immoral men, not a helpless woman.) The Levite—as individual, as Israel—has no comprehension of an honorable covenantal relationship between the sexes.

In Gen. 19.4, the entire spectrum of men came to Lot's house, 'from young to aged, people from all parts'. The description effectively includes all temporal and spatial possibilities. In contrast,

Judges 19 limits the Benjaminite ruffians to 'men of the city, sons of Belial [worthlessness]'. . . a particular element. The Judges text implicitly recalls Abraham's protest to Yahweh in Gen. 18.23-33 immediately prior to the angel's visit to Lot, in which Abraham reasons against the utter destruction of Sodom lest as few as ten good men be inadvertently destroyed. The precise wording of Judg. 19.22 allows that the worthless men in no way encompass the whole of the city's population. There are men in this city worth saving. Nevertheless, the entire city will be destroyed. That judgment is made by man.

When the Sodomites 'surrounded the house and called to Lot', demanding the visitors that they might 'know them' sexually, Lot went out to the intruders and closed the door behind him to protect his guests. He risked his well-being to preserve that of his guests. The old man, who imitates Lot's actions, apparently knowingly, fails to comprehend the moral basis of Lot's behavior. The old man mimics the outward action only. In this passage, he, like Lot, goes 'out to them' (parallel phrase), but he fails to close the door as Lot had done. The Ephraimite fails to protect his guests.

In his response to the Benjaminites, the old man's first statement is a paraphrase of Lot's in which no element has been left out.

Gen.   19.7   Not please my brothers (do) evil. . . .
Judg. 19.23   Not my brothers not (do) evil please . . .

The reader might be somewhat encouraged that the old man knows his tradition and may act accordingly. And he does, imitating the *number* of women to be offered to the ruffians, even if he abuses the honor of the guest tradition in so doing. Lot had offered his own two virgin daughters rather than subject his guests to a forbidden sexual act. Rape, though condemned and punishable by death, is not an unnatural act in the sense that sodomy is.[10] The old man, fixed on the literal, on 'two' women, offers his own virgin daughter and, to make up the lack, the concubine of his guest—neither presumably virgin nor his to offer. He fails to recognize the point of the Lot narrative: the guest must be protected as a matter of righteousness.

Gibeah is depicted as a latter-day version of Sodom. Yahweh punished the former city by total destruction, only Lot and his immediate family saved by the divine messengers. Gibeah is also destroyed, but in this case the judgment and destruction are not Yahweh's and they are not effected through nature. This time, man judges and man destroys.

At this point, the narratives diverge markedly. In Genesis, three separate pieces of information/action originate with the men of Sodom:

> Gen. 19.9 (1) And they said, 'Stand back!'
> And they said, 'The one came to
> sojourn (*gar*) and he must judge.
> (2) Now we will [do] evil to you
> [rather] than to them'.
> (3) And they pressed on the man, upon Lot,
> exceedingly, and almost broke the door.

In the parallel version, the drama is distanced by narration; and the response—not threat but negation—is greatly mitigated:

> Judg. 19.25 And the men were not willing to listen to him.

The men are not commanding in their speech. The old man is never *paṣar*, 'pressed' by the men, nor is the Levite—although his father-in-law had earlier *paṣar*, 'pressed' him to stay (19.7). Most striking is the complete absence of reference to 'judging' that the Sodomites had made: 'This one came to sojourn, and he must judge' (Gen. 19.9). The Sodomites want the visitors to decide whether they wished to be 'known'. They accuse Lot of not letting the sojourner 'judge' for himself, in that Lot had shut the door behind him. In fact, the guests *did* 'judge'; they pulled Lot back in with *their hand* (power)—in the singular, as one—and closed the door. The angels struck all the men outside with blindness so that they struggled but could not find the door.

The Judges sequence pointedly omits reference to the guest judging for himself. This host has not shut the door, so that the rabble could not complain that the guest could not 'judge'. Then, in an ironic inversion of the angels' ethical judgment, the Levite *does* judge. He 'takes a hold on his concubine' and brings her outside to them. In terms of the Sodomites' complaint, it is ironic that the angels *do* judge, which makes the Levite's 'judging' doubly ironic: it is uninvited and unjust.[11] The angels could judge; the Levite cannot, but presumes to do so. Although the Benjaminites are not as threatening as the Sodomites, the Levite protects his own person by sacrificing his concubine to their forbidden and brutal practices.

The inconsistencies in the Levite's behavior become somewhat comprehensible. He pursues the concubine because he misses her (presumably sexually), but in masculine company— her father's presence or even that of his servant—he ignores her. The concubine is a sexual object, not worthy of speech, not 'human'. The Levite cannot pretend to the Levite calling or to affluence with his father-in-law, who knows that the Levite lives in a tent; but with the old man he intimates position (priesthood) and wealth (food, provisions) with supplies that possibly came from his father-in-law. The Levite is later consistent with this gleaned image—sham, egotistical and mendacious—in his recounting of the events of this night.

The narration of the multiple rape of the young woman is one of the rare passages in Judges where the narrator's objectivity is sufficiently abridged so that a narrative attitude may be discerned. Condemnation is conveyed in the central verb:

> Judg. 19.25b . . . and they *knew* her and they *abused* her all the night and *sent her away* when the dawn rose.

'Abused' is conveyed with the Hithpa. of *'ll*: 'to exert oneself against anyone; to abuse, insult'.

It is not a girl or young woman, *na'ārāh*, but a woman, an *'iššāh* who reappears in the morning; and it is a bitter irony that is implicit in the change of terms. The woman falls at the door of the house where her *master* is. This change of nomenclature emphasizes that the concubine is his slave; he is no longer referred to as her husband, as in 19.3, even though he was her father's 'son-in-law' in 19.5.[12] In his actions, the Levite has shown himself to be a master of a female slave, not a husband in a secondary kind of marriage; and the more accurate term subtly replaces the more honorific. Curiously, the concubine's master is referred to in the singular except with regard to his relationship to the woman, and the inconsistency is repeated, from both points of view.

> Judg. 19.26   And she came, the woman, at the turning of the morning, and she fell [at] door of [the] house of *the man* where her *masters* [were] there, until the daylight.
>
> Judg. 19.27a   And *he* rose up, her *masters*, in the morning, and *he* opened the door of the house and went out to go *his* way. . . .

When the woman falls at the door of the house where her *masters* are, the reader is not sure whether the host is included as another 'master'. But when the Levite (sing.) rises and opens the door, and 'he' is pluralized as masters of the concubine, the point becomes clear. In giving his singular right over the woman to other men to *master* her, the Levite implicitly partakes of their abuse.

Condemnation is also conveyed in an image unusual in its clarity:

> Judg. 19.27b   ... and behold, his concubine had fallen [at] the door
> of the house, and her hands [were] on the threshold.

The entire figure of the woman is concentrated in her hands, stretched toward the door. The image of mute helplessness, even before she is surmised to be dead, is in dramatic contrast to the singular independence shown by the woman in leaving her husband. In as much as the text condemns the husband in his callous sacrifice of his concubine, the fact that she dies as a result of illicit sexual relations (even though 'authorized' by her husband) is an explicit comment on her 'unfaithfulness'to him. The nature of her unfaithfulness is irrelevant. Although both man and concubine have been remiss, the point is heavily made that women must live faithfully within the covenantal tradition. Disobedient, the concubine dies in an excess of unlawful sexuality. We cannot infer that the Levite had any other motivation than self-protection in casting her out to the worthless men, but the woman's 'unfaithfulness' is punished, and her death is worse than stoning. This is the only, however ironic, element of justice in the Levite's 'judging'.

The Levite's callousness, his disdain for humanity, is fully revealed only in the scene at the doorstep. This passage is dramatized, and the reader experiences the pathetic clutching of the concubine at the step of the house where her husband has 'made his heart merry', the reader hears the aloofness with which the Levite greets the immobile figure. And once again, Genesis 19 is alluded to. The Levite remains the night, and the men abuse the concubine

> Judg. 19.25   ... until the *morning*, and sent her away in the *rising*
> *of dawn*
> 19.26   And the woman came at the turning of the *morning*. . .
> until it was light
> 19.27   And he rose up her masters in the *morning* . . .

The repetition of the time of day as 'morning' isolates and calls attention to the paraphrase, 'rising of dawn', which appears in the Genesis passage:

> Gen.   19.15   And when the *dawn arose*, then the angels urged Lot,
> saying 'Up . . .'

The rapists *finish*, send the woman away with light, which makes manifest; in contrast, the angels *begin* their activities with the ascent of light.

Repetition of the verb *qûm* also links the two passages. With the angels' warning of impending destruction to Sodom, Lot said to his sons-in-law, *qûm*, 'up and go forth from this place' (Gen. 19.14), but his warning was laughed at. The angels urged Lot, using the same verb, *qûm*, 'Up, take your wife and your two daughters'. The Levite uses this verb when he speaks to his prostrate and immobile concubine: *qûm*, 'Up, let us go'.[13] The allusion keeps the saving action of Yahweh's angels in contrastive relationship with the selfish and destructive actions of the Levite. Genesis 19 establishes the Yahwist standard of guest-host behavior, against which Judges 19 is counterposed. The situation in Genesis is used for parody; it is copied and inverted. The ironic inversions depict the inverted moral condition of Israel, the utter perversity to which the Israelites have sunk, at the conclusion of the period of the judges.

With his presumably dead concubine, the Levite returns to his home: he completes his circle. Closer identification of the remote place where the Levite resides is avoided: he went to his 'place' and came to his house.[14] An element of unconsidered haste is conveyed in the series of brief conjunctive clauses of the next verse:

Judg. 19.29   . . . and came to his house
and took the knife
and lay hold on his concubine
and cut her in pieces [according] to
her bones into twelve pieces
and sent her into all
the territories of Israel.

With the dispatch of the dismembered concubine, the narrative shifts briefly between the reaction of Israel and the testimony of the Levite, which constitutes the trial to determine the cause of the evil.

It is profitable to compare the narrative of the Levite and his concubine, the last narrative concerned with individual Israelites, and that of Caleb, Achsah and Othniel, the first narrative in the book of Judges. In the resolution, allusion to the narrative of the paradigm judge, Othniel, effects a closure in that episodes of sexual relationships, marital and non-marital, begin and end the book. The ideal relationship is preceded by a Yahweh-sanctioned war. Husband and wife belong to the same people, the same tribe. Achsah is a *promised* reward, and Othniel *earns* his wife (in lieu of a bride price) by conquering enemy territory. Achsah suggests her husband *ask* her father for a field, and Achsah herself *asks* for water. Caleb grants both; harmony and fertility are implicit in the marriage. In the resolution narrative, the *gēr* Levite has *taken* a wife-concubine of another tribe. The concubine commits adultery; that is, insted of being a fertile field to her husband, she either outright abandons her husband and his potential progeny or she harbors the seed of another man, subsequently returning to her father. Either denies righteous procreation. This union—to differentiate it from marriage—leads to the death of the concubine, to internecine war, very nearly to eradication of a tribe. The tribe's continuance and the integrity of the sons of Israel are maintained by overpowering young virgins—kidnapping (violently taking) and, implicitly, rape. Although concubine marriages have been socially acceptable to guarantee procreation, this text denies the practice legitimacy as *replacement* of traditional marriage. The Levite's non-marriage has ended in the opposite of fertility: brutality and death.[15]

It has been suggested that Achsah is not only a wife to Othniel but also serves as a symbol of Israel, bride to Yahweh. She represents faith (she 'asks') and fertility (she provides fields and water). Counter to Achsah, the concubine can be understood as a symbol of dishonored Israel. Neither faithful nor fertile,[16] the concubine cannot be a bride to Yahweh because she is a slave, just as Israel has become a slave to power and passion. She is poor and her master, in several senses, is poor. The Levite plays a significant role in the turn of events, but the 'marriage' which he contracted is the basis of the death of the woman and the internecine war which follows. The concubine is sacrificed to her own passion, be it sexual or merely 'doing what is right in [her] own eyes', and she is literally reduced to pieces. The threat is implicit: Yahweh's bride, Israel, will be divided, reduced from a functioning whole to its 'dead' components. It must cease its 'whoring'.

Although the major narratives relate the diminishing capacities of the judges to deliver the Israelites, the opening and closing narratives lay great stress on the kinds of relationships—between man and woman, man and man, man and Yahweh—that are the basis of the ensuing morass. In a similar fashion, recurrent names, phrases, situations and actions serve as links, often ironic, between the initial and final chapters. The exposition begins with Yahweh war (1.1-11);

the resolution closes with a war that is the diametric opposite, even though Yahweh takes an active role. It is to that war and Yahweh's role in it that we now turn.

Irony

The penultimate chapter concentrates its irony on human relationships. Evoking the paradigm marriage of Achsah and Othniel, the narrative of the Levite and his concubine discloses a correlation between Israel's relationship to Yahweh and Israel's human interactions. In harmony with Yahweh, Achsah and Othniel promised fruitfulness and harmony between the generations. The Levite, estranged from man and Yahweh, abuses the guest tradition with his father-in-law; and the old Ephraimite abuses the same tradition with his guests's concubine. The Levite's concubine relationship can only be regarded as an ironic inversion of marriage. The dismembering of the woman whom the Levite had put out to the 'sons of Belial' is brutally ironic—and symbolic of Israel.

Chapter 10

RESOLUTION III

Judgment

Individuals do not dominate the final chapters of the book as they have the previous ones. In the opening chapters, the protagonists of the book are identified by name, relationship, and tribe; and each judge is seen to symbolize an apsect of the entity of Israel. Other terms for Israel—'sons of Israel', 'tribes of Israel', 'men of Israel'—likewise bond the relationships of 'son', 'tribe', and 'men' into Israel in the early part of the book.

In the sequence of narratives, the traditional designations of Yahweh's chosen people have been substituted with human oriented terms like 'clan', and in the Resolution even that designation increasingly disappears. (Micah is an example of a named character who has no patronymic at all, either tribal or familial). Terms which link the individual with his posterity fall away. Even the proper names of protagonists are replaced by simple, essentially tribal designations (Levite priest, Levite) and these designation are consistently ironic. The tribal names may be used for individuals who are *gēr*, without family (clan), but these people have no names or their names are withheld. In the closing narratives, the participants are identified as 'men', only barely placed in the ranks of Israel.

The final step in transformation of individual sons of Israel to 'man' that has taken place in the first chapter of the resolution is, in chs. 20–21, extended to the collective sons of Israel. All the sons of Israel respond *as one man* to the Levite's gruesome message, to sit as self-proclaimed judge. And when they have heard the Levite, they judge. That it is hasty is suggested by their not seeking to hear the accused. The judgment is made without asking Yahweh, and it is not made by the *sons* of Israel. With its judgment, Israel acts once again as one *man*. And with this judgment, reference to the community of

Israel changes both in quantity and in kind. The traditional terms of the book, which *unified* all elements, now function ironically, to the opposite effect: they polarize. The terms become more specifically weighted, so that 'sons' of Israel depicts a relationship to *Yahweh*, the 'tribes' of Israel a confederation among the *men*, and 'man' of Israel an even more individualistic attitude (even in unified actions). The chosen people is totally abstracted from its relationship to Yahweh as 'Israel' or 'Benjamin'.

Chapter 19 tells a tale about essentially nameless men, 'the old man', further qualified as 'the master of the house'; 'the Levite', his 'young man', and 'the men of the city', but the characters are so manifest that their namelessness is not particularly noticeable. The Levite is only twice so named; otherwise he is 'husband', 'son-in-law', 'master', or simply, and most often, 'the man'. The narrative concludes with an allusion to 'the sons of Israel' who 'came up out of the land of Egypt', an allusion to a time when men had names and genealogy.

With the exception of Phinehas the priest, traditionally identified, not one individual is introduced in the last two chapters.[1] Instead, nameless men identified only by varied but specific epithets govern the action. The narrative it tells generates from the activity of groups and, in a dramatic shift of style, these groups are carefully, even precisely named, with fluctuating genitive adjectives ('son of', 'man of'), or the specific names rendered as an abstraction. After the namelessness of ch. 19, ch. 20 invokes one appellation or another for 'Israel' and 'Benjamin' over a hundred times.[2] This chapter also gives new significance to the terms 'sons of Israel' and 'Israel'.[3] I have annexed an analysis of the final chapters with regard to these appellations (Appendix II).

The action of the penultimate chapter follows directly upon that of its predecessor. Confronted with the Levite's unexamined version of the events, the people are shocked. In their perplexity, they turn to their leaders, not to Yahweh.

> 19.30   Everyone who saw it said, 'Not was and not was seen [anything] such as this since the day [when] the sons of Israel came up from [the] land of Egypt to this day. Set yourselves upon it, counsel, and speak'.

They assemble 'as one man' before Yahweh at Mitzpah, and their chiefs take their places in the 'assembly of the people of God' (20.1-2). It is worth noting that these tribal spokesmen are not called 'judges' or 'leaders' or 'elders' or 'heads' of the people. A new word for this function is introduced in this chapter, a word without any suggestion of ethical judgment. *Pinnot* is understood figuratively as 'chief, ruler' in the sense of a '*corner* (support or defence)' (*BDB*, 1979: 819). These are more like war chiefs than judges. Yahweh is the only judge specifically so named (11.27).[4] This is the moment *par excellence* when Israel should turn to Yahweh and ask him to judge. But no. The Levite charges the *sons* of Israel, but 'all the people rose as one *man*'. An army is culled from the *tribes* of Israel, but every *man* of Israel joined against the city, united as one *man*. The *sons* of Israel assemble before Yahweh. It is still the *sons* of Israel who ask the Levite to state his case, and the Levite makes his charge to the *sons* of Israel, but it is 'all the *people*', the '*man* of Israel', the '*tribes* of Israel' which respond. The trial, which presents the Levite as accuser and the Gibeaites of Benjamin as the accused, is called for by the '*sons* of Israel' (20.3) but judged by '*man*' (20.7, 8).

The congregation of (the remaining tribes of) Israel questions the accuser but makes no effort to hear the accused. The Levite's version of the fateful night, however, has skirted the truth at best. He claims '*the men* of Gibeah': were responsible when only the 'sons of Belial [worthessness]', a *limited* part of the population, came to the Ephraimite's house. Furthermore, the Levite attributes to the men of Gibeah the intention to kill him, an outright lie. He does not mention their apparently homosexual intentions. Without explanation or justification, the Levite submits that 'they humbled my concubine, and she died'.[5] That the judges fail to perceive the lack of causal relationship between the given 'intent to kill' and the act of 'humbling' is an implicit judgment of the judges. The Levite dismembered and distributed the pieces of his concubine, he maintains, because the Benjaminites had committed unchastity[6] in Israel. The discrepancy between his words and the reader's knowledge of his deeds creates an inescapable dramatic irony.

It seems evident that anyone in a position to 'judge' would naturally ask how the primary intent (to kill the Levite) was transformed into 'humbling' the concubine. That the question is never put to the Levite condemns the judge as well as the judgment. Exploration of that loophole would have revealed that the Levite himself had thrust his concubine on the 'sons of Belial'. Consistent with his character, the Levite protects himself, even though this time he ultimately sacrifices not only one woman, innocent or not, but many men of the tribes, the substance of Israel.

Judgment is made. The sons of Israel make a hasty judgment to exact retribution for the murder of the Levite's concubine. It is a masterstroke of irony that the sons of Israel, who have been drawing apart into ever-smaller units—from tribes to clans to family groups to individuals—act as a unity in the role of 'judge':

> 20.8   And rose up all the people
> as one man, saying
> let us not go, any man, to his tent
> and not let us turn, any man, to his house
> and this [is] the thing
> which we shall do to Gibeah.

The Benjaminites hear of the assembly, but the reader is not told of their reaction. Not until 20.12 do the tribes of Israel send men to the tribe of Benjamin, and the men do not ask for confirmation of the Levite's testimony. They have already judged, and they demand the culprits:

> 20.13   And now, give up the men the worthless sons which [are] in Gibeah, and let us kill them and we shall remove evil from Israel.

Because judgment is passed by 'all the people . . . as one man' (20.8), each man, in effect 'speaks'.[7] They respond in accord in presuming to judge and in actually making judgment; and they are all, each and every man, in error. Each man commits himself to 'not go home . . . not return to his house' (20.8). The Israelite *men* (20.8) will not return to their homes (their private lives, their wives, their chidren) until the affront to the Levite and his concubine has been rectified. They determine their offensive by lot, assemble an army, make provisions, and determine to punish Benjamin in Gibeah. That they subsequently assemble before Yahweh and pose a question is disclosed as empty ritual by the nature of the question raised, by their disregarding Yahweh's answer, and by the fact that they have determined their actions prior to the ritual.

They cannot judge themselves, yet they presume Yahweh's prerogative to judge. This may be the 'last straw' and an explicit impetus for Yahweh to sanction (20.18), even to direct (20.23) their entry into battles that will devastate them. Contrasting Yahweh's intentions (knowledge) and Israel's interpretation (naïveté), the author depicts Yahweh giving partial answers which the sons of Israel construe from their (Israel's) point of view. Yahweh's answers are inconclusive, but there are no grounds to presume that Yahweh acts ambiguously in these chapters.[8] The text suggests that Yahweh intentionally allows Israel to lose two battles. Yahweh's will is done, and it is done through the tribes of Israel even though the people's intent may be far different. Only when a humbled Israel appeals to Yahweh do the goals of Israel and Yahweh, however briefly, coincide. When the submissive question is presented with fasting and sacrifice, priest and ark, Israel finally achieves a predictive response. A complex justice is achieved, if only momentarily.[9]

Tribal War of Eradication

At the opening of the book, the sons of Israel inquire of Yahweh:

1.1b   Who shall go up (*'alāh*) for us
       against the Canaanite
       as the initiator[10]
       to fight against him?
1.2a   And Yahweh said,
       Judah shall go up (*'alāh*);
       Behold! I have given the land into his hand.

The resolution posits a similar situation. The sons of Israel ask Yahweh:

20.18b Who shall go up (*'alāh*) for us
        as the initiator
        to the battle against [the] sons of Benjamin?
        And Yahweh said,
        Judah, as the initiator.

Despite Yahweh's answer, there is no mention of Judah in the Israelite's actions. And once again, the variations convey as much meaning as the allusions. In the opening verses, Yahweh tells the tribes the consequences of Judah's being the initiator of the conquest, and success is assured by Yahweh's words. In the closing verses, Yahweh's statement is abrupt; his promise is heavily missing. And the enemy has changed from non-Israelite Canaan to a part of Israel, the tribe of Benjamin. In the first chapter, the sons of Israel partially disregard Yahweh's advice in that Judah invites his brother Simeon to fight with him.[11] In the penultimate chapter, they have remembered to ask Yahweh, but their questions are empty formalities since their plans have already been set. They ask, but not the right questions;

and they are not prepared to accept that advice. The counsel sought and received is not even acknowledged in the actions of the tribes:

> 20.19   And the sons of Israel rose up in the morning and pitched against Gibeah.

Only with an assembled army do the tribes send envoys to Benjamin demanding surrender of the 'wicked men of Gibeah'. Judged without a hearing, the Benjaminites turn a deaf ear to 'their brothers' and they too mobilize an army. Curiously, the army includes two special forces, seven hundred each:

> 20.15   seven hundred chosen men from Gibeah.
> 20.16   Among all these soldiers there were seven hundred chosen men who were left-handed, each of whom could sling a stone at a hair and not miss.

The seven hundred left-handed Benjaminites recall the first post-paradigm judge, the left-handed Benjaminite Ehud.[12] Ehud was not 'raised' by Yahweh, he acted deviously, and he never received the divine spirit. Abstracted and magnified by a round number, the mark of Ehud reappears as the glory of the insubordinate tribe. The seven hundred left-handed Benjaminites may be sharp-shooters, but they are all literally 'left-handed sons of the right hand', 'crippled' in some sense and inferentially not up to Yahwist standards.

The Samson narrative, with its repeated use of the number 'seven', secures an ironic association of sacredness with this number. In the final battles of the book, 'seven' is 'seven hundred *chosen*'—to fight against Yahweh's '*chosen*'. This is an inversion of both the sacredness of 'seven' and that of 'chosen'. This use of the holy number, in conjunction with the 'left-handed' deviousness of Ehud and 'exploded' to a great 'chosen' force, also yokes Yahwist and anti-Yahwist oppositions. Through allusion, multiple ironies convey multiple meanings.

Having first determined their action by lot and then assembled an army, the people ask God (although Yahweh answers) *who* shall initiate the battle. Ignorant of a perspective other than their own, the Isralites ignore Yahweh's answer and follow their pre-established plan. They attack *en masse*, adopting a fairly simple and direct battle plan: *all* the forces arrayed before the city. Benjaminite losses are not mentioned, but twenty-two thousand men of Israel fall.

Nevertheless, the Israelites do not question either themselves or Yahweh; they bolster their courage and plan the next day's battle just

as they had for the first battle. The people, the men of Israel, do not
learn from their losses. Only *after* they have strengthened their
courage and 'set' the next day's battle plan do they adhere to the
ritual of appealing to and weeping before Yahweh. Fully prepared,
and with their courage strengthened, they once again ask Yahweh;
but the force of the question has shifted from *who* shall initiate battle
to:

> 20.23b   Shall I again
>   draw near to battle
>   with the sons of Benjamin,
>   my brother?

This time they ask Yahweh *whether* they should battle their brothers
again. The question they ask—'*Shall I* go up again to battle with
Benjamin my brother?'—seems after the fact in view of their
preparations. Hesitancy is suggested in the substitution of verbs—
from *alah*, 'go up', in the first question to *nagash*, 'draw near' or
'approach', in the second—and is concentrated in the final phrase of
the second question, 'my brother', which emphasizes kinship. Unable
to 'hear' even a clear command, they fail to recognize that Yahweh's
support, his assurance of victory, is *not* implicit in his response, 'Go
up against him'.

Yahweh answers their question without elaboration, and again the
Israelites suffer heavy losses: eighteen thousand armed men, with no
mention of Benjaminite losses. Granted, Israel reveals hesitation in
its second question to Yahweh, and the casualties of the second battle
are somewhat less than those of the first. Cause and effect cannot be
claimed, but the relationship is suggestive. Despite the odds, for the
second time the Benjaminites have a resounding success. The reader
is reminded that Yahweh can lead the Israelites or their enemies to
victory under unlikely circumstances: as with Gideon, the few have
routed the many. The repeated losses and the repeated contrast with
the opening verses of the book (1.1-4) raises questions about the
implications of Yahweh's answers and his intent. A careful reading
discloses that *man* of Israel strengthens *himself*—without recourse to
Yahweh—and repeats his battle position (plans) of the prior day
before the *sons* of Israel go up to weep before Yahweh. The *men* act
independently; the *sons* defer to Yahweh. This distinction accrues in
significance in the ensuing action.[13]

Finally, the people do not behave as men, isolated in time; but as
sons of Yahweh, linked in tradition and belief. They do not bolster

their own courage; they turn to Yahweh; and not only the army but *all*—the menfolk and their families, 'even all the people'—go up to Bethel, pay proper tribute, fast, and ask for guidance through a proper agency: Phinehas, son of Eleazar, son of Aaron, standing before the ark of the covenant. This time the question is even more hesitantly phrased:

> 20.28b   Shall I again
> come out to battle
> with the sons of Benjamin,
> my brother,
> or shall I cease?

One important term is variant in the three questions. In 20.18, the assumption of attack is posed by the verb *'alāh*, 'go up'. In v. 23, although attack is still intended, a more cautious verb, *gešet*, 'draw near', is added. In the last question (20.28), Phinehas uses the verb *yāṣā'*, 'to go forth',[14] and a new element appears, the suggestion that the battle be abandoned. The increasing doubts of the sons of Israel are recorded in the verb fluctuations.

The Israelites assemble at Mizpah to judge and to declare war, but they go to Bethel to consult Yahweh. The distinction of the two sites also distinguishes the independent judgment of Israel from that of Israel under God. The 'Israelites, all the people' go up to the altar at *Bethel*.[15] They fast and present burnt- and fellowship-offerings to Yahweh through an uncorrupted Levite priest ministering before the ark of the covenant. Preparations for battle have not been made, and the question they raise is even more tentatively phrased. The sons of Israel are finding their judgment costly, and they sound willing to drop the issue. But Yahweh's will will be done, and with proper observances, Yahweh gives assurance of victory.

As the questions of the Israelites become more hesitant, Yahweh's answers reveal consistency through increasing (but always incomplete) information. Syntax as well as import convey the initial want of information. Yahweh's first answer lacks an explicit verb; the second supplies the verb—the imperative form of *'alāh*—but nothing else; the third repeats the verb (in the same verb form) and adds assurance of success in the battle. Only when all the people return to Yahweh at Bethel and petition through a faithful priest does his answer have certitude.

> 20.28   Go up, for tomorrow I will give him into your hand.

This inclusion of a promise makes its omission in the first two responses manifest. Nevertheless, Yahweh doesn't promise victory. He promises the Israelites that they will have the Benjaminites in their hand, in their power. They will have the *potential* for victory.

Comparison with the opening verses of the book discloses a further variation, a change of tense in Yahweh's promises:

1.2   Behold, I *have given* the land into his hand.
20.28   Go up,
         for tomorrow I *will give* him into your hand

Formerly, he had given the land into the hand of Judah even before the battle; here, though Israel is assured of power over Benjamin, the sons of Israel must fight before they will get what they wish. Significantly, how the Israelites exercise their power over Benjamin is left open. Yahweh does not promise to eradicate the tribe of Benjamin—only to give it into Israel's power.

Nevertheless, the Israelites change their military tactics, suggesting that they are still unwilling to rely altogether on Yahweh. After all, Yahweh told them who was to lead the first battle and advised them to fight a second battle, and both were lost with heavy casualties. They fail to consider that they had not asked the right questions and had not obeyed the first answer, and that this time Yahweh has assured success. Israel practises the necessary formalities but not the necessary faith.

The critical battle of the resolution is presented from two points of view—Yahweh's and Israel's—corresponding with the two points of view of the exposition. With a force arrayed *before* the city, as earlier, the Israelites post ambushers *around* the city.[16] The Benjaminites come out, unaware that the array is a decoy, and this time they are drawn away from the city. The Israelites seem to be retreating, but they are drawing the Benjaminite warriors away from the walls of the city and into the open highways and fields. This segment of the third battle narrative exhibits the immediacy and detail characteristic of the Israelite point-of-view: specificity of time (third day), of place (roads to Bethel and Gibeah), of number of men felled (about thirty), and of thoughts (as words spoken by Benjamin and Israel [20.32]).

The following passage (20.33-36a) recounts the same action with interpolations of the divine point-of-view[17]. Even though *all* the men

of Israel (a non-specific number) take up position at *Baal Tamar*, a
reduced number (the ones ambushing) move into the ambush. Only
then is the main battle fought. The narrator does not restrict the
conquest to the frontal attack, saying 'Yahweh defeated Benjamin . . .
on that day', but Yahweh's name is not involved with the ambush.
Yahweh's perception of the battle describes ten thousand chosen
warriors of Israel in a *direct* attack on Gibeah.

Particularly interesting are the juxtaposed points of view:

Yahweh:	20.35a	And *he* defeated, Yahweh, Benjamin before Israel
Israel:	20.35b	and *they* struck down, sons of Israel, from Benjamin on that day, 25,100 sword-bearing men . .

The text suggests that in Yahweh's perception both Benjamin and
Israel have estranged themselves from their god, but the Israelites are
unaware of the significance of their judgment. Even though they
have lost two battles which Yahweh enouraged, they think they are
still Yahweh's 'sons'. And, in a sense, they are: this battle is a direct
confrontation in which they are once more the agents of Yahweh's
will.

The following verses (20.36-46) recount the same battle, once
more from the Israelite point-of-view, and this account stresses the
advantage of the ambush. This portion of the narration is again
much more vivid: it is full of concrete details of the action.

Yahweh's promise is kept. Israel has Benjamin in its hand, in its
power. Interestingly, the Israelite version specifies (in both the cited
total and the tally of the Benjaminite causualties) a somewhat
smaller number of Benjaminite dead than does the Yahwist
account.[18] Israel reports 'round numbers' which minimalize; Yahweh
is accurate.

	Israel	*Benjamin*
Pre-battle	400,000	26,000
		+ 700 Gibeahites
	400,000	26,700
Battle Casualties:		
Battle #1	22,000	?
Balance	378,000	
Battle #2	18,000	?
Balance	360,000	26,700

		[*Yahwist*]	[*Israelite*]
Battle #3	30	25,100	25,000
Balance	359,970	(1)600	(1)700[19]

The battle is severe, but Benjamin is unaware of his position:

20.34   ... and not they knew that touching them the evil (*rā'āh*).

The phrase is ambiguous. The 'evil' may be understood as abstract: 'evil' has struck. It may also be taken to suggest that the forces of Israel, which are striking the Benjaminites down, are themeselves evil, that Yahweh uses the reprehensible forces of Israel to conquer iniquitous forces of Benjamin. The 'evil' (*rā'āh*) which is striking will purge the 'evil' (*rā'āh*) in Benjamin. The phrase alludes to 20.13, wherein the Israelites demand 'the men of sons of Belial so we may kill them and we may purge evil (*rā'āh*) from Israel'. The core of the phrase is repeated again in 20.41 when the Benjaminites do realize that 'evil' (*rā'āh*) is upon them. Yahweh's will is done, and the Israelites are victorious, but the victory of the greater forces belongs to Yahweh—not the men, not the ambush. Israel's judgment of and attack on Benjamin courts Yahweh's punishment of the tribes for their presumption in making war with Yahweh's people. When they are chastized and make proper observances, Yahweh uses Israel to punish Benjamin for its valuing tribal ties over those of the covenant. These battles make it evident that Israel's will may serve Yahweh's in ways that are opposed to the people's intentions.

The varied and controlled use of nomenclature calls attention to shifts in perception; the reader perceives the viewpoint of each of the interested parties—Israel, Benjamin, and even that of Yahweh. The multiple perspectives of the resolution complement that of the tri-partite exposition with the difference that in the resolution the reader is involved in judgment of the war between the tribes. The action of this penultimate chapter is concerned with the act of judgment, for the entire action devolves upon the judgment of the leaderless people. The action of the final chapter arises from the rash judgment and from the fulfillment of that judgment.

Unity without Integrity

The last chapter of the book of Judges discloses a structural tie with the first: these two chapters use the device of flashback to supplement information already given. In 20.8-10, the people, the men of the tribes of Israel, determine in concert to punish Benjamin, but there is no mention of a vow or an oath. Suddenly, in the opening verse of the last chapter, a flashback to Mizpah discloses that oaths had been taken. In the exposition, the flashback distinguished the human and divine points-of-view, setting up a polarity which functions throughout the book. In the resolution, the flashback reinforces the reader's knowledgeable position *vis à vis* the Israelites. Yahweh is silent, but the reader is invited to an ethical point-of-view.

Chapter 21 begins with a flashback to the assembly scene at Mizpah which opened ch. 20, and this flashback introduces new aspects of the earlier scene. In 20.8, the people respond to the Levite's testimony by gathering an army to eliminate the evil from Israel; the leaderless people acting on a tacit judgment. In the flashback of ch. 21, another, heretofore undisclosed, response to the Levite's testimony is revealed:

20.8   And he rose,
         all the people as one man,
         to say not (he) will go man
         to his home,
         and not (he) will return man
         to his house.
21.1   And man of Israel
         he took oath at the *Mizpah*
         to say not one of us,
         (he) will give his daughter
         to Benjamin as wife.

The narrator reveals that the assembled Israelites had also taken an 'oath' not to give their daughters as wives to any Benjaminite, and in 21.5b that they had also taken a 'solemn oath' that whoever who did not assemble for the judgment must die. In 21.7 the sons of Israel recall the oath prohibiting giving their daughters to any Benjaminite as wives. These oaths were taken not at *Bethel*, before the third battle, but at the very beginning of the episode, at *Mizpah*, when they made judgment; and these oaths were made with the root *šābā'*, 'to swear', *'to seven oneself*, or *bind oneself by seven things'* (BDB, 1979:989) familiar to us from Samson's narrative. Once again the Israelites use the holy number for unholy purposes.

The hasty vow of Micah's mother (17.2) generated anti-Yahwist

idolatry, first on a family scale and subsequently, after the theft of
the idols by the migrating tribe of Dan, on a tribal scale at the
sanctuary of Dan at Shiloh. The concluding chapter, opening with
the scene of another hasty vow, alludes to the earlier one and
expands the province of the unconsidered vow to include all Israel.[20]
This vow is made not by the 'sons' of Israel, nor by the 'man' of Israel
acting in the plural, united; it is made by the 'man' of Israel—each
individual, each man, without relationship—acting in the singular.
The oath that was taken, even before the battles, precludes giving a
daughter from any of the Israelites to a Benjaminite as wife. The
Israelites took this oath at Mizpah, before Yahweh; *after* the battles
they go to Bethel to bemoan to Yahweh the realization of that which
they desired.

At Bethel the people cry out to Elohim, weep bitterly and ask:

21.3   Why Yahweh, God of Israel,
         happened this to Israel,
         to be missing the [this] day
         one tribe from Israel?

This time there is no answer. Repeatedly, the people have not sought
counsel fom Yahweh, presuming to know what to do, as in 20.8-10.
Here Israel asks Yahweh a question that Israel could better ask itself,
since Israel made the judgment and made the vow. Yahweh's silence
invites Israel to answer its own question. That it does not do.

The people respond to Yahweh's silence less hastily than they did
to the Levite's words. They build an altar and present burnt-
offerings and fellowship-offerings before they seek a solution on their
own. They do not acknowledge their own responsibility for the near-
elimination of a tribe, let alone try to understand the justice of that
loss. They seek a loophole by which they need not break the vow and
can nevertheless provide wives for the remaining 600 Benjaminites.
The dilemma, as they see it, is keeping the vow and losing a tribe or
circumventing the vow. They choose to do the latter. Though they
technically maintain the vow, they betray Yahweh in doing so;
however, the question of the ethics of their actions is not brought
up.

Their first consideration is to survey the fighting forces for any
missing groups, and indeed they find that Jabesh-Gilead is not
represented. Since those men have not been present, they have not
taken the vow precluding giving their daughters, but nevertheless fall
under the secondary vow (21.5b), which demands the death of

whoever did not assemble for the judgment. Without consulting Phineas, the assembly directs the murder of all living members of Jabesh-Gilead with the exception of its virgins. This action recalls that of Numbers 31, wherein the sons of Israel execute the 'vengeance of Yahweh on Midian'. Moses demands that the captive women and children be killed and only the virgin girls kept:

Num. 31.15   Have you saved all the women alive?
     31.16   Behold, these caused the sons of Israel,
           through the counsel of Balaam,
           a treacherous deliverance against Yahweh.

The men of Midian were killed as a 'vengeance of Yahweh' and the women because they lured the sons of Israel to act against Yahweh. The destruction of the Midianites served Yahweh's purposes; the destruction of Jabesh-Gilead to abduct the virgins is entirely against those purposes. In the first instance, the virgins were nothing more than an acceptable booty for the men; in the second, they are the purpose of the exploit. The massacre at Jabesh-Gilead is not holy war; it is not war in any sense. All the men and all the women and children are *murdered*, while the virgins are abducted and given to Benjaminite warriors as 'wives': in essence, child-bearers. Ironically, it is the people who did not respond to the Levite's injustice who are murdered.

But even this 'solution' fails to provide a wife for each of the Benjaminites. With the Benjaminites only partially paired, continuance of the tribe remains threatened and the people grieve for Benjamin because

21.15   Yahweh made [a] gap
       in the tribes of Israel.

Not only do the people fail to recognize their own responsibility in the judgment and the ensuing developments, but they end up blaming Yahweh for their getting what *they* wanted: to punish Benjamin for its protection of those who committed evil in Gibeah. Even the narrator's economy contributes to the irony as Israel righteously modulates from tribal judgment

20.9   And now this [is] the thing
      that we will do to Gibeah:
      [go] against her by lot.

to questioning Yahweh

21.3   Why Yahweh, God of Israel,
         happened this to Israel,
         to be missing the [this] day
         one tribe from Israel?

to putting the blame on Yahweh for the realization of its wishes

21.15b   he made Yahweh [did] a gap
         in [the] tribes of Israel.

Thus the two actions of this chapter are each preceded by reference to Yahweh's responsibility for the destruction of the tribe of Benjamin, as if the tribes of Israel had made no judgment, no vow:

21.3   Why, Yahweh, God of Israel,
         [has] happened in Israel
         to be missing [this] day
         one tribe from Israel?
21.15   And the people grieved
         for Benjamin because
         he made Yahweh [did] a gap
         in [the] tribes of Israel.

This closing narrative continues the opposition of the points-of-view of Yahweh and Israel; indeed, it demonstrates how Israel's point-of-view changes as the occasion demands. In the above-cited passages, Israel's own judgment (20.9) is distorted into a *question* (21.3), and the answer the people construe for themselves is the destruction of Jabesh-Gilead for the purpose of seizing the maidens. The second time the destruction of Benjamin is mentioned, the blame is placed squarely on Yahweh, '*he* made a gap in the tribes of Israel'. Not only are ethics in flux, but facts can also be reconstructed. If Israel has not eradicated Benjamin, it has eradicated its own sense of ethical judgment and displaced its errors on Yahweh.

Confronted with their own prohibition against *giving* their daughters to Benjamin, the remaining tribes propose that the Benjaminites *take* daughters of Israel. The concern with 'taking' and 'giving' recalls the opening narrative of the resolution, when Micah and his mother abuse covenantal laws in the restricted circle of the family. In the expanded milieu of the closing narrative, an opportunity for 'taking' presents itself at the festival of Yahweh at Shiloh—the same Shiloh sanctuary which houses Dan's stolen idols.[21] Even if the consequences were not violent and unethical, the event would nevertheless be anti-Yahwist in that it evolves out of concealment, not direct confrontation. Each Benjaminite is to hide, seize one of the girls, and take her to his home in Benjaminite territory. In response to the anticipated protests of fathers and brothers, the elders propose an appeal to 'compassion': the males of Shiloh could not be found guilty of breaking the vow since they have not given their daughters, and the girls were not seized in hostility, which would warrant reprisals. Therefore, the men of Shiloh are appealed to for merciful toleration of the kidnapping in the name of preservation of the tribes. The difference between 'taking and tolerating' and that of 'giving' is not scrutinized, nor is the preservation of tribal unity by immoral, anti-Yahwist means. After the Shiloh incident, as after other narratives of anti-Yahwist actions (Abimelech, 9.35; Micah, 18.26), the Israelites meekly return to their homes.[22]

The book closes in an ironic inversion—literally multiplied six hundred times—of the narrative of Othniel and Achsah. That story, a narrative of a promised bride won by a hero in a Yahweh battle, gave assurance of fertility in the people and the land. The events developed with respect between the generations: the father of the bride was asked for land and water, and he was generous to the betrothed couple. The closing tale is a reversal of that pledge. Instead of generosity between the generations, there is war; instead of fertility, there is murder of the men, women, and children of a city; instead of a betrothal, there is kidnap and rape. The book has reversed its initial premises: it has taken a full turn.

The resolution of the book of Judges is clearly delineated by the disappearance of judges and the appearance of the coda paradigm. Nevertheless, the book of Judges does not resolve; it devolves in disorder. There is no king in Israel, and everyone does what he thinks right. The narratives of the resolution project a series of doing 'what is right in his/her own eyes': Micah and his mother; the Levite priest and the tribe of Dan; the Levite, his concubine, the Ephraimite host; the tribe of Benjamin and the sons of Israel—each determines for himself what is right and acts upon his decision, his judgment. The vision of a moral state under a single god of right and might has become a chaos of 'flexible' right, technical loopholes and brutal behavior, including murder of 'brothers', blamed on Yahweh. All the anticipation of the tribes standing on the threshold of the promised land has come to nothing because each man is his own judge and does what is right in his own eyes. As each of the judges—major and minor—discloses new human limitations for ethical judgment, it becomes increasingly clear that Yahweh is the only judge in the book of Judges. At the conclusion of the book of Judges, there is no judge in Israel, and there is no right in Israel.

Irony

Building on the non-ironic base of the opening of the book, the sequence of narratives increases in instances and intensity of irony until the resolution fairly redounds with levels of presumed knowledge under that of the master ironist, Yahweh. Humanity is ignorant before the knowledge of Yahweh, but is not victimized by that knowledge.[23] In the resolution, the presumed knowledge of man, embraced without asking for guidance from Yahweh, repeatedly leads Israel to victimization. But despite the many 'levels' of irony in the resolution, the point of view of the book is consistently 'vertical', 'from the ironist's point of view' (Muecke, 1983:412). The reader is invited to share that point of view.

Irony permeates the resolution. And it is primarily dramatic irony, which invites the perceptive reader to recognize the ignorance of the protagonist and also invites that reader to self-recognition. Ironic effect is created through allusion to earlier biblical narratives and to earlier narratives in this book. There are also instances of irony which arise out of the immediate situation: e.g. Micah's mother perverting the restored silver, vowed to Yahweh, into anti-Yahwist idols *in the name of Yahweh*, and the further theft of these idols to found a temple *to Yahweh* in a city conquered in an *anti-Yahwist* war.

The use of *gēr* to describe the nameless, fatherless, leaderless, often tribeless protagonists consolidates an ironic contrast with the figure of Othniel, the paradigm judge. The strategies to preserve the tribe of Benjamin ironically recapitulate on a grander scale and with even more brutality the stimulus for the wars: the rape of the Levite's concubine. Levi, the priestly tribe; Benjamin, the 'son of the right hand'; and Dan, the judge, dominate the last narratives—in bitter contrast to the promise of their names.[24] Through irony, the reader is invited to share Yahweh's judgment of Israel during the period of the holy wars of territorial conquest. The ironic structure dramatizes the interaction of human will, free but naive, and Yahweh's will and knowledge.

Through literary form—exposition, main narrative, and resolution—and the structure of ironic opposition, the book of Judges creates out of opposition and succession a 'fiction of concord' (Kermode, 1966:63-64); and it achieves concord even though it depicts a series of crises and concludes in an ethical abasement. Artistic harmony is created through an intricately reinforced structure which brings into concordance beginning and end, myth and history. Those elements which remain disparate—ethics and power, divinity and humanity—are the burden of human life.

APPENDIX I

A major claim of this book is that the book of Judges is a unity, one in which structure—including those figurative devices which contribute to structure—conveys meaning. In this regard, a few words on two components of structure, narrative form and irony, which I find to be particularly relevant to Judges, may be useful to the reader.

Narrative Form
One essential aspect of narrative form is the narrative itself, the main (or central) narrative, as distinguished from exposition and resolution, which respectively introduce the reader to the 'fictive world of the story' and resolve the issues presented in the main narrative (Sternberg, 1978:1). These non-essential aspects may be minimized to such an extent that their functions can only be conjectured. A story which begins *in medias res* requires the reader to infer the circumstances from the action. Such absence of expositional material generates a narrative 'fraught with background', in Erich Auerbach's oft-quoted phrase (1953:12). Unresolved narrative is more familiar: it leaves the reader 'hanging' and demands reader involvement in concluding the action of the main narrative. But the central or main narration, with its plot of conflict, is essential to narrative form.[1]

This tautology is invoked so that the *non-essential* aspects of narrative may be examined. Meir Sternberg has explored the conventions of expositional text which distinguish it from the main narrative. In exposition of time, place and circumstances in the fictive world, *represented* time (duration of an event in the text) differs markedly from *representational* time (the time required to read the text). In other words, events which may involve a long span of time are summarized in providing background or exposition. In a main narrative, important elements demand detailed presentations, which takes up representational (reading) time. Expositional narration is, by comparison, less significant; it serves to introduce the reader into the narrational milieu—the nature of that world, the particular situation and the principal personae. Exposition, therefore, tends to summarize represented time; and in so doing is generally non-specific and non-concrete in its presentation. It describes a static world in general terms; in contrast, the central narrative introduces scenes of dynamic action which bring about change and movement and complications.[2]

The central narrative presents specific individuals in unique situations, with concrete incidents or action involving change in the causal chain of the story. With the first such *scene*, the main story establishes its own dominant relationship of represented (duration in story) to representational (reading) time. This 'time ratio' is distinct from that of the expositional material and constitutes its own 'time norm'. Furthermore, expositional material has naturally occurred before the action of the main narrative can begin; its events precede those of the first scene of the main story. The reader can thus distinguish expositional elements (whether preliminary or delayed) from scenic elements of the main narrative by using several parameters of differentiation: (1) the time norm of the main narrative, (2) specificity and concreteness, (3) the pastness of events of exposition, (4) the sense of present time—the 'fictive present', (Sternberg, 1978:21)—in the main narrative, and (5) the causal dynamics of action which constitute plot. The author may complicate the reader's task by varying the expositional time ratio, usually in order to move gradually toward the first scene proper. The author may also wish to dramatize, and thereby emphasize, certain expositional points especially relevant to the ensuing action. The criteria of concreteness and dynamic action expose the true nature of such quasi-scenes. Apparent concreteness may serve to exemplify an authorial generalization or to vivify a static state of affairs, but it leads nowhere. Similarly, actions that are summarized in non-specific, non-concrete text are expositional rather than scenic; they serve to establish themes and motifs of the main narrative.

Elements of exposition may be interwoven at any juncture within the main narrative, providing new insights and causing the reader to re-evaluate his or her understanding of the text. Resolution lacks this extreme flexibility, but though the relationship of main narrative to resolution is generally chronological, the sequence of narrative action to resolution may be shifted about. Aspects of resolution may be introduced in advance: for example, symbolically, by 'foreshadowing' subsequent discovery; or dramatically, in partial resolution.[3] In neither instance, however, is the complication of the plot completely untied; it remains for the chronologically last element of resolution to unravel the manifold consequences of the actions of the main narrative. The essential function of the resolution is to work out the effects and the meaning of the narrative conflict. The resolution introduces no new themes of conflict; it draws out those of the narrative to their consequences. Narrations which omit the resolution force the reader to work out the conflict. Accordingly, exposition and resolution usually provide the background to and the effects of the actions of the main narrative; but they are not essential to narrative form.

The essential narrative form, then, is the main narrative, composed of narrative scenes. Because the technical, more accurate terminology (scenes) may be distracting, I choose to use the more familiar term 'narrative' for those textual units which exhibit some degree of plot structure, even in exposition or resolution; and the term 'episode' for incidents, plot-related or digressive, primarily within a longer narrative. 'Story' retains the familiar sense of a sequence of events.

Irony

One valuable distincton that characterizes irony is its instantaneous, momentary nature. Irony cannot be grasped until the statement has been read (or heard) completely, at which moment the non-ironic meaning first springs into existence, all at once. The opposite and ironic meaning likewise comes into existence not over a period of time, but immediately upon comprehension of the original statement.[4] Thus, although ironic elements are contrary, irony does not 'begin in conflict': the 'perception of the distance between pretense and reality' is an *opposition*, not a conflict.[5] Conflict, like any event, takes place in time; it demands action if it is to be resolved. The opposition of irony, on the other hand, is an 'opposition of perception' as well as a 'perception of opposition'; it occurs in a moment in time. Irony is expressed in moments of ambiguous, (literal versus ironic) knowledge, whereas conflict, dependent upon cause and effect, evolves in time. Narrative plot, based on conflict, enacts a progression; in contrast, irony is a 'simultaneous apprehension' (Mansell, 1985:637; Frye, 1957:77-78). Both conflict and irony are based on opposition, but they are distinguished by their actions relative to time.[6]

Douglas Muecke describes three 'formal requirements of irony': (1) it has two levels, (2) there is opposition between the levels, and (3) there is [usually] an 'element of innocence' (1969:19-20). The primary opposition, between knowledge and ignorance, may be conceived as a vertical line of polarity, with knowledge in the position of power:

Knowledge

↓

Ignorance
(Innocence)

Knowledge (and its counterpart) is not a simple matter. Accordingly, the composite characteristics of the ironic poles may be described as:

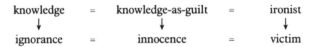

knowledge	=	knowledge-as-guilt	=	ironist
↓		↓		↓
ignorance	=	innocence	=	victim

Such vertical irony is essentially uni-directional and non-dialetical: there is no exchange between the poles, but at best there is a 'smiling down' (1983:403).[7] The vertical opposition is also the axis of power:

> the archetypal ironist is God because he is omnipotent, omniscient, transcendent, absolute, infinite and free. The archetypal victim is man... trapped and submerged in time and matter, blind, contingent, limited, unfree, the slave of heredity, environment, historical conditioning, instincts, feelings and conscience... unaware of his being in these prisons (Muecke, 1983:402).

Because an element of naïveté adheres to one of the poles of meaning, one character is rendered either unaware of a differing interpretation of the relevant words or situation (victim) or pretending to be unaware (ironist). Furthermore, the innocence of a character may be deceptive or real to himself or to the observer.

Inasmuch as ironic opposition is based on incongruity, 'irony may be made more striking either by stressing the ironic incongruity or by stressing the ironic "innocence"' (Muecke, 1969:32). In any case, as an ambiguous expression, irony involves judgment; it invites interpretation of the opposing perspectives encoded in the message or situation in order to make sense of the ambiguity (Kaufer, 1983:451-64).

Ironic opposition may arise through verbal expression or situation, and the irony may interact with the reader in different ways. Muecke classifies irony according to *modes*, which differentiate the *kind of agent* used for the ironist's disclosure of information. Muecke's first three modes posit an ironic character in some relationship to the other personae. I have grouped these as *speaker* irony. The first mode Muecke calls 'impersonal' irony, because the character of the ironist is irrelevant; the irony resides in what is said rather than the person who speaks. A second mode is 'self-disparaging' irony, whereby the ironist is ignorant, credulous (*eiron*) or over-enthusiast (*alazon*). The self-disparaging ironist understates or overstates himself. In this mode, the irony resides in the character rather than in the spoken content and thus is the opposite of impersonal irony. These modes are expressed through speakers, as opposed to those modes which arise through incongruity of situation. (Muecke's third mode, 'Ingenu Irony', which uses a wise fool as ironic agent, is not a biblical mode.)[8]

Muecke's fourth mode, which he calls 'dramatized' irony, presents 'in drama or fiction . . . such ironic situation as we may find in life' and allows the characters to act; the ironist has withdrawn completely (1969:63).[9] There is no ironic speaker, *per se*, although irony may be expressed by a speaker. This mode of irony has long been termed 'irony of situation'; and since Muecke's 'dramatized' mode may be confused with 'dramatic', one of his categories of ironic situations, I propose to designate 'dramatic irony' as that form of irony which may include the verbal and the situational (Muecke's 'dramatic' and 'dramatized'). Dramatic irony is distinguished from speaker and situation irony in that the *reader alone* observes the play of irony between two poles. Naturally, all irony is directed at the reader or observer; the difference is whether the reader gains this ironic knowledge directly (dramatic), through the ironic speaker (speaker) or through a character who recognizes the irony of situation (situation).

The victim of dramatic irony does not fully comprehend the implications of his own words (or situation). Muecke says that dramatic irony (of ironic situation) is 'immediately ironical' because the 'observer already knows what the victim has yet to find out' (1969:104–105). Extending Muecke's observation to include both verbal and situational modes of dramatic irony, I might add that even though the victim's words or situation present the irony, the reader, being knowledgeable, is placed in the vacant role of ironist, which is characteristic of this mode.[10] Dramatic irony is differentiated from irony of situation by the locus of ironic knowledge: whereas in dramatic irony it resides in the reader/observer, outside the narrative, in irony of situation someone within the narrative becomes aware of the ambiguity, becoming ironist.

Muecke codifies five kinds of ironic situations: (1) irony of simple incongruity, (2) irony of events, (3) dramatic irony, (4) irony of self-betrayal, and (5) irony of dilemma. The varieties of situational irony are regarded as 'modes' of this category, comparable to those of speaker irony.[11] The first involves incongruous juxtaposition within a situation, without further comment. Irony of events entails a disparity between the expectation and the events which do take place. 'It is ironic when we meet what we set out to avoid' (1969:102). (Dramatic irony is discussed separately). Muecke's fourth ironic situation, irony of self-betrayal, is expressed by a character innocently exposing his own failures, weaknesses; it is a mode often used for comic effect. The fifth and last is irony of dilemma. Dilemma presents an impossible situation, one in which either choice is negative. The character confronted with this choice may be unaware that he is in a dilemma, which is in itself ironic. On the other hand, the character may be immobilized by the dilemma, another kind of irony of situation, so that we can distinguish between victims of dilemmas and victims of irony of dilemma.

I have schematized this re-working of Muecke's classification as follows:

> A. = locus of knowledge (ironist)
> B. = *kind of irony*
> C. = mode: kind of agent

A.	Speaker-Ironist	Reader-Ironist	Character-Ironist
B.	*Speaker*	*Dramatic*	*Situation*
C.	impersonal self-disparaging	speaker (victim) situation (victimizes) events (self-betrayal) dilemma	simple incongruity

Dramatic irony has probably been the kind most frequently used as a structural device. Due to the momentary nature of irony, it contributes to narrative structure either by significantly related and repeated moments of irony or by a final inclusive moment, or both.

> One has to remember, of course, that in literature . . . the victim, though a single character, may in fact be playing the role of

Everyman, and his predicament, though a particular one in the story, may be universalized as a symbol or allegory of the predicament of all men. In such a case the irony may be General though it has the appearance of being Specific. On the other hand, if the protagonist, even in his role of Everyman, is presented as being 'in the wrong' *vis-à-vis* the gods with the implication that he would have been safe had he been less hubristic or more circumspect, the irony is still on Specific. For General Irony, the gods would need to be shown as utterly implacable or utterly indifferent or as capable of being moved only by such abject piety as would seem to be worse than any punishment they might inflict (Muecke, 1969:120).

The ironic forms classified in the above discussion are regarded by Muecke as kinds of 'Specific Irony', differentiated from 'General Irony'. Specific irony is primarily corrective or normative; it prevails in the literature of a society 'whose values are more or less established'. In contradistinction, general irony places us 'all in the same hole and there is no way of getting out of it' (1969:120-21). General irony is directed not against a particular circumstance, but against all of life at any time or place; it arises with the development of doubt as to the purpose of life. Only specific irony is relevant to biblical literature.

To summarize: irony is expressed in moments of ambiguous knowledge, generated by incompatibility between opposites. The force of irony may be sharpened by stressing either the incompatibility or the opposition (innocence is the variable factor). *Speaker* irony is generated by any one of a variety of knowing characters (ironist). *Irony of situation* arises when the irony is dependent not upon spoken words but upon incongruity arising from a situation. The victimization by situation is likewise recognized by a character within the narrative. Thus, in both speaker and situational irony, the irony is recognized by a knowing character in the narrative. *Dramatic* irony arises when a literary character is ignorant of the meaning implicit in his/her own words, which irony may be compounded by concomitant ignorance of the real situation, but the reader is aware of that significance—when the reader, more knowledgeable than the character, assumes the role of ironist, which cannot be vacant: irony requires that someone grasp both poles of ambiguous knowledge. Finally, Specific irony occurs in a society with established values, whereas General irony arises when values are in flux or doubtful.

APPENDIX II

The final narrative (chs. 20, 21) is concerned with interaction between Israel, Benjamin and Yahweh-Elohim. I can discover no differentiation between the divine names in this text, but the various significations of the human groups do suggest meaning. The term 'sons' emphasizes the relationship between Yahweh and his people, through Jacob-Israel. 'Sons of Israel' admits of relationship to Yahweh, but 'man of Israel' implies independence of Yahweh. 'Man' is a collective noun, but is construed in this text with either singular or plural verb constructions, which variations convey additional information. The 'sons of Benjamin' have, however, separated themselves from the chosen people, so that 'sons of' has a different connotation with reference to Benjamin. Finally, the use of abstracted 'Israel' or 'Benjamin' has a significance perhaps unique in these chapters.

I shall begin exploration of the pattern of naming in ch. 20 with the various names for Israel. There are sixteen verses concerned with the 'sons' of Israel in this chapter. In three, the phrase functions as object of a preposition or appositive of an object:

20.13   ... to listen to the voice of their brothers, sons of Israel.
20.14   ... to fight against sons of Israel.
20.25   ... they cut down in sons of Israel ....

In these passages the sons of Israel are rendered passive, objects of actions by their brothers, the sons of Benjamin. 20.13b is particularly interesting:

20.13b   ... but not wanted they [sons of] Benjamin to listen to
           voice of their brothers, sons of Israel

Most Hebrew manuscripts have the *Qere* (vowel pointing) for 'sons of' (Benjamin) without the *Kethib* (consonant) form, so that the verse reads 'not wanted they *Benjamin* to listen'. Refusal to listen to their brothers is anti-Yahwist; curiously the Yahwist designation of 'sons of' has been largely elided.

In one passage, the appositive phrase is object of an imperative:

20.7   Now all of you sons of Israel give word. . .

Even when action is demanded of the sons of Israel, the term is in apposition and the sons of Israel are objects of actions or wishes. In the first verse in which 'sons' of Israel functions as subject of a verb,

20.1   And they came out, sons of Israel,
         and assembled as one man . . .
         before Yahweh at Mizpah.

the action is in *response* to the Levite's challenge.

Two active verbs are used several times with 'sons of Israel',— 'went up' (*'ālāh*) and 'said' (*'āmar*), and they both occur in verse 20.3:

20.3   And they heard, sons of Benjamin, that the sons of Israel
         went up to Mizpah and they said, sons of Israel, tell us how
         this awful thing happened.

In the first clause, the action of the sons of Israel is embedded in a noun clause as the *object* of the verb 'heard'. In the second clause, the sons of Israel ask what has happened, but they have not yet acted to pass judgment. When the sons of Israel ask, they do so as sons of the founding father, Israel, in the context—at least formally—of a relationship to Yahweh: his chosen people. Thus when they consult Yahweh, asking,

20.18   And they said, sons of Israel, who shall go up as
         initiator . . . .

they do so as 'sons'. Their asking may be empty ritual but it is not independent of or against Yahweh. Though they will ignore Yahweh's answer, they prepare for battle:

20.19   And rose, sons of Israel, in the morning . . . and they
         pitched camp.

After being defeated, the *man* of Israel strengthens himself and takes (plans) battle positions, but the *sons* of Israel turn to Yahweh:

20.23   And they went up, sons of Israel, and they wept before
         Yahweh.

Yahweh instructs them to 'go up' again to battle against the sons of Benjamin,

20.24   And they *approached*, the sons of Israel, to sons of Benjamin on the second day.

The verb is unusually restrained for a battle engagement; it conveys a tentative quality, a lack of realization of the goal. The sons of Israel only 'approach' their brothers, but in the next verse, it is 'Benjamin' that slaughters eighteen thousand of the 'sons of Israel'. After this second devastating battle,

20.26   All of the sons of Israel and all of the people went up and they came to Bethel and they wept and they sat before Yahweh . . . .

20.27   . . . and they inquired sons of Israel of Yahweh. . . .

In these passages, the sons of Israel behave in a commendable manner, and they are consistently 'sons'.

The passage which seems least to conform with the suggested pattern is

20.32b   and sons of Israel, they said, let us retreat and let us draw him away from the city to the roads.

In this verse, *speech*—observances, not action—is presented, and presented from the point-of-view of the Israelites, who consider themselves 'sons of Israel' even when they are being deceptive or anti-Yahwist. Even so, consistency is maintained: the plan to retreat is not the incentive for the ambush on the city, which has already been set (20.29).

In the third battle, the 'sons of Israel' are fighting for Yahweh and the verbs of battle become stronger. In earlier verses, they *rose* or *approached*; with Yahweh's assurance of victory they *strike down*.

20.35   And they struck down, sons of Israel, from Benjamin. . . .

No relationship is implied for Benjamin: the 'sons' strike down 'Benjamin'. Yahweh acts through the 'sons' of Israel when they strike down the major fighting force of Benjamin, and that battle is a 'frontal attack on Gibeah', not part of the ambush (20.34-35).[1]

20.29   Then Israel set ambushers around Gibeah.

20.30   And they went up, the sons of Israel, against the sons of Benjamin on the third day and they took positions against Gibeah as before.

Israel sets ambushers; the sons of Israel take positions for direct attack.

As 'sons of Israel' either the people are passive, objects of plans and aggressions and remarkably restrained in their activities, or they behave in a manner consistent with Yahwist principles and are vigorous. The second term for Israel, 'man' of Israel, appears as antecedent to both singular and plural pronouns. Used with a plural pronoun, 'man' of Israel depicts a collective action. It indicates that the people are acting as a unit but, like the 'man' of the last chapter, without relationship to Yahweh. In this mode, five actions are undertaken:

20.17	*. . . they* were mustered, man of Israel
20.20	*. . . they* took positions . . . man of Israel
20.33	*. . .* every man of Israel, *they* moved
20.36	*. . . they* gave way, man of Israel
20.48	*. . . they* went back, man of Israel

With one exception, the actions undertaken with plural reference are not aggressive. The strongest verb, 'mustered', is rendered in a passive form, and the others range from deliberate ('take position', 'move') to retreating ('gave way', 'went back'). Only in 20.48 is the plural 'man of Israel' shown in a context of aggression. In this verse, 'man of Israel' carries out *ḥerem*—destruction of everything forbidden to Yahwist devotion—against Benjamin: 'all the towns, including the animals and everything else they found'. With bitter irony, what Israel failed to do with its Canaanite neighbors it does with its own. Collective 'man of Israel' is depicted as inconsistent at best.

With a singular antecedent, 'man' of Israel conveys the individual actions of the men, even though they all may be doing the same thing. Instead of a unit, there are separate men, separate actions. The relationship to Yahweh is gone, and the relationship to one another is minimized. There are six such actions associated with the singular (one is cited twice):

20.11	And *he* assembled himself, each man of Israel, against the city.
20.20	And *he* went out, man of Israel, to the fight . . .
20.22	And *he* encouraged the people, man of Israel . . .
20.39	And *he* turned, man of Israel,

20.41   And man of Israel,
         he turned . . .

Of the five verbs used with 'man' of Israel in the singular, two are in
verb forms which emphasize the reflexive quality of the action:

20.11   . . . and he assembled himself,
         each man of Israel
         [Niphal, reflexive]
20.22   . . . and he strengthened himself,
         the people,
         man of Israel
         [Hithpael, reflexive]

Because no sign of a direct object precedes 'the people' (20.22), it is
read as the subject of the preceding verb, and 'man of Israel' as an
appositive. The actions originate from each man; there is no sense of
a divine cause and the sense of unity has been subtly displaced. One
action occurs both in the singular and in the plural, but with diffrent
verbs:

20.11   . . . and he assembled himself, man of Israel
20.17   . . . and they were mustered, man of Israel

The verb root *'sf*, when used in the Niphal (usually passive) has a
reflexive sense, so that the men act individually, each to assemble
himself (to the others) in 20.11. In 20.17, the verb root *pqd* is used in
the Hithpael, probably with a passive sense. The singular action of
collective man is consistently passive, so that individualism is
undermined.

'Tribes of Israel' is used only three times:

20.2   And they took places,
         chiefs of all of the people
         of all of the tribes of Israel. . . .
20.10   Now we will take
         ten men from each hundred
         from all the tribes of Israel. . . .
20.12   And they sent, tribes of Israel,
         men through all of tribes of Benjamin. . . .

This formulation has several implications. It calls attention to
the inclusiveness of the tribes: 'all the tribes'. The discrepancy—
'all' the tribes are, in fact, minus the tribe of Benjamin—is
reinforced by the obvious misrepresentation in 20.12: 'all' the tribes

of Benjamin. Finally, the formulation calls attention to the term
itself. In the development of the book, a word that was initially
unnecessary, 'tribes', has become not only necessary but vague in
meaning.[2] Initially, 'Judah' signified the person and the tribe. In
20.12, 'tribes (plural) of Benjamin' can only mean the 'clans',
although the word 'tribe' is used. Even this slight connotation
reinforces the image of instability in the world of the judges.

The last major designation of this group, 'Israel', is not new to this
chapter, having been frequently used in the earlier narratives. In this
last chapter, however, amid concentrated naming, even 'Israel' takes
on new significance. In ch. 20, the Levite refers to 'Israel', and
though his first use of the abstraction suggests territory rather than
people, the second could refer to place and/or people:

> 20.6   . . . and I sent her to each region of inheritance of *Israel* for
> they committed lewdness and disgrace in *Israel*.

The response of the assembly is to judge and to condemn what has
happened in Israel.

> 20.10   Now we will take. . . men. . . for the army to attack Gibeah
> of *Benjamin* because of all the vileness he did in *Israel*.
> 20.13   . . . and we will kill them and we will purge evil from
> *Israel*.

The people wish to purge an evil from 'Israel' and presume they can
do so by eliminating the evil element of Gibeah. Implicitly, without
relationship to Yahweh, and as evidenced by the initial battles, evil is
in Israel as well as in Benjamin.

> 20.21   And they came out sons of Benjamin from Gibeah and they
> slaughtered on that day from Israel twenty-two thousand
> men on the battlefield.

On the following day, even though Yahweh has assured them that
they will have success in battle, a new strategy is used: ambush. A
direct frontal attack is made on Gibeah by the 'sons of Israel' when
Yahweh leads them to strike down over 25,000 Benjaminites. In
contrast, all the actions of the ambush are undertaken by 'man' of
Israel, 'Israel', or by an abstraction, 'the ones ambushing' (20.33, 36,
37, 38).[3] The ambush has been considered the one militarily sound
action of the entire book, and it may be so; but it is anti-Yahwist in
that it is deceptive, intended to delude. This final ruse recalls Ehud's
deceptive method with the king of Moab. Both instances demonstrate

Israel's lack of faith that Yahweh will provide the sought-after victory; here the ambush demonstrates that the sons of Israel are not willing to be utterly reliant on Yahweh. Yahweh's word will be realized, but the participants in the ambush battle are not 'sons' to him. 'Israel', like 'man of Israel' connotes man's separation from Yahweh. Discounting Yahweh's power, Israel discounts the relationship.

The second main designation of the people is the tribe of Benjamin. This constituent is referred to as 'sons' of Benjamin and 'Benjamin' in almost equal frequency (thirteen and fourteen times respectively), and once each as 'tribe' of Benjamin and 'man' of Benjamin. This last presents a marked disparity with such references to Israel:

Sons of Israel:	16	Sons of Benjamin:	13
Tribes of Israel:	3	Tribes of Benjamin:	1
Israel:	9	Benjamin:	14
Man of Israel:	15	Man of Benjamin:	1

Although references to 'son', 'tribes' and proper nouns remain roughly equal for the opposing forces, 'man' of Benjamin is employed only once, compared to fifteen instances of 'man' of Israel. This is perhaps related to the nature of the insurrection. The text implies that 'sons of Benjamin' is roughly parallel in significance to 'man of Israel': both terms *minimize* relationship. Implicitly, only the sons of Israel can be 'sons' to Yahweh; the 'sons' of Benjamin are not tribal but clan, and therefore 'sons of Benjamin' has the connotation of 'man of Israel'. The interpretation is reinforced by the curiously plural 'tribes of Benjamin', which can only refer to 'clans'.[4] The 'sons' of Benjamin represent a faction of Yahweh's people, but they separate themselves from the rest of the people, making themselves great and putting the interests of the tribe above those of Israel.

Furthermore, the separation divides not only the people, but the sons of Jacob-Israel from the sons of the next generation, of Benjamin. Even though the antagonists may be of the same generation, the 'sons' of Israel are a generation older than the 'sons' of Benjamin. In this sense, Benjamin is in revolt against his father; he prefers to protect his own interests rather than those of his father, and through his father's relationship to Yahweh, those of Yahweh.[5] The text invites the reader to recognize this apsect of the war by calling the rebelling forces the 'sons' of Benjamin, and the actions undertaken with this designation parallel those of 'man' of Israel.

Man of Israel	Son of Benjamin
20.11 and he **assembled** himself, man of *Israel* (Niphal, reflexive)	20.14 and they **assembled** themselves, sons of Benjamin (Niphal, reflexive)
20.17 and man of *Israel*, they were **mustered** (Hithpael, passive)	20.15 and they were **mustered**, sons of Benjamin . . . (Hithpael, passive) they were **mustered** seven hundred of chosen men (Hithpael, passive)[6]

Both of these verbs describe actions independent of Yahweh. In 20.15, the second use of the passive verb 'mustered' is associated with a shift in pronoun antecedent from 'sons' to 'chosen men'. The irony implicit in 'chosen' assigned to rebels from Israel and Yahweh is made explicit: these men, the next verse describes, are the left-handed 'sharpshooting' (stone slinging) Benjaminites—'sons of the right hand'. That the holy number is magnified to quantify these men lends further irony.

The 'sons' of Benjamin are comparable not to the 'sons' of Israel but to 'man' of Israel. The sons of Benjamin are estranged from the sons of Israel as the disparity of generations and the 'tribes of Benjamin' makes clear; they defend their own tribal individuality against Yahweh's people. The correlation of 'sons' of Benjamin and 'man' of Israel—both involved in anti-Yahwist activities—is endorsed by the two identical actions cited.

Only when Benjamin realizes that evil is upon him does he become a 'man' of Benjamin:

20.41   and he was terrified, man of Benjamin.

Terrified, 'man' is depicted as an abject creature.

A last category, proper noun without genitive adjective, 'Benjamin' has further significance. The abstraction of the tribe characterizes 'Benjamin' as a rebellious son, at war with 'Israel', father of the tribes.[7] When the assembly condemns the men of Gibeah, 'Benjamin' is unwilling to hear. Thus 'Benjamin' does not acknowledge Jacob-Israel, the father, parallel to Israel's lack of faith in the god of Israel's father, Yahweh.

The 'sons of Israel' ask Yahweh who should initiate the action, and the 'sons of Israel' pitch camp; but the 'man of Israel goes against 'Benjamin' (20.20). The change in name suggests that the battle expresses *Israel*'s will, even though Yahweh uses it to punish his intractable people. In the first battle it is the 'sons' of Israel who pitch camp, but because they have made all their plans without consulting Yahweh (and, incidentally, ignore his answer), it is 'man' of Israel who goes into battle against 'Benjamin'. The 'sons of Benjamin' slaughter 'Israel' (20.21), but Yahweh defeats 'Benjamin' before 'Israel'—wording which emphasizes the conflict of generations.

Before the second battle, the 'sons of Israel' again act independently, bolster their courage and make plans for the next battle, but they do ask Yahweh *whether* they should fight their brothers, 'sons of Benjamin'. When, in response to Yahweh's affirmative command, they do so, they act as 'sons of Israel'. Obeying Yahweh's command to battle, the 'sons of Israel' approach the 'sons of Benjamin' (perspective of Israelites), but 'Benjamin' comes out to oppose them (perspective of Yahweh). Israel only loses its 'sons' appellation when, after Yahweh has promised conquest, Israel sets ambushers (20.29) and the ambush of Israel charges from its place (20.33). The ambush is led not by men but a substantive form of the verb, the 'ones ambushing'. Yahweh needs no ambush to be victorious, and the ambush evidences lack of faith. Only direct confrontation is fought by the 'sons of Israel'. The rebel tribe, however, remains 'Benjamin' until 20.48, when the remnants of the tribe have fled to the Rock of Rimmon. 'Benjamin' fights; defeated, he is once more partially redeemed, a 'son of Benjamin'.

The varied and precise references to Israel and Benjamin are continued in the final chapter, albeit less intensively than in ch. 20. The total number of references to the opposed forces remains approximately equal, but there is greater disparity within the segments:

sons of Israel	4	sons of Benjamin	3
tribes of Israel	4	tribe of Benjamin	0
man of Israel	1	man of Benjamin	0
Israel	3	Benjamin	7

With one exception, 'Benjamin' is represented as an object of others' actions or concerns, and the single activity he undertakes is acquiescent: to return from the Rock of Rimmon when his victors offer peace. The 'sons of Benjamin' are likewise, with one exception, recipients of others' words:

21.13   . . . and they *spoke to* sons of Benjamin who [were] at
         Rock of Rimmon and they said to them, peace.
21.20   so they *commanded* [the] sons of Benjamin saying. . .

The last mention of the sons of Benjamin in the book seems to reverse the image of passivity. The sons of Benjamin *do* something:

21.23   And they *did* that, sons of Benjamin, and they each
         carried off a girl from those dancing which they *caught*. . . .

When the sons of Benjamin were initially confronted with an ultimatum from the sons of Israel (20.12, 13), they *rejected* it immediately; this time they *accept* their 'command' (21.20-21), again without evaluation. The judgment of the rebelling tribe is shown to be consistently faulty. Earlier, they refused to listen or consider; here, by complying with the suggestion of their brothers, they are compounding their sins. At this juncture, when they should protest, they accept the false reasoning of their brothers and meekly agree. The responses are opposite in effect—rejection, acceptance: whether proud or beaten, the Benjaminites are lacking in judgment. This is reinforced by the consistent image of Benjamin as object of others' intentions. Even in activity, the sons of Benjamin are passive.

The narrator describes the '*man* of Israel' as having taken the oath to isolate his family from Benjamin (21.1), but the wise men (21.16)—the 'elders'—reveal that the '*sons* of Israel' took the oath (21.18). This disparity distinguishes between the narrator's point of view, which regards the oath as anti-Yahwist, and that of the Israelites. Like their judgment, their vow is unconsidered and hasty. And, like Jephthah, they 'know' in ironic ignorance that a vow must be kept.[8]

The term 'tribes of Israel', like 'tribe of Benjamin', is the subject of discussion rather than of action:

21.5   Who did not from all the *tribes of Israel* come up to the
         assembly. . .?
21.8   Which one of [the] *tribes of Israel* (that) did not come
         before Yahweh [at] the Mizpah?
21.15   And he grieved the people for Benjamin because Yahweh
         he made [a] gap in the *tribes of Israel*.

'Israel' is likewise an object of prepositions in discussions:

21.3 Why Yahweh, God of Israel, has this happened *to Israel* to be missing this day one tribe *from Israel?*

Indeed, only the 'sons of Israel' are the subject of actions:

21.5 And they asked, sons of Israel. . . .
21.6 And they grieved, sons of Israel. . . .
21.18 . . . since they took an oath, sons of Israel. . . .
21.24 And they left from there, sons of Israel. . . .

The author allows only the 'sons of Israel' to initiate action. Without the relationship to Yahweh, the people are, inferentially, merely subject of discussion, incapable of action.

The action of the penultimate chapter is concerned with the act of judgment, for the entire action devolves upon the judgment of the leaderless people. The action of the final chapter arises from the rash vow that ensues from that judgment and the fulfillment of that vow. The varied and controlled use of nomenclature calls attention to shifts in viewpoint so that the reader perceives the attitude of each of the interested parties—Israel, Benjamin, and even that of Yahweh. The multiple perspectives of the resolution complement that of the tri-partite exposition with the difference that in the resolution the reader is involved in judgment of the war between the tribes.

NOTES

Notes to Chapter 1

1. Robert Polzin's commentary on Judges does read the book as a whole. See *Moses and the Deuteronomist*, Part I (1980). Unfortunately, I have not been able to see Barry Webb's recently published book, *The Book of the Judges. An Integrated Reading* (Sheffield: JSOT, 1987) before submitting his manuscript.

2. Some theoretical comments on narrative form and irony appear in Appendix I, but that section might well be read first.

3. The resolution of Gideon's narrative provides a transition to that of Abimelech and is somewhat more developed (8.28-35), and the narrator's comments in the resolution of the latter attribute the outcome to Yahweh, but there is no significant development of resolution in the individual narratives.

4. The distinction between 'author' and 'editor' or 'redactor' so aptly clarified by Adele Berlin is welcomed. Nevertheless, since the more exact terminology stresses a factor which has no significance in this interpretation, we will forgo that determination, crediting the last writer with artistry, with authorship (Berlin, 1983:128-29).

5. The exposition not only sets the time and place of the main action to follow. It employs a variety of forms of foretelling: overt statement, covert analogy, paradigm, dramatic forecast. For a perceptive discussion of these functions of exposition, see 'Mode of Shaping the Narrative Future' in Meir Sternberg's *The Poetics of Biblical Narrative* (1985), pp. 285ff.

6. See Appendix I, pp. 193-95.

7. 'Dynamics' refers to the force that generates action.

8. For the distinction between 'episode' and 'narrative', see Appendix I, p. 195.

9. Contrary to commentary (e.g. *New Oxford Annotated Bible*, 1973:296) which finds the story of Othniel 'vague' and misplaced—'Othniel's true place seems to be in 1.12-13'—I find the author has structured the narrative carefully.

10. Caleb also presents model behavior as father-figure, but not as warrior-leader-judge.

11. The 'minor' formula is concentrated not on the sins of Israel, but on the figure who rose to save/judge Israel and died: Tola (10.2), Jair (10.3), Jephthah (12.7), Ibzan (12.8-10), Elon (12.11-12), Abdon (12.13-15), and Samson (15.20, 16.31).

12. The spirit of Yahweh and the death of the judge.

13. Ehud, for example, leads and delivers the tribe of Benjamin but is also, symbolically, Israel.

14. See also Alan J. Hauser: 'Israelite society' during this era [constituted] little more than a multifaceted category of peoples all of whom had some form of allegiance to the god Yahweh' (1979:303).

15. I concur with Hauser that 'any attempt to make these men into figures of national significance is doomed to failure' (1979:302).

16. See Appendix I, pp. 195-99 for discussion of irony.

17. See Chapter on Exposition.

18. See Appendix I, p. 199 for discussion of these terms.

Notes to Chapter 2

1. Perfect tense, thus completed action.

2. Yahweh's regard is that of knowledge, the ironist who looks down on ignorant man. Accordingly, man can avoid being a victim only by according with Yahweh's will.

3. Scrutiny proves the coalition far less effective than the single tribe.

4. Burney's interpretation is perhaps more determinate than the available information justifies. In a more recent examination of the problems associated with this name, Soggin offers a similar, if more guarded, interpretation: 'It is perhaps a play on words, producing a taunt-name' (1981:21-22).

5. We can recognize in Adoni-bezek's response an example of 'horizontal irony' of the 'Speaker-ingenu' mode, naive Adoni-bezek ironizing himself as victim.

6. For the distinction between 'episode' and 'narrative' see Appendix I, p. 195.

7. I am indebted to Meir Sternberg for calling to my attention (in private correspondence) the subtlety of the language in this passage.

8. In a culture based on primogeniture, Caleb is not only in a position to give land to his sons (if he has any), but to his daughter as well.

9. The italicized words in the quotation are additions to the Joshua text.

10. J.A. Thomson, in an article entitled 'Israel's Lovers', points out that the connotation of 'love' and 'lover' in the context of a covenant is specialized, and that

> 'lover' is a 'political metaphor ... of vital importance ...: the terms 'love' and 'lover' occur, namely, in the situations where Israel abandoned Yahweh her God to worship other gods. That situation, like the political one in which Israel entered into political alliances with the nations, was also described as an act of adultery (*VT* 26:479-80).

11. This is reminiscent of the restitution of Job's wives and children and sheep after his epiphany.

12. The tribe of Joseph is included in the 'forced labor' charge, but is excluded from the more severe charges leveled against the remaining tribes. Joseph is not mentioned again in the book of Judges.

13. Intermediate level 3 is not reiterated in this unit, which quickly returns to the level of anti-Yahwism.

14. The Septuagint has 'Bethel' in the place of 'Bochim', which reading connects this passage with Judg. 1.22 and accords with the Ark being in Bethel in 20.27. We may infer that 'unto Bethel' was the reading of the Hebrew original of the Septuagint. At any rate, 'Bochim' is questionable.

15. In comparison with the sequence in Joshua, 24.29 is only modified to eliminate the introductory phrase, 'And it came to pass, after these things', there being no referent in the Judges text. One alteration in the third verse of the quoted Joshua text may be evidence of *haplography*—a subordinating 'which' or 'who' (*'aser*) is omitted—but the alteration of the place named *Timnat-serah* in Joshua to *Timnat-heres* in Judges has been considered an intentional *metathesis* (possibly to eliminate reference to the sun with its idolatrous implications [Burney, 1970:56; Martin, 1975:34]. But see Boling [1969:72], who attributes 'popular etymology' as the basis). In the final verse of the series, Josh. 24.31 (Judg. 2.7), 'Israel' is changed to 'the people', already identified in verse 6 as the 'sons of Israel'. The dropping of a conjunctive *waw* before the subordinating *'aser*, 'which', is perhaps an accidental scribal *lapsus*.

16. These emendations of the Joshua text do not, of course, alter the validity of that text. Allusion imparts meaning by modifications which do not obscure the original context and offer additional perceptions.

17. Compare Hos. 2.19-20; Isa. 54.6.

18. This pattern is often compressed into its essential components, e.g. Boling: 'apostasy, hardship, moaning, and rescue' (1975:74); Sternberg: 'Evildoing→Punishment→Outcry→Deliverance' (1985:272).

Although both are used for allusions of the 'theme and variation' variety, it is useful to distinguish between 'pattern' and 'type-scene'. In the former, a series of *narrated* actions are a scaffold for variations; in the latter, a *dramatized* set scene serves the same function. Although the Book of Judges draws from narrated, dramatized and other (non-paradigmatic) passages for purposes of allusion, only the narrated 'pattern' paradigm, which functions to structure the narrative sequence, will be generally be distinguished as such. An exception is the Samson narrative, which uses the dramatized 'type-scene' extensively.

19. What Sternberg aptly calls 'a variation on the theme of the incongruous deliverer' (1985:273).

20. Presumed to be a jesting modification of a form of '*Cushite*' (Burney, 1970:64).

Notes to Chapter 3

1. Boling notes 'the vivid stylistic contrast between the Othniel unit and this one with its wealth of detail and obvious narrative humor' (1975:85, n. 15).

2. Cf. Exod. 15.6, 12, where Yahweh uses it to destroy enemies.

3. True, later in Judges there is mention of seven hundred left-handed Benjaminite warriors, but that episode, widely separated from this narrative, can only exert influence retrospectively.

4. A *hapax legomenon* in this form.

5. One may infer that the servants' hesitation to enter king's chambers is not based on the locked doors as a 'known signal' that the king was 'relieving himself' (Martin, 1975:49), but on the resultant *smell* of incontinence, which adds to the scorn heaped on the enemy-king.

6. Taking of the Jordan fords is a motif which will be recalled in the Jephthah narrative.

7. It has been argued that Ehud must be an ethical judge because he claims Yahweh's support and achieves success. I maintain that Yahweh's support can only be ascertained when *Yahweh* has confirmed it. Israel's perception is often clouded by earthly concerns; the judges (hence, Israel) are often unethical, anti-Yahwist, manipulatively dishonest. And success in battle is no indication of Yahweh's guidance. Humankind exercises free will; and unless it is counter to Yahweh's *word*, it can—and does—fight its own battles.

8. 'Flash of lightning' is also a possible meaning for 'Lappidot', but that the two men are one and the same is considered unlikely.

9. The term 'prophetess' is not anachronistic in a book of the Major Prophets. Prophets had been promised to Moses (Deut. 18.9-19); indeed, Judg. 6 introduces a prophet.

10. 'Honey' is mentioned thirty-nine times in the Bible; 'honeycomb' an additional nine times.

11. This great goddess created a son without need of a phallus; she created out of herself the first male as her son, Ophion, the snake. The son became his mother's lover but could not become her master; when he demanded participation in authority, the mother-lover chopped his head off. This reflects in symbol and myth the prevalent human understanding of the earth's eternal capacity to create and destroy its products in Spring and Fall.

Of the many analogies with this parallel between nature and human existence, that of the bees was the most telling. This 'natural' social structure is ruled by a queen bee, who is served by a hierarchy of female bees. This reduces the males to passive drones living on the products of the female society and forming a reservoir for the annual selection of a single impregnator. The act of fertilization involves castration of the male, for the queen takes the male genitals with her, and the 'winner' of this contest dies immediately after fulfilling his single independent function. In the cells prepared by her 'vestal virgins', the queen returns to lay the eggs from which the next queen will arise. The superfluous male drones are killed and cleaned out of the hive by the females.

The Cretan worshippers of the Mother Goddess took this image in nature as a model for humans. The Great *Melisse*, or priest-queen, had a hierarchy of Melissa priestesses as servants of purity. Men functioned as servants of the female society and not as their masters—as subjects of the Great Melisse until one was chosen for a 'secret marriage' culminating in the death of the consort. And 'Melissa' in Hebrew is 'Deborah'.

In a land of distinctly patriarch-oriented nomads the symbol of the 'queen bee' was in direct opposition to the symbol of the 'shepherd of the flock' and references to the bee were repugnant. 'No one has a good word to say about the bee' (Margulies, 1974:48).

In the patriarchal version of creation, the earth and mankind were created by a masculine figure without benefit of a female womb: in Genesis 2 Adam is born into a womanless world and named 'Adam' after the ground, the land, *'adāmāh*. The land, not woman, has the feminine version of this name for man. The word for woman has nothing to do with the reproductive earth; it is the feminine form (*'iššāh*) of an abstract word for man (*'iš*). The role of the woman in Hebraic tradition is neither the Babylonian, to sexually serve the male gods, nor the Aegean, to master men—but to serve them. Naturally, the servant has no right to demand or to call the male master to come to her. But these are the actions of Deborah.

The name of Deborah recalls not only the woman to whom the men of the tribes come to be judged and who calls Barak to come to her, but also the Cretan queen bee. Margulies suggests that references to bees were all but eliminated from the Hebrew text in order to avoid association with the hated Cretan-Philistine cult practices (1974:75). The story of Deborah, and hence her name, could not be eliminated, but it is surrounded by male figures of fire which symbolically keep this 'queen bee' within *their* limits. Bees can route men, but fire routes bees. I propose that Barak's name is historical and that the meaning of this name suggested the possibility of another name of fire, Lappidot, Deborah's husband—with which to master the dreaded feminine image.

The association of Cretan 'Melissa' with 'Deborah' suggests a contradictory reason why the spirit of Yahweh is not explicitly given to Deborah: the name is too ambiguous, too close to the Melissa spirit. However, the fact that Deborah already acts through the spirit of Yahweh claims our primary attention. Perhaps both were contributing factors.

12. In fact, the guest-host motif recurs sufficiently and significantly enough to suggest a 'theme and variations': it appears in the narratives of Deborah, Gideon, Samson, Micah-Jonathan, and the unnamed Levite.

13. A *hapax legomenon*; other possible translations are 'mantle', 'rug'.

14. Jože Krašovec's concern with biblical antithesis draws attention to the opposition of curse (5.23) and bless (5.24) in the Song, and attributes this, among other curse-blessing passages to 'the compulsion to construct antitheses, and that as directly as possible' (1984:31). Krašovec finds Jael a 'paradigmatic figure, as clearly indicated in the Song: God acts through a weak person to humble the powerful enemy. But this fact also implies that Jael personifies all the willing tribes that were mentioned before' (30). He also says 'Jael kills Sisera in a most dishonorable manner . . . '(33). It is not creditable that Yahweh lead a weak person to act in a dishonorable manner. This consideration leads back to the speakers of the poem: first Deborah and Barak, then Israel, through the narrator. I submit that the Song does *not* express Yahweh's version, in *his* vision.

15. Sternberg effectively develops the play, with reversal of sexual roles depicted by Deborah (female deliverer) and Barak (male follower) as 'variation on the theme of the incongruous deliverer' (1985:273ff).

16. Although in other biblical books feminine sexuality need not be derogatory, it is consistently so presented in Judges.

Notes to Chapter 4

1. M. O'Connor discusses 'The Word-Level Trope of Repetition' in Chapter Four of his *Hebrew Verse Structure* (1980:360-70).

2. With regard to god, 'fear' has the sense of 'reverence', 'worship'.

3. This angel/messenger, like that of 2.1, speaks in the first person as Yahweh (6.14).

4. A complete call pattern recurs in Jer. 1.5-10; incomplete call patterns are also found.

5. Gideon's hiding in a cave is another link between the judge and the people: the sons of Israel also 'made shelters for themselves in the caves and strongholds of the mountains' (6.2). (The word translated as 'shelters' is a *hapax legomenon* and it is difficult to ascribe an exact meaning.)

6. Martin notes that Canaanite sanctuaries were often associated with trees; here the terebinth may suggest conversion of an existing sanctuary to one of Yahweh and foreshadow conversion of Baal's temple (1975:83).

7. The question of historical sequence of the naming is not relevant to our purposes. In the narrative as it stands, Gideon is renamed Jerubbaal.

8. The importance of vv. 36-40 is indicated by the extended use of first person narration—indeed, Gideon delivers a monologue.

9. The sequences preparatory to Gideon's first battle project humanity as free to accept or reject the opportunities Yahweh may present.

10. The site has not been discovered.

11. The analogy is not explicit but this action may foreshadow Judg. 21.6-

7; 21.15-18, in which other Israelite populations are decimated and *men* are left without *women*.

12. Jether's fear, his inability to act, also introduces background for the developments of the next narrative, after Gideon's death.

13. 'According to the ideology of holy war, the enemy was offered as a sacrifice to the Lord' (*NOAB*, 1962:205n).

14. The narratives of Jephthah and Samson conform to both major and minor paradigms in varying ways and degrees.

15. Ehud uses verbal irony; Gideon may use verbal irony in protesting his powerlessness (6.15), but he is primarily involved in situational irony, an irony which dramatizes character.

Notes to Chapter 5

1. As in making Saul king over Israel (1 Sam 15.10, 30). Subsequently, Yahweh chooses a successor to Saul, but it is many events and years before he indeed becomes king.

2. The total of seventy silver shekels uses a holy number, seven, for unholy purposes.

3. From the root *g'l*, 'abhor, loathe'—an abhorrent man whether his name is pointed to read 'dung-beetle' (Wellhausen) or 'a black and ugly and small man, or a contentious one' (Moore), both cited by Burney (278, n. 26).

4. Shechem violated Jacob's daughter, Dinah; Shechem and his father were slain by Dinah's brother, Simeon and Levi.

5. Jotham also uses repeated rhetorical questions but his appeal, even though expressed in the form of a parable, is based on morality and logic rather than on blood lines. Ironically, the appeal based on these grounds fails.

6. Boling stresses this point, contrasting this scene 'sharply with the standing theme of legal protection and cultic participation by the disadvantaged elements of society, required repeatedly in Ugaritic and Hebrew' (1975:177).

7. Or 'a stirring up' (Burney, 1970:282); 'alienating' (Boling: 1975:178).

8. 'The feelings of the Israelites against the Bene-Hamor of Shechem and the Cana'anites of the neighboring cities must have been intensified by the fact that the assassination of Jeruba'als Israelite sons was a Cana'anite movement; and, hostile at heart as they must have been to Abimelech as the Cana'anite nominee, they would naturally support him when it came to a conflict with the Cana'anites; and they probably formed the bulk, if not the whole of his army' (Burney (1970:288-89, n. 55).

9. The covenantal relationship was forged in the desert by a homeless folk. The abstract conception of that relationship must be realized in time

and space—the ethics of Yahweh embedded in history and the promised territory.

10. That Israel had peace for the lifetime of the judge is predetermined by the paradigm (2.18).

Notes to Chapter 6

1. Abimelech is included among the major judges because, as an ironic inversion of a judge, he more closely approximates the major than the minor figures. The evil spirit confirms the suitability of this designation.

2. See Num. 26.23. See also Burney's comments (1970:289).

3. Issachar is a 'half-tribe', so designated to maintain tribal number.

4. *Tola*
   1: name
   2: genealogy
   3: tribal, clan affiliation
   4: occasion of judgeship: 'rose' to save Israel
   5: (city), (tribal) territory of residence
   6: duration of judgeship
   7: death, place of burial.

   Jair:
   4: occasion of judgeship: 'follows' prior judge
   1: name
   5: territory of residence
   3: clan affiliation
   6: duration of judgeship
   2: genealogy: future generations
              (individualizing detail about family)
   7: death, place of burial

5. For example, see Boling (1975:189); Martin (1975:132).

6. This translation is counter to the standard reiteration of the cyclical pattern. See Robert Polzin's convincing argument (1980:177-78), to which I might add that the verb *kaṣar* is always used in a negative sense. Compare Num. 21.4; Zech. 11.8.

7. See Burney with reference to cities as individuals (1970:134, 304).

8. See E. Neufeld (1944:127).

9. The text has taken care to identify non-Israelites. There is no basis for assuming that the mother is other than Israelite.

10. Mizpah is also the site of a cult shrine, a detail which will have significance in the resolution.

11. Soggin distinguishes Mizpah of Gilead from a town of the same name associated with Benjamin (1981:204). Polzin discusses this 'deliberate, even stylized' spatial ambiguity (1980:180-81).

12. For discussion of this point, see Stanley A. Cook (1926:268-83).

13. Some major positions:
Boling, *Judges*:

> Because there were rooms built on three sides of a court, there was plenty of space to house such animals as sheep, cows, goats. It was reasonable, therefore, for Jephthah to assume that the first creature to wander out of his house when he returned would be an animal acceptable for sacrifice, and not his daughter (Illustration 8c).

Burney, *Book of Judges*:

> ... *human* sacrifice is contemplated. It is an extraordinary sacrifice, offered in a great emergency as a supreme bid for the active co-operation of the deity (1970:319-20)

Douglas, *The New Bible Dictionary*:

> Jephthah intentionally promised Jahweh a human sacrifice, probably intending a slave, because a single animal would have been as nothing from a people's leader (1962:605).

Elliot, 'Exposition: "Trying to Buy God's Favor"' *Interpreter's Bible*:

> Eager for victory ... he was fearful lest God should not be completely with him. If he were given the victory he would offer as sacrifice the first living thing to meet him as he returned home (1952:769).

Martin, *The Book of Judges*:

> The reference here, however, cannot be simply to animal sacrifice, since that would not have been anything unusual. Jephthah must have envisaged human sacrifice, though not, presumably, his daughter (1975:145).

Myers, 'Exegesis: "Defeat of the Ammonites"', *Interpreter's Bible*:

> The language of the vow suggests that he had a human sacrifice in mind. The purpose behind the vow appears to have been that since great things were expected of the Lord, the best at one's command must be given to him (1952:769).

Oesterly, *Abingdon Bible Commentary*:

> ... the Hebrew can only mean 'whosoever', which is further borne out by the words 'to meet me'; this could be said only in reference to a person. The most likely person to welcome the returning victor would be a woman, and Jephthah must have expected this person to be his daughter; it is just herein that the essence and significance of his vow lay (1929:357-76).

New Oxford Annotated Bible:

> He takes the extreme step of vowing a human sacrifice (1962:310 n.).

14. In his book on *Sacrifice in the Old Testament*, George Buchanan Gray makes the point that

> the story of Yahweh's trial of Abraham by demanding of him the sacrifice of Isaac, seems to be, or to be based upon, the (ἱερὸς λόγος) of some sanctuary

where, according to tradition, at one time human sacrifice was offered, but for which later the sacrifice of rams was substituted... Nor again is it necessary to determine in detail what may be the historical nucleus or the exact nature of the myth or legend underlying the story. As the story now stands it is a study in human character and God's demands.... Abraham in the story never imagines for a moment that Yahweh has become alienated from him. No room can be found in the story for a propitiatory sacrifice. ... where God is wholly pleased with Abraham and Abraham wholly devoted to God..., sacrifice is pre-eminently the gift of men to a God who has deserved their gratitude and receives their devotion (1971:91-92).

15. Gray does find Jephthah's sacrifice to be one of gratitude for victory, but overlooks the grotesque effect such a celebration would create (1971:92-93).

16. Burney cites the Moabite king's sacrifice of his firstborn son to win the support of Chemosh in war (1970:320).

17. Everything that opens the womb
        of all flesh, among man and among beast,
        which they offer to Yahweh,
        shall be yours; nevertheless
        the first-born of man
        shall you certainly redeem ... (Num. 18.15)

18. In order to test this claim, let us examine those texts in which Yahweh speaks with respect to human sacrifice:

Demanded by Yahweh	*Negated/forbidden by Yahweh*
Gen. 22.1-2:	*Gen. 22.12-13*:
... *testing* Abraham, Yahweh said.... Take your son ... and offer him as a burnt offering....	Do not lay your hand on the boy... for now I know that you fear God....
Exod. 13.2:	*Exod. 13.13b*:
Set apart every firstborn to me... among men and among livestock; it [shall] belong to me.	And every firstborn of man among your sons you shall redeem.
Exod. 22.28-30:	
You shall give to me the firstborn of your sons. So you shall do to your oxen, to your sheep: it shall be seven days with its mother; on the eighth day you shall give it to me. And you shall be holy men to me.	
Exod. 34.19a:	*Exod. 34.21*:
Every [one] opening the womb [is] mine.	You shall redeem every firstborn of your sons.
	Lev. 27.4-5
	... when a man makes a special vow

of persons to the Lord . . . then your
valuation shall be. . . .

Num. 18.15:
. . . the firstborn of man you shall
redeem. . . .

Deut. 12.31:
You shall not do so to Yahweh your
God . . . everything hateful which he
detests . . . for they have even burned
their sons and their daughters in the
fire to their gods.

Deut. 18.10:
. . . there shall not be found in you
one who causes his son or his daughter
to pass through the fire. . . .

Jer. 7.31:
They have built high places . . . to
burn their sons and their daughters in
the fire; which I did not command
nor did it come into my heart. (Cf.
Jer. 19.4-6; 32.35.)

Ezek. 16.20-21:
And you have taken your sons and
your daughters, whom you have borne
to me . . . and you gave these to them
for food. . . . You have slaughtered my
sons and gave them, to cause them to
pass through [the fire] for them.

Ezek. 23.39:
And when they had slain their sons to
their idols, then they came into my
sanctuary in that day to profane it.

19. Object of construct-verb, 'became'.

20. *BDB* translates *rîb* as 'strife, dispute . . . of public hostilities' (1979:937).
Other words which convey this meaning (all from *BDB* are): *m^{e}rîbāh* strife,
contention (193); *madôn*, strife, contention (663); *māṣāh*, strife, contention
(663); *nāṣāh*, struggle (663). Jephthah chooses his words—*rîb, šibbolet*—
carefully.

21. That this incident is correlated with that of the sacrifice of Jephthah's
daughter—human sacrifice—is suggested by the identification of Tammuz or
Adoniz as a corn-spirit. In his chapter on 'The Sacrament of First-Fruits',
Frazer says that 'the corn-spirit is represented sometimes in human,
sometimes in animal form, and . . . in both cases he is killed in the person of
his representative and eaten sacramentally' (1963:479-80).

22. René Girard emphasizes that 'ritual in general, and sacrificial rites in
particular, assume essential roles in societies that lack a firm judicial system'
(1977:18).

23. In isolating Jephthah, this tale marks the beginning of namelessness.

24. The mother of Jephthah's daughter plays no role and is not mentioned. Her absence clarifies the relationship.

25. At death, Tola is simply 'he' ('he died'); Jair is reduced from 'Jair the Gileadite' to 'Jair'; Ibzan is similarly 'Ibzan'. Only Elon the Zebulunite bears the name of his tribe at his death.

26. The Calibites were descended from the Kenites (Edom). Moses' Kenite father-in-law (Ruel or Hobab) participated in the forty years' wandering in the desert and in Judg. 1.16, he 'went up from the city of palms [Jericho] with the sons of Judah to the wilderness of Judah'. The tribe of Simeon was also assimilated into Judah.

27. Othniel is described as the 'son of Kenaz, Caleb's younger brother' (3.9). Caleb is the eponymous ancestor of the clan which will be known as the Calebites, but there is no suggestion of clan or family. The context identifies these verses with the tribe of Judah. See 1.8-13.

28. One may object to inference based on the scant verses which mention Shamgar. The single verse in 3.31 and the very brief reference in 5.6 do not allow us to associate Shamgar with tribal Israel, but neither do they suggest the clan orientation of the later minor judges (12.8-10, 13-15). Shamgar is not remembered for his personal circumstances, whether descendants or ass-colts; but for his having won a victory with insufficient means—an ox goad—and for delivering Israel. Though probably not an Israelite, the apparent orientation of Shamgar's known actions do not contrast with those of the early tribal narratives, and may be taken to correlate with them.

29. Burney notes that in Gen. 46.13 both

> Tola and Puah appears as sons, i.e., doubtless *clans* of Issachar [and] Jair the Gileadite . . . is the same as Jair the son or *clan* of Manasseh . . . . Elon is a son of Zebulun . . . in Numb. 26.26, founder of the *clan* of the Elonites. . . . That Ibsan and Abdon are clan names may be inferred (1970:289; Burney's italics).

These observations support the claim that clan names largely replace the tribal names of the early narratives, but fail to note that in some instances (Tola and Elon) the text does not make reference to clan affiliations.

30. See Hauser (1979:303); Mendenhall, (1973:225). The thrust of Mendenhall's argument is that 'The conflict between ancient Israel and the non-Israelite population . . . was a conflict with an old political regime . . . because they valued *power more than ethic, and valued property and wealth more than persons*' (my italics). It seems that though the Israelites took over the land, the foreign values took over the Israelites: Judges shows that just these values encroached upon Yahwist ethics.

31. A sample of commentaries:

> (a) Moore (1912:316n): '. . . the Manoahites of Zorah (observe the preservation of the name) traced their origin . . . to the Calebite clans'.

(b) Cook (1926:373): 'Manoah is the eponymous ancestor of a family which is incorporated in the tribe of Judah'.

(c) Burney (1970:341): '... the connexion in form between Manoah and Manahites is merely accidental'.

32. For a discussion of value and control systems in the biblical tradiion, see Mendenhall (1975:169-80).

Notes to Chapter 7

1. This is effectuated by a shift in point-of-view from objective to partial omniscience.

2. The four heroic origins: 'a beginning from conception, from birth, from conversion, and from—as we say—nowhere. The resulting narratives are the annunciation-story, the birth-story, the call-story, and the allusion (for no 'story' can develop here) to the obscurity or exceptional unlikelihood of the candidate for heroism, or to the hero's oddity ... ' (Nohrnberg: 1981:36).

3. In 1 Sam. 19, Hannah's prayers are answered without an annunciation or a visit:

> 1 Sam. 1.19b And Elkanah knew Hannah his wife and Yahweh remembered her
>
> 1.20a And it happened, when the time had come around, that Hannah conceived and bore a son ..

4. *AHCL*, 1951:70: 'to have connection with a woman'; *BDB*, 1979:98: '*coire cum femina*'.

5. The sons of both annunciation-conception theophanies are attributed to the human fathers, Abraham and Manoah. Whatever the divine role in the impregnation, there is no mixing of divine and mortal species.

6. Greenstein (1981:240) reviews how Samson 'deviates in diametric fashion' from the judge prototype; Gros Louis (1974:161) shows how Samson 'epitomizes the judges'.

7. Though the narrator is reliable, it is an Israelite, *human* justification of Yahweh's actions. The author uses direct speech when an idea is to be attributed to Yahweh.

8. Humanity may exercise free will by free submission to god or by independent action.

9. Ideally, Yahweh's will and man's are one, as in the Othneil and Deborah narratives.

10. This is not to imply that Yahweh cannot create a worthy judge, but that the material at hand—the condition of Israel, the man of the covenant— is insufficient thereto.

11. The title The Book of Judges is from the Vulgate, *Liber Judicum, Hebraice Sophetim.*

12. Only the Samson and Deborah narratives, at the beginning and end of the book, present women in roles and situation which imply power over men.

13. Robert Polzin argues that Manoah, after initial ignorance, finally does know 'who it is who speaks' and that the wife is ignorant (1980:184). I can agree insofar as Mahoah seems to know tradition and ritual, but he is skeptical; his wife consistently demonstrates the knowledge that comes with faith.

14. Although the root of 'Delilah' is generally held to be *dalal*, 'languishing' (*AHCL*, 1981:151)—and the name has been variously interpreted as 'sacred prostitute' (Burney, 1970:407), 'flirt' (Boling, 1975:248), 'darling' (Crenshaw, 1978:92), 'falling curl' (of hairstyle) or 'humble, submissive' (Soggin, 1981:253)—it is suggested that the concurrence of consonants in *dlylh* 'Delilah' and *lylh* 'night' created an association of sound and meaning. Ithamar Gruenwald comments that the 'relationship between words established by the *sound-pattern* is frequently regarded by *Midrashim* as parallel to the relationship between the *meanings* of these words. Various nouns and verbs are linked in this way, by a process of free association, in total disregard of their different etymologies and designations (1968:763).

15. For defense of Delilah as Philistine, see note 30, below. As a Philistine, Delilah's genealogy is inconsequential for an Israelite narrative. That neither her father (nor her husband, if any) nor her city is cited, however, makes her virtually rootless in time (no male line) and place (no place of origin). This is suggestive in a literature which emphasizes the continuity of genealogy, distinguishing the 'sons of Israel' from the rootless foreigners.

16. Even though *BDB* gives the root of *nahal* as 'unknown', Burney finds the root 'obviously' allied with *halal* in the sense of 'to pierce' and states that *nahal* 'properly denotes a cutting or boring' (Burney, 1970: Addenda: xiii). These linguistic links anticipate both the sexual and the cutting (of Samson's hair) activities in Delilah's identification with the *nahal*.

17. Granted, Manoah's wife does not tell her husband all the details of what was said to her, but she is open and direct with the central aspect of the encounter: 'A man of God came unto me' (13:6).

18. Burney finds that, philologically, the connotation of 'this name . . . can hardly be mistaken. Delilah must have been a sacred prostitute devoted to the service of the goddess [Ishtar]' (1970:407). The insinuations surmised from philology and double-entendre reinforce each other.

19. Greenstein suggests comparison with Ehud (3.15), Barak (4.6), Gideon (6.11), Abimelech (9.1), Jotham (9.5), Gaal (9.26), Jephthah (11.1) (1981:240-41).

20. 'Manoah' comes from the root *nuah*: 'rest, quiet' (*AHCL*, 1981:540), and means 'resting place, state, or condition of rest' (*BDB*, 1979:629).

21. Gideon also recognizes the implicit danger, but he expresses his concern with manly presence: 'Alas, Lord Yahweh! for I have seen the angel

of Yahweh face to face' (6.22). Compare Manoah's complaint *to his wife*: 'we shall surely die, for we have seen God' (13.22).

22. Cf. Gideon (6.24).

23. Martin suggests that the camp of Dan in 14.24 and that in 18.12 'represent separate Danite settlements associated with the period when the tribes were still semi-nomads and practiced seasonal migrations with the flock (1975:160).

24. Burney finds *'Ešta'ol* a rare Hebrew form, 'in the sense [of] "ask for one self," and so may mean "place of consulting the oracle"'. (1970:353).

25. These root forms are not used. *'Dan'* is the Qal preterite.

26. Manoah's statement uses the noun in the construct form so that 'of' is implied, making 'judgment' an attribute of the following noun.

27. Alter retains the Hebrew syntax ('What will be the regimen for the lad and his deeds?') but fails to discern the ambiguity (1981:101).

28. Samson says as much to Delilah, and when she cuts his hair, he is 'like other men'.

29. In the narratives of the judges, Yahweh has punished Israel through oppression from its neighboring powers. In the resolution, Yahweh punishes Israel directly.

30. I can discover no basis for inferring Delilah to be Israelite, and there is at least the suggestion that she is Philistine. After his disdain of his parents' charge that he find a woman of his own people and his subsequent escapades with non-Israelite women (the Timnite woman and the prostitute of Gaza), Samson's love for Delilah and her association with Philistines are consistent with his earlier behavior, all of which strongly supports that she is not an Israelite and is a Philistine.

31. Samson's wife may not be a harlot, but neither is she a wife to Samson, as evidenced by her betrayal of her husband before the marriage is even consummated.

32. Soggin recapitulates a series of translator's interpretations based on the possible roots of this name (1981:253); I suggest that Delilah, based on the sound association, is 'a woman of the night', at least for Samson.

33. Whether or not Samson actually slept with Delilah is irrelevant. He loved her, though she was a Philistine and a harlot (ethically if not physically, though both are strongly implied).

34. E.G. Burney, 1970:75; Cundall and Morris, 1968:172; Moore, 1976; 106, 345.

35. The Philistines are oppressing Israel in 10.7, 8; but the subsequent defense led by Jephthah is directed against the Ammonites.

36. That bees never, in nature, approach dead flesh is discussed by Margulies (1974:57).

37. The allusion to bees, which creates a link between the Deborah and the Samson narratives, reinforces the motif of the influence of the Minoan-Mycean culture: 'Deborah' means 'bee' (*Melissa*). This subtle recollection of

the Deborah narrative suggests that foreign influence (Deborah-Melissa) can have a positive effect when it is under Yahwist control (in the former narrative); but foreign influence can get out of control (Samson's bee and riddle episode), with marked ironic effect.

38. Samson's parents may or may not be under life-long Nazirite proscriptions, but Samson implicates them in his sin by 'sharing' it with them.

39. We may presume that Gideon also 'turned aside' to the enticements of his non-Israelite concubine, but the circumstances are not dramatized.

40. I disagree with Polzin's argument that 'the knowledgeable Manoah remains ignorant' (1980:183). Knowledge and ignorance are concentrated in the Jephthah narrative; Manoah and his wife contrast, perhaps, skepticism and belief.

41. The 'soothsayer's terebinth' of the Abimelech narrative (9.6) recalls the sacred terebinth in the Gideon narrative (6.1).

42. Samson's story is, however, not tragic. The nature of Yahweh disallows this possibility. See Paul Ricœur (1967:218-26). Furthermore, Samson lacks the qualities of a tragic hero. Finally, the narrative lacks 'the necessary balance between fate and flaw that sustains the tragic vision' (W. Lee Humphreys, 1985:68).

43. The text strongly suggests that Achsah and Othniel also have a fruitful marriage.

44. Alter includes: (1) 'the annunciation [using] the term from Christian iconography precisely to underscore the elements of fixed convention of the birth of the hero to his barren mother'; (2) 'the encounter with the future betrothed at a well'; (3) 'the epiphany in the field'; (4) 'the initiator trial'; (5) 'danger in the desert and the discovery of a well or other source of sustenance'; (6) 'the testament of the dying hero'.

45. It was noted above (p. 115) that not all divinely announced births produce heroes for Israel. However, annunciations to barren women *do* produce such heroes—until the Samson narrative uses the type-scene for ironic effect.

46. It is important to remember that though Samson the individual represents Israel the people, they are separate elements in the narrative. It is not logical that 'Samson does not fight *for* Israel because Samson *is* Israel', as Greenstein claims. Samson epitomizes Israel, but he remains Samson (1981:253: author's italics).

47. The third passage of particular intensity is, of course, the concluding scene at the temple of Dagon.

48. See Polzin (1980:188) for the sequence of cause-and-effect actions.

49. That the Samson cycle incorporates elements of the folk-tale has often been remarked. I wonder if the narrative observes the formalities of structure

set forth in Propp's *Morphology of the Folk-Tale*, with the exception of the last function, Propp's thirty-first: 'The Hero is married and Ascends the Throne (Definition: *wedding*)'. If Proppian functions are fulfilled in the Samson narrative, the displacement of the expected folk-tale conclusion by death renders the wedding a self-sacrifice. Irony generates the *opposite* of expectations; the Samson cycle might be using the folk-tale ironically. This conjecture, however, awaits further study.

Notes to Chapter 8

1. Burney discounts RJE as redactor because he is assumed to live 'at the time of the idolatrous reign of King Manasseh', which would not esteem kingship as 'moderating' influence, favoring a 'relative purity of cultus'. His view of the formula is more closely allied to the constitutional and priestly aspect—post-exilic like the Chronicler—than to highly spiritualized characters of prophetic thought of the 7th cent. BCE. Burney offers an overview of other positions, summarized below:

a. 'the form of expression used by the editor implies without a doubt that when he wrote there *was* a king in Israel . . . (Kue., Bu., Cor., Driver, LOT.9, Cooke)'.

b. 'an exilic or post-exilic editor may [have distinguished between] pre-monarchic and monarchic times, regarding the former . . . as an unsettled and disorganized period'.

c. 'The statement in 17.6 is clearly called forth . . . by the irregularities of cultus which the old narrative relates is the work of the latest redactor, Rp. (1970:410-11)'.

—Soggin, accepting H.-W. Juenglin's theory that there is no connection between this phrase and Dtn/Dtr, rejects Veijola's argument from Deut. 12.8-12 to the contrary. 'In our texts, the figure of the monarch appears in place of the centralization of the cult . . . the driving force behind the centrality of the cult' (1981:265).

2. Talmon's view is supported by subsequent studies. See Martin S. Rozenberg, who notes that the term *šōfet* 'as a leader or ruler reflects the more basic meaning of the verb *šft*, which is 'to exercise authority, rule, govern', and not the extended meaning 'to judge; . . . the emphasis is on leadership in general and not on judicial functions specifically' (1975:75-86). See also I. Ishida (1973:514-30).

3. For instance, the Danites ask the Levite priest to consult his oracles that they might know whether their mission will be successful.

4. Boling 'restores' a verse from the end of verse 3 in MT to verse 2 (1975:417). Moore finds 'extensive interpolations . . . aggravated . . by corruption of the text and secondary glosses (1895:366-67). Gray comments:

The text 'may be complicated by the use of two variant sources (1967:363)'.

5. The concluding narratives intensify the trend toward unnamed characters begun with Jephthah's daughter. Manoah's wife is unnamed, as are all other characters in that narrative sequence—except Samson and Delilah.

6. Burney: 'clearly disarranged' (1970:417); Boling: 'displacement triggered by confusion of 'archaic' and 'modern' uses of prepositions' (1975:255-6); Martin: 'original unity [has been] distorted by subsequent additions and alterations' (1975:183-84).

7. *Wayašēb*, to cause to return: Hiphil imperfect with waw consecutive of *šûb*, to return.

8. Micah has (twice) taken the silver from his mother, and the mother takes it back from him. Micah (twice) returns the silver to his mother and she promises to return it to him. Micah's mother also promises to make an 'image' and an 'idol' from the silver, the silversmith makes them, and Micah makes an 'ephod' and 'terraphim'.

9. 'Flat': essentially predictable, as distinguished from 'round', complex characters.

10. Indeed, Micah's mother is an ironic reversal of Samson's: one accepts the conditions of bearing a Nazirite from conception without making a vow; the other makes a sacred oath for mundane purposes.

11. Burney (1970:418) allows that the oath may be 'a curse which results *from the violation of such an oath*' (Burney's italics).

12. Exod. 20.7a: 'You shall not take the name of Yahweh your god in vain'. 20.12: 'Honor your father and your mother...' 20.15: 'You shall not steal'.

13. Hendiadys: the expression of an idea by two independent terms. See Boling (1975:256).

14. We note that the kind of work involved in *making* has been reversed for two idols: the *maṣṣēbāh*, normally 'cast', is here 'hewn'; just as the *pesel*, normally 'hewn', is here 'cast'. The conflation underscores the consistency of condemnation. The words for 'image' or 'idol' which have *not* been used stress some other aspect—the shape, material or quality of the idol, be it the iniquity of the thing or the fear invoked:

'abēn	idolatry, associated with trouble, sorrow
'alil	worthless gods, idols
ašerāh	goddess figure, possibly stone shaft
imāh	idols as dreadful, shocking
eṣev	image, idol; associated with pain, hurt, toil
galgul	log or block idol; shapeless thing
mepleṣet	horrid thing; or some object of idolatry
maṣṣēbāh	pillar; stone anointed as divine memorial
mascit	image; imaginative image
ṣelem	image, especially as in God's image
se'er	images, idols; their form
temûnāh	likeness, representation, or apparition

15. Yahweh uses the verb *'aśāh*, 'to make' when he speaks of his intentions ('let us make man', Gen. 1.26); 'I will make him a helpmeet', Gen. 2.18) or when he makes something out of existent materials ('did Yahweh make garments of skins', Gen. 3.21). The verb *bārāh*, 'to create'—always a divine activity—is used for 'creation'. *Ṣelem* is also used to denote images: molten images (Num. 33.52), carved images and painted pictures of men (Ezek. 23.14). This passage suggests the contrast between the empty images a human *makes* from existent materials and the reality of man *created* by Elohim/Yahweh in his likeness, 'image'.

16. Yahweh has designated the Levite tribe as his priestly tribe.

17. The protagonist of the last narrative is a Levite who has even lost connection with his assigned territory. His only connection with the Yahwist covenant is a tribal designation which has ceased to be relevant to his life. He too is a resident alien.

> 19.1   . . . there was a man, a Levite, *gar* [sojourning]
> on the far side of the hill country of Ephraim.

18. As in the Samson narrative, the text refers to the tribe of Dan as a 'family, clan'. See 13.2.

19. This allusion to differing tribal accents recalls Jephthah's catchword, *šibbolet*, by which the Ephraimites were recognized (12.5-6). The allusion anticipates similarly negative developments, and indeed they are soon evident.

20. For discussion of *elohim* as *terraphim*, see Burney (1970:426).

21. Boling (1975:263) reads *kᵉmišpaṭ* as 'An obvious double entendre, recalling the Yahwist's public allegiance to the "ruling" of the Yahwist judge, and the wider sociological nuance of *mišpaṭ* as 'custom'''.

22. See A.A. Macintosh, *VT* 35, (1985), p. 73, for a variant reading, one which does not change the burden of the description.

23. Instead of reading this problematic phrase literally, as a construct of 'opening of gate', I interpret it metaphorically, as the 'door' or 'entrance' of the space within the gate, the 'place where justice is decided'. This interpretation is supported in an article by Robert M. Good: 'The Just War in Ancient Israel', *JBL* 104 (1985), p. 397. The suggested translation eliminates the problem presented by the entrance of the gate 'of an unwalled village' (Cooke, cited by Burney, 1970:432), or even of the 'gate of a courtyard' (Burney (1970:432).

24. In the sense of 'aggressive entry', Burney (1970:432).

25. Admittedly, 600 men is quite a crowd to have before the house, but once again the symbolic significance of the gate—associated with justice—transcends the illogic of the crowd of men. Note that although 'men', 'priest', 'warriors' and 'spies' are described, none is a 'son of Israel'.

Notes to Chapter 9

1. For the Levite priest, the spatial corresponds to the ethical—he travels 'away' from Yahwist ties and ethics. The Levite travels in a circle but this does not bring him 'back' to Yahweh. There is no initial tribal link to which to return. Instead, he involves the rest of Israel in his compass.

2. Raphael Patai clarifies the distinction between a wife and a concubine that can be gleaned from the literature. Unlike a wife, a concubine was acquired without any protracted bargaining between the families involved. A concubine could be a slave girl purchased from a poor Israelite father or a woman captured in war. A free man could purchase slave girls to serve 'the purpose of sexual gratification, just as he could purchase a male or female slave for the purpose of doing any kind of work in the home' (Patai, 1959:41).

3. 'Of all the component features of Middle Eastern social organization, the family is undoubtedly the most fundamental and most important. Beginning with the most ancient times from which historical records are extant and down to the present day, the Middle Eastern family has remained basically the same, has been composed of largely the same personnel, structured along the same lines, fulfilled the same functions, and commanded the same loyalty of its members' (Patai, 1969:84).

4. The many exceptions to patrilocality (Jacob and Moses, to name just two) suggest another aspect of the 'exceptional' motif, like the youngest son, the left-handed warrior.

5. *Patrilocal*: A newly-wed couple resides with the family of the male. *Patriarchy*: Social organization marked by supremacy of the father and legal dependence of wives and children in the clan or family, including descent and inheritance in male line. *Patrilineal*: One aspect of patriarchy: descent traced through paternal line.

6. This verb is translated as 'played the harlot' or 'betrayed' in the Hebrew, but as 'became angry' in Greek and Old Latin manuscripts. Despite longstanding support of the LXX version, I submit that the ambiguity of the Hebrew reinforces the bride-whore-idolatry motif recurrent in Judges, and implicitly faults the Levite for not adhering to covenantal law, thus preparing for the development of his character in the narrative. For contrary argument, see Soggin, p. 284.

7. Plaza (*reḥob*): '*broad open place, plaza . . . broad open place* in city, (usu. near gate)' (*BDB*, 1983:932; author's emphasis).

8. The old man is not identified as an Ephraimite, though he is often referred to as such.

9. T. Desmond Alexander cogently argues that 'Lot's Hospitality [is] a Clue to his Righteousness'. It is against Lot's (and Abraham's) hospitality (and righteousness) that the old man and his guests are measured (1985: 289-300).

10. 'The duty of hospitality is, in fact, so much more important than the preservation of the womenfolk even from sexual abuse that in the narratives about Lot and the Gibeah incident we can discover no traces of the conflict which may have preceded the decision to sacrifice the daughters [sic], rather than the guests, to the lust of the mob' (Patai, 1959:138). 'What they [the authors of the passages] condemn and execrate is the intended violation by the Sodomite and Gibeahite mobs of the visiting strangers. This would have been rape and, as such, just as sinful as the rape of a woman, and, in fact, worse, because it would have been also a flagrant violation of the sacred institution of hospitality' (*ibid.*, p. 169).

11. There is an ironic element of justice: the concubine suffers from an excess of *zōnāh*, harlotry, and is punished for her sin.

12. The Levite has appropriately been master to his young man (19.11, 12).

13. The verb *qûm* recurs throughout the final chapters.

14. That his place of residence is here called 'house' is not a contradiction of 19.9, where the father-in-law refers to it as a 'tent'. The meanings of the word *b't*, 'house', are very broad, including 'house, dwelling; temple, palace; household' among others. The broader term has been qualified and the qualification need not be repeated.

15. In the narrative of the anti-climax, Abimelech—product of a concubine marriage—has no marriage, no fertility; his is a dead end.

16. The turn the narrative has taken suggests that the concubine was sexually unfaithful to her husband—or that *any* unfaithfulness (non-sexual; including leaving, going home to her father) is 'whoredom'.

Notes to Chapter 10

1. The Levite is carried over from the prior narrative.

2. One could dispute some instances. For instance, verse 20.10 vows to give to 'Gibeah of Benjamin' what it deserves. Although it could be argued that this term refers to the city, I have included this use of 'Benjamin' among the non-'sons-of' references to the tribe. Similarly, many uses of 'man' as warrior are conventional. The sudden proliferation of 'man', nevertheless, drives homes that the warriors are merely men, left-handed, chosen or not.

3. In the chapters of the exposition, 'sons of Israel' refers to actions of the individual in a collective, and 'Israel' to the collective—the people. Chapter 1 opens with the 'sons of Israel' and makes no mention of 'Israel'. Chapters 2 and 3 have eleven references to 'sons of Israel' and nine to 'Israel'. Altogether, the three chapters of exposition have twelve references to 'sons of Israel' and nine to 'Israel'. In chapter 20 alone, 'sons' of Israel occurs sixteen times and 'sons' of Benjamin thirteen times. In addition, 'tribes of Israel'

occurs three times and 'tribes [sic] of Benjamin' once. Without a qualifying genitive adjective, 'Israel' is used nine times and 'Benjamin' fourteen times. Furthermore, 'man' of Israel is used with a verb in the singular, in the plural, or as an object a total of fourteen times; and 'man' of Benjamin is used once, in the singular. 'Man' or 'men', with no other distinction, appears twenty-seven times. Finally, one term is specific to this text: the 'ones ambushing' is used six times. ('Sons' of Israel or Benjamin is used a total of twenty-nine times; all other appellations total seventy-six.) This sudden eruption of designations, not always necessary to delineate the movements of the opposing forces, implies information. I offer a closer examination of these appellations in Appendix II.

4. Deborah has functioned as judge but is not so named.

5. The report of the Levite has mitigated the action from the narrator's 'abused' to 'humbled'.

6. 'Unchastity' is also a metaphor for idolatry.

7. The 'chiefs' apparently do not serve this function.

8. In a lecture, J. Cheryl Exum proposed that the Book of Judges depicts 'problems in the presentation of God', questioned God's 'ambiguous answers' and found his rule 'ineffective and destructive' (SBL:1986).

9. Robert M. Good has shown that Yahweh's role as warrior can be subordinated to his role as judge, and his authority as judge made subject to the general duty of law to function in accordance with standards of justice. In matters of war, Yahweh seems not to have been conceived as a might-makes-right deity (1985:399).

10. This word, *vathillah*, (from the root *hll*, Hiphil future defective, 'to open, begin' [*AHCL*, 1981: 260]) is usually translated as 'at the first', or 'at the beginning'. Because both of these words have implications (number; time of creation) that are not relevant here, I prefer to use a neutral word with this meaning.

11. Nevertheless, the land falls only to Judah.

12. This is one of several undeveloped allusions to the opening narratives which bring about closure in these final chapters.

13. See Appendix II.

14. In the Hebrew the implications are clearer. *'Ālāh* has the implication of rising *up*, ascending, increase; and *yāṣa'* the sense of coming *out* of a place, a land, a generation.

15. In Judg. 20.18, there is no 'assembly' at Bethel: 'They rose and they went up to Bethel and they inqiured of Elohim . . . .'

16. 'Before' the city, direct frontal attack, is implicitly Yahwist. 'Around' the city, in ambush, is devious, non-Yahwist. It is ironic that the first two battles, in direct frontal attack, were lost (to punish Israelite 'judgment'); and that the last battle, in which Yahweh defeated the Benjaminites in direct frontal attack, was credited in the Israelite point-of-view to the non-Yahwist ambush.

17. The thoughts of Benjamin are narrated, not quoted.

18. 20.44 18,000 Benjaminites slain; 20.45 5,000; 2,000; 20.46 total: 25,000.

19. Kimchi evens the tally by attributing 1000 casualties to Benjamin in the first two battles (quoted by Burney, 1970:475). Boling interprets the inflated numbers as representing contingents of ten men each: 22,000=22 contingents, etc. (1975:285). The significance remains the same.

20. Like several of the preceding narratives, this one is, in Frank Kermode's apt phrase, an 'end-determined fiction': one that 'has continually to be modified by reference to what is known of the divine plan . . ., is perpetually open to history, to reinterpretation' (1966:5-6).

21. The dancing festival suggests that anti-Yahwist idolatry and theft, which were the basis of the sanctuary, have been amplified by Canaanite patterns of celebration. Gray observes '*dances*: usually associated with primitive religion, man dancing out his religion before thinking it out. . . . Here it may have been connected with sexual excitement in a rite of imitative magic in the fertility cult' (1967:395).

22. Though we may wish it, there is no indication that they have learned anything.

23. In the first two battles of the resolution, the tribes of Israel are victims of Yahweh's knowledge because they have presumed knowledge: they decide first and ask later. Yahweh invites them to discover the limitations of their perceptions.

24. Ephraim is mentioned several times, but as a territory, not a tribe. Micah and the Levite live in the hill-country of Ephraim, but their tribal affiliations are not given (17.1; 19.1). The old man who hosts the Levite was 'from the *hills* of Ephraim',—the territory, not the tribe, which implies that he was not necessarily an Ephraimite—and he was *gar* in the Benjaminite territory of Gibeah.

Notes to Appendix I

1. That conflict is essential to plot is a basic concept. See any introductory college reader, such as Perrine, *Literature: Structure, Sound and Sense* (1983:421).

2. 'Dynamic' refers to the action of a force that produces motion and thereby plot development. Expositional 'action' is not dynamic.

3. As example of the latter, Faulkner's *The Sound and the Fury* introduces aspects of the resolution within each of the narrator's accounts.

4. For a relevant discussion, although not specifically concerned with irony, see the article by Darrel Mansell, '"Time"—in Language', in *Poetics Today* (1985:627-42).

5. I hesitate to disagree with Edwin M. Good. His *Irony in the Old*

Testament is an unusually valuable contribution to literary criticism of the Bible. However, Good claims 'irony . . . begins in conflict' (1981:14).

6. To advance this discussion of irony, I draw freely from Douglas Muecke's work on this subject, *The Classification of Irony* (1969) insofar as Muecke's discussion of irony is relevant to biblical texts. For clarity, I have re-shuffled and schematized Muecke's classification.

7. Muecke describes other kinds of irony—a second, 'horizontal' image, which make the ironic positions relative, potentially interchangeable; and a third image, involving self-irony—'Protean'—which effects a 'loss of contact with the ironist' (1983:412). These do not accord with biblical literature and are not discussed.

8. Muecke's third mode, 'ingénu' irony, projects the voice of the ironist onto a naive, simple character. Because the character is unknowing and the ironist is not present, the reader does not observe irony but becomes the ironist, and ingénu irony qualifies as an aspect of dramatic irony.

9. Norman Knox offers a number of cogent objections to Muecke's classification, among which is his comment on the withdrawn ironist: 'In dramatized irony the ironist does not, surely 'withdraw completely', though he often does 'present' his irony without overt comment' (1972:55). Nevertheless, in the absence of a better classification, Muecke's is a valuable frame of reference.

10. In situational irony, the character is either aware of his situation and acts accordingly (ironist) or is not aware (victim).

11. A standard definition of 'irony of situation' indicates a circumstance in which there is incongruity between appearance and reality, or between expectation and fulfillment, or between the actual situation and what would seem appropriate. These are all dramatized irony, without an ironic speaker.

Notes to Appendix II

1. That Yahweh defeats 'Benjamin' before 'Israel' will be considered shortly.

2. 'Tribes of Israel' occurs for the first time in the book of Judges in ch. 18.

3. The word 'ambushers' is the object of an action by Israel: 'And Israel set ambushers against Gibeah' (20.29).

4. The tribe of Benjamin has not warranted sub-division into tribes like the tribe of Joseph.

5. Such rebellion is against the commandment of Exod. 20.12: 'Honor thy father and thy mother'.

6. The verb for 'assemble', *'sf*, appears in the bible a total of twenty-four times in the Niphal, with varying degrees of passive or reflexive stress. It

would be risky to estimate just how many times the verb is used in exactly the same nuance as in these verses. The verb for 'muster', *pqd*, in the Hithpael, appears in this form only in this chapter of Judges, twice in verse 15, both times referring to the sons of Benjamin as *being* mustered.

7. Sometimes 'son of Benjamin' is used to emphasize the difference in generations.

8. Num. 30.2 When a man vows a vow to Yahweh
   or has sworn an oath
   to bind his soul with a bond
   he shall not break his word;
   all that has gone out of his mouth
   he shall do.

BIBLIOGRAPHY

Ackerman, James S., 'Prophecy and Warfare in Early Israel: A Study of the Deborah-Barak Story', *BASOR* 220 (1975), pp. 5-12.

Alexander, T. Desmond, 'Lot's Hospitality: A Clue to His Righteousness', *JBL* 104/2 (1985), pp. 289-300.

Alonso-Schökel, L., 'Erzählkunst im Buche der Richter', *Biblica* 42 (1961), pp. 143-72.

Alter, Robert, *The Art of Biblical Narrative*, New York: Basic, 1981.

Auerbach, Erich, *Mimesis: The Representation of Reality in Western Literature*, trans. Willard Trask; New York: University Press, 1953.

Bar-Efrat, S., 'Some Observations on the Analysis of Structure in Biblical Narrative', *VT* 30/2 (1980), pp. 154-73.

Berlin, Adele, *Poetics and Interpretation of Biblical Narrative*, Bible and Literature Series, 9; Sheffield: Almond, 1983.

Blenkinsopp, J., 'Structure and Style in Judges 13-16', *JBL* 81-82 (1962-63), pp. 65-76.

Boling, Robert G., *Judges*, AB; Garden City, NY: Doubleday, 1975.

Booth, Wayne, C., *A Rhetoric of Irony*, Chicago: University of Chicago Press, 1974.

Brown, Francis, with S.R. Driver and Charles A. Briggs. *The New Brown-Driver-Briggs-Gesenius Hebrew and English Lexicon* (BDB), n.d.; rpt, Christian Copyrights, n.p., 1979.

Burney, C.F., *The Book of Judges*, 1903; rpt. New York: KTAV, 1970.

Cazelles, H., 'Deborah (Jud. V. 14), Amalek et Makir', *VT* 24/2 (1974), pp. 235-38.

Childs, Brevard S., *Memory and Tradition in Israel*, SBT 37; London: SCM, 1962.

Cook, Stanley A., 'The Theophanies of Gideon and Manoah', (1926) *JTS* 27 (1965), pp. 368-83.

Crenshaw, James L., *Samson*, Macon: Mercer University Press, 1978.

Culley, Robert C., 'Themes and Variations in Three Groups of OT Narratives', *Semeia* 3 (1976), pp. 3-11.

Cundall, Arthur E. and Leon Morris, *Judges and Ruth: An Introduction and Commentary*, TOTC; London: Tyndale 1968.

Davidson, Benjamin, *Analytical Hebrew and Chaldee Lexicon* (*AHCL*), 1850; rpt, Peabody, Mass.: Hendrickson, 1981.

Davies, G. Henton, 'Judges VIII 22-23', *VT* 13 (1963), pp. 151-57.

DeVries, Simon J., 'Temporal Terms as Structural Elements in the Holy-War Tradition', *VT* 25/1 (1975), pp. 80-93.

Douglas, J.D., *The New Bible Dictionary*, Grand Rapids: Eerdmans, 1962.

Driver, S.R., *Introduction to the Literature of the Old Testament*: 'Judges, Samuel, and Kings', 9th edn; ITL; Edinburgh: T & T Clark, 1913.

Elliot, Phillips P., 'Exposition: "Trying to Buy God's Favor"', IB; New York: Abingdon, 1953, pp. 769-70.

Encyclopedia Judaica, 16 vols.; Jerusalem: Keter, 1971. (*EJ*)

Exum, J. Cheryl, 'Promise and Fulfillment: Narrative Art in Judges 13', *JBL* 99/1 (1980), pp. 43-59.

—'Narrative Strategies in Judges', SBL International Meeting, Jerusalem, 18 Aug. 1986.

—'The Theological Dimension of the Samson Saga', *VT* 33/1 (1983), pp. 30-45.

Feldman, Shammai, 'Biblical Motives and Sources', *JNES* 22 (1963), pp. 73-103.

Fensham, F.C., 'The Son of a Handmaid', *VT* 19 (1969), pp. 317-21.

Frazer, James George, *The Golden Bough*, 1 vol., abr. New York: Macmillan, 1949.

Fritz, Volkmar, 'Abimelech und Sichem in Jdc. IX', *VT* 22/2 (1972), pp. 129-44.

Frye, Northrup, *Anatomy of Criticism: Four Essays*, Princeton: Princeton University Press, 1957.

—*The Great Code: The Bible and Literature*, New York: Harcourt, 1982.

Genette, Gérard, *Figures of Literary Discourse*, trans. Alan Sheridan; New York: Columbia University Press, 1982.

Girard, René, *Violence and the Sacred*, trans. Patrick Gregory; Baltimore: Johns Hopkins, 1977.

Golka, Friedemann W., 'The Aetiologies in the Old Testament', Part 2, *VT* 27 (1977), pp. 36-47.

Good, Edwin M., *Irony in the Old Testament*, 1965; rpt (Bible and Literature, 3), Sheffield: Almond, 1981.

Good, Robert M., 'The Just War in Ancient Israel', *JBL* 104/3 (1985), p. 397.

Graves, Robert and Raphael Patai, *Hebrew Myths: the Book of Genesis*, New York: McGraw-Hill, 1963.

Gray, George Buchanan, *Sacrifice in the Old Testament: Its Theory and Practice*, 1925; rpt (LBS), New York: KTAV, 1971.

—'The Nazarite', *JTS* 1 (1900), pp. 201-11.

Gray, John, *Joshua, Judges and Ruth*, CB, new edn; London: Nelson, 1967.

Greenstein, Edward L., 'Biblical Narratology', *PT* 1/2 (1981), pp. 201-208.

—'The Riddle of Samson', *PT* 1/3 (1981), pp. 237-60.

Gros Louis, Kenneth R.R., 'Ch VIII: The Book of Judges', *Literary Interpretations of Biblical Narratives*, ed. Kenneth R.R. Gros Louis; Nashville: Abingdon, 1974, pp. 141-62.

Gruenwald, Ithamar, 'A Technique of the Midrash: Linkage by Sound Patterns', *Hasifrut* 1 (1968-69) (Hebr.), pp. 726-27 (Engl. abstr: p. 763).

Gunn, D.M., 'Narrative Patterns and Oral Tradition in Judges and Samuel', *VT* 24/3 (1974), pp. 286-317.

Habel, N., 'The Form and Significance of the Call Narratives', *ZAW* 77/1 (1965), pp. 297-323.

Halevy, A.A., 'Irony in Talmudic Exposition', *Proceedings of Fifth World Congress of Jewish Studies*, ed. Pinchas Peli et al.; 5 vols.; Jerusalem: Hacohen, 1969, III, p. 91.

Handelman, Susan A., *The Slayers of Moses: The Emergence of Rabbinic Interpretation in Modern Literary Theory*, Albany: State of University of New York Press, 1982.

Hart, R. van der, 'The Camp of Dan and the Camp of Yahweh', *VT* 25/4 (1975), pp. 720-28.

Hauser, Alan J., 'The "Minor Judges"—A Re-evaluation', *JBL* 94 (1975), pp. 190-200.

—'Unity and Diversity in Early Israel before Samuel', *JETS* 22/4 (1979), pp. 289-303.

—'Judges 5: Parataxis in Hebrew Poetry', *JBL* 99/1 (1980), pp. 23-41.

Hehn, Johannes, *Siebenzahl and Sabbat bei den Babyloniern und im Alten Testament*, Leipziger Semitische Studien II/5; Leipzig: n.p., 1907.

Hertzberg, H.W., 'Die Entwicklung des Begriffes מִשְׁפָּט im AT', *ZAW* 41 (1923), pp. 16-76.

Humphreys, W. Lee, *The Tragic Vision and the Hebrew Tradition*, Philadelphia: Fortress, 1985.

Interpreter's Dictionary of the Bible (IDB), 4 vols. and supplement (*IDBSup*); Nashville: Abingdon, 1962.

Ishida, I., 'The Leaders of the Tribal Leagues: "Israel" in the Pre-Monarchic Period', *RB* 80/1 (1973), pp. 514-30.

Jones, 'Holy War or Yahweh War?', *VT* 25/3 (1975), pp. 642-58.

Kaufer, David S. 'Irony, Interpretive Form and the Theory of Meaning', *Poetics Today: The Ironic Discourse*, 4, No. 3 (1983), pp. 451-64.

Kermode, Frank, *The Sense of an Ending: Studies in the Theory of Fiction*, London: Oxford University Press, 1966.

Knox, Norman, 'On the Classification of Ironies', *Modern Philology* 70 (1972/72), pp. 53-62.

Krašovec, Jože, *Antithetic Structure in Biblical Hebrew Poetry*, Leiden: Brill, 1984.

Labuschagne, Casper J., 'Teraphim—A New Proposal for its Etymology', *VT* 16 (1966), pp. 115-17.

—'The Pattern of the Divine Speech Formulas in the Pentateuch: The Key to its Literary Structure', *VT* 32/3 (1982), pp. 268-81.

Lasine, Stuart, 'Guest and Host in Judges 19: Lot's Hospitality in an Inverted World', *JSOT* 29 (1984), pp. 37-59.

Licht, Jacob, *Storytelling in the Bible*, Jerusalem: Magnes, 1978.

Long, Burke O., ed. *Images of Man and God: Old Testament Short Stories in Literary Focus*, Sheffield: Almond, 1981.

Macintosh, A.A., 'The Meaning of *MKLYM* in Judges XVIII 7', *VT* 35/1 (1985), pp. 68-77.

Mansell, Darrel, '"Time" in Language', *Poetics Today*, 6, No. 5 (1985), pp. 627-42.

Margalith, Othniel, 'Samson's Riddle and Samson's Magic Locks', *VT* 36/2 (1986), pp. 225-34.

Margulies, Heinrich, 'Das Rätsel der Biene im Alten Testament', *VT* 24/1 (1974), pp. 55-76.

Martin, James D., *The Book of Judges*, CBC; Cambridge: Cambridge University Press, 1975.

Matthews, Victor H., 'Entrance Ways and Threshing Floors: Legally Significant Sites in the Ancient Near East', *FEH* 19/3 (1987), pp. 25-40.

Mayes, A.D.H., 'The Historical Context of the Battle against Sisera', *VT* 19 (1969), pp. 352-60.

McKenzie, John L., *The World of the Judges*, London: Chapman, 1967.

Mendelsohn, I., 'The Disinheritance of Jephthah in the Light of Paragraph 27 of the Lipit-Ishtar Code', *IEJ*, 4 vols.; Jerusalem, 1954, I, pp. 116-19.

Mendenhall, George E., *The Tenth Generation: The Origins of Biblical Tradition*, Baltimore: Johns Hopkins, 1973.

—'The Conflict between Value Systems and Social Control', *Unity and Diversity: Essays in the History, Literature, and Religion of the Ancient Near East*, ed. Hans Goedicke and J.J.M. Roberts; Baltimore: Johns Hopkins, 1975.

Miller, J. Maxwell, 'Geba/Gilbeah of Benjamin', *VT* 25/2 (1975), pp. 145-66.

Moore, George E., *Critical and Exegetical Commentary on Judges*, ICC, 1895; rpt Edinburgh: T & T Clark, 1976.

Muecke, Douglas, *The Compass of Irony*, London: Methuen, 1969.

—'Images of Irony', *Poetics Today: The Ironic Discourse* 4, No. 3 (1983), pp. 399-413.

Mullen, E. Theodore, Jr, 'The, "Minor Judges": Some Literary and Historical Considerations', *CBQ* 44 (1982), pp. 185-201.

Müller, Hans-Peter, 'Der Begriff "Rätsel" im Alten Testament', *VT* 20 (1970), pp. 465-89.

Myers, Jacob M, 'Exegesis: "Defeat of the Ammonites"', *IB*, Vol. II, New York: Abingdon, 1953, p. 688.

Neufeld, E., *Ancient Hebrew Marriage Laws*, London: Longmans-Green, 1944.

New Oxford Annotated Bible: Revised Standard Version (NOAB), ed. Herbert G. May and Bruce M. Metzger; New York: Oxford University Press, 1973.

Niditch, Susan, 'The "Sodomite" Theme in Judges 19-20: Family Community, and Social Disintegration', *CBQ* 44 (1982), pp. 365-78.

Norhnberg, J., 'Moses', *Images of Man and God: Old Testament Short Stories in Literary Focus*, ed. Burke O. Long; Sheffield: Almond, 1981, pp. 35-57.

Noth, Martin, 'The Background of Judges 17-18', *Israel's Prophetic Heritage: Essays in Honor of James Muilenburg*, ed. Bernhard W. Anderson and Walter Harrelson; New York: Harper, 1962.

Oesterly, W.O.E., *Judges*, ABC; New York: Abingdon, 1929.

Patai, Raphael, 'The Goddess Asherah', *JNES* 24 (1965), pp. 37-52.

—*Golden River to Golden Road: Society, Culture, and Change in the Middle East*, 3rd edn; Philadelphia: University of Pennsylvania Press, 1969.

—*Sex and Marriage in the Bible and the Middle East*, Garden City: Doubleday, 1959.

Pederson, John, *Israel: Its Life and Culture*, III-IV, London: Oxford University Press, 1940.

Polzin, Robert, *Moses and the Deuteronomist: A Literary Study of the Deuteronomic History*, Part One, New York: Seabury, 1980.

Porter, J.R., 'Samson's Riddle: Judges XIV.14, 18', *JTS* 13 (1962), pp. 106-109.

Raviv, C., 'Alien Cities in the Bible', *Proceedings of the Fifth World Congress of Jewish Studies*, ed. Pinchas Peli: Jerusalem: Hacohen, 1969, I, p. 240.

Revell, E.J., 'The Battle with Benjamin (Judges XX 29-48) and Hebrew Narrative Techniques', *VT* 35/4 (1985), pp. 417-33.

Reventlow, Henning Graf, 'The So-Called "Short Prayers" in Old Testament Narrations', SBL Annual Meeting, 1983; Abstract from Ch. 2 of forthcoming book, *Das Gebet im Alten Testament*.

Ricoeur, Paul, *The Symbolism of Evil*, Boston: Beacon, 1967.

Roesel, Hartmut N., 'Die Überleitungen vom Josua- ins Richterbuch', *VT* 30/3 (1980), pp. 342-50.

Rozenberg, Martin S., 'The ŠŌF\`ṬÎM in the Bible', *EI* 12 (1975), pp. 75-86.

Sawyer, John F.A., 'Place of Folk-Linguistics in Biblical Interpretation', *Proceedings of the Fifth World Congress of Jewish Studies*, ed. Pinchas Peli et al.; 5 vols.; Jerusalem: Hacohen, 1969, IV, pp. 109-13.

Schild, E., 'On Exodus III 14—'I Am That I Am', *VT* 4 (1954), pp. 296-302.

Scholes, Robert, *Structuralism in Literature*, New Haven: Yale University Press, 1974.

Segert, Stanislav, 'Paronomasia in the Samson Narrative in Judges XIII-XVI', *VT* 34/4 (1984), pp. 454-61.

Simon, Uriel, 'Secondary Characters in the Biblical Narrative', *Proceedings of the Fifth World Congress of Jewish Studies*, ed. Pinchas Peli et al.; 5 vols.; Jerusalem: Hacohen, 1969, I, pp. 226-27.

Smolar, Leivy and Moses Aberbach, *Studies in Targum Jonathan to the Prophets*, New York: KTAV, 1983.

Soggin, J. Alberto, *Judges: A Commentary*, Philadelphia: Westminster, 1981.

—'Das Amt der "Kleinen Richter" in Israel', *VT* 30/2 (1980), pp. 245-47.

—'Heber der Qenit: Das Ende eines biblischen Personen-namens?', *VT* 31/1 (1981), pp. 89-91.

Sternberg, Meir, *Expositional Modes and Temporal Ordering in Fiction*, Baltimore: Johns Hopkins, 1978.

—*The Poetics of Biblical Narrative: Ideological Literature and the Drama of Reading*, Bloomington: Indiana University Press, 1985.

—Repetition Structure in Biblical Narrative: Strategies of Informational Redundancy, *Hasifrut* 25 (1977), pp. 109-50.

Talmon, Shemaryahu,. 'In Those Days There Was No King in Israel', *Proceedings of the Fifth World Congress of Jewish Studies*, ed. Pinchas Peli et al.; 5 vols.; Jerusalem: Hacohen, 1969, I, pp. 242-43.

Taubler, Eugen, *Biblische Studien: Die Epoche der Richter*, Tübingen: Mohr (Paul Siebeck), 1958.

Thompson, J.A., 'Israel's "Lovers"', *VT* 27/4 (1977), pp. 475-81.

Thomson, H.C., '*Shophet* and *Mishpat* in the Book of Judges', *Transactions of the GUOS* 19, Leiden (1963).

Torczyner, Harry, 'The Riddle in the Bible', *HUCA* 1 (1924), pp. 125-49.

Trible, Phyllis, *Texts of Terror: Literary and Feminist Readings of Biblical Narratives*, Philadelphia: Fortress, 1984.

De Vaux, Roland, *Studies in Old Testament Sacrifice*, Cardiff: University of Wales Press, 1964.

Vickery, John, 'In Strange Ways: The Story of Samson', *Images of Man and God: Old Testament Short Stories in Literary Focus*', ed. Burke O. Long; Sheffield: Almond, 1981.

Weinfeld, M., 'The Moloch Cult in Israel and its Background', *Proceedings of the Fifth World Congress of Jewish Studies*, Jerusalem: Hacohen, 1969, I, pp. 227-28.

Weingreen, J., *A Practical Grammar for Classical Hebrew*, 1939; 2nd edn, Oxford: Clarendon, 1959.

Wharton, James A., 'The Secret of Yahweh: Story and Affirmation in Judges 13-16', *Interp* 27 (1973), pp. 48-65.

Wilkinson, Elizabeth, 'The *Hapax Legomenon* of Judges IV 18', *VT* 33/4 (1983), pp. 512-13.

Wilson, William, *Wilson's Old Testament Word Studies*, rpt McLean, Va.: MacDonald, n.d.

Wood, Leon, *Distressing Days of the Judges*, Grand Rapids: Zondervan, 1975.

INDEX

INDEX OF BIBLICAL REFERENCES

INDEX OF AUTHORS

INDEX OF SUBJECTS

JOURNAL FOR THE STUDY OF THE OLD TESTAMENT

Supplement Series

*   Out of print